Bonnie Smith has been a writer all her life but had to earn a living for her family instead of writing the sentences that rattled around in her head nearly every day and night. She still has many short stories and essays that were never published due to time restraints.

Several years ago, she wrote and published a nonfiction book entitled *Our Rank, Our Freedom, Our Power*, plus she has written numerous newspaper articles, as well as editorials, and feature stories.

Smith published *Black-Eyed peas and Turnip Greens* about eight years ago to test the market. Her real estate business required too much time to follow through to expand, re-edit and finalize it into a marketable book until after retirement. It is her first book to be published at ninety-two years old.

Everyone who read the book urged her to publish it. A literary professor was extremely excited about it, describing it another *To Kill a Mockingbird*. Smith's talents include a part-time career as a professional artist in watercolor, oil, and pastels, and computer graphic arts.

The author is a lifetime nature worshiper who loves fishing, gardening, photography, and painting. She also is political 'news junky' who is fascinated by history and politics.

Dedicated to my mother, who made me believe that "there ain't no such thing as *can't*".

Bonnie Smith

# BLACK-EYED PEAS AND TURNIP GREENS

## A MEMOIR

AUSTIN MACAULEY PUBLISHERS™
LONDON • CAMBRIDGE • NEW YORK • SHARJAH

Austin Macauley is committed to publishing works of quality and integrity. In this spirit, we are proud to offer this book to our readers; however, the story, the experiences, and the words are the author's alone.

**Ordering Information:**
Quantity sales: special discounts are available on quantity purchases by corporations, associations, and others. For details, contact the publisher at the address below.

**Publisher's Cataloging-in-Publication data**
Smith, Bonnie
Black-Eyed Peas and Turnip Greens

ISBN 9781647504885 (Paperback)
ISBN 9781647504892 (Hardback)
ISBN 9781647504908 (ePub e-book)

Library of Congress Control Number: 2020911857

www.austinmacauley.com/us

First Published (2020)
Austin Macauley Publishers LLC
40 Wall Street, 28th Floor
New York, NY 10005
USA

mail-usa@austinmacauley.com
+1 (646) 5125767

# Chapter 1

My great grandfather, Samuel Layton, was lured to the Mississippi Delta in the 1830s by the promises in a brochure that praised the incredible opportunities for farmers to migrate to the Mississippi Delta to farm the rich soil. It was dreams come true for sixteen-year-old Sam. He had become the head of a family of seven brothers and sisters after their parents died, and their eastern Tennessee farm had to be sold for taxes.

The promises made in the brochure, *The Call of the Alluvial Empire,* convinced the young family that they must go there and start a new life, especially since they had no other option.

When the orphans first set foot on the Mississippi soil, they were sure they had made a good decision and had found the Promised Land.

The Mississippi Delta is a long, wide valley with black soil that the Great Mississippi River deposited there during its frequent overflows. When rain fell into streams in the hills to the east, it joined the mighty river until the banks filled and overflowed, carrying black soil from its bottom onto the red clay. It created some of the richest cotton lands in the world. The river's thick brown waters boiled and raged, destroying everything in its path. Houses and barns and wild-eyed pigs and cows went floating down the river and were lost. For days afterward, the stench of rotting flesh could be smelled for miles. When the river finally spent its fury, it left multiple bayous and ponds filled with eels, cottonmouth snakes, turtles, catfish, bass, and carp. Once in a while, some of the lost animals were found alive in the hazelnut bushes on islands left by receding waters, or stuck in wild gooseberries, struggling to free themselves from thorns. Ferns and moss hung under banks and in the underbrush, with still clinging debris left by rushing waters. A primordial odor of mud, dead leaves, and decaying matter permeated the area. When the soil dried out, wild grapes and muscadines[1], chestnuts, hickory nuts, and plums sprouted out of the rich soil and grew at astonishing speed in the humid air. Huge maple, sweet gum, and oak trees grew to 100 feet or more almost overnight, sheltering wolves, bears, skunks, snakes, turtles, and thousands of other animal life. The skies were dark with ducks, geese, egrets, herons, doves and bluebirds, cardinals, nightingales, quail, and pheasant and the air was alive with their song. Bats chased swarming mosquitoes at night-fall and fireflies lit the soft evenings.

Leaders of the new frontier called the area the Yazoo Valley, to avoid the connotation of floods in the previous Yazoo Delta, as it had been called. Illinois Central railroad land commissions, along with a consortium of big planters and civic leaders, sent a train loaded with Delta products and free passes to farmers all over the country, praising Delta opportunities. They distributed tens of thousands of copies of a pamphlet, *The Call of the Alluvial Empire* that cited six-foot-high cotton and an experimental demonstration plot that yielded 220 bushels an acre of corn, while elsewhere 40 bushels an acre was considered excellent. It was a scheme to import good, cheap labor to work on the plantations. Immigrants were pouring into the country in the millions, and Delta leaders believed that any nationality would be superior to the thousands of Negroes who were now working the rich planters' fields. Unfortunately, many blacks had purchased and worked their own land, so the Delta/railroad consortium sought hordes of any kind of laborers they could induce to come to work.

The group decided on another inducement—a share-crop contract in which owners would supply seed, mules to pull the plows, and a dwelling to anyone who would come in exchange for their labor. Advances would be repaid at the end of the harvest and income would be divided 50-50 or perhaps 60-40 if the tenant supplied his own mules, plows, and seed.

According to old family stories, my great-grandfather Samuel Kindle was in love and refused to leave his twelve-year-old sweetheart, Mollie Short, so he negotiated with her father for her hand.

Unfortunately, the young family was unable to negotiate a contract after they arrived in the delta because they were considered too young to be responsible. Further, none of the houses available were large enough to accommodate their large family. They were forced to search for land in the hill country a few miles to the east, where they were able to find an acceptable farm where they settled.

The land and its 300-day growing season, with 50 or more inches of rain a year, favored the growing of cotton, corn, and other crops, but is heavily forested and had to be cleared, but they reasoned that the timber would be useful for building homes. Eventually, each sibling took mates and farms nearby. They settled near their brother and sister's homes and farms. Sam built his comfortable log cabin there, and his siblings spread out with their many children on nearby lands.

Then, the civil war erupted. The battle between Shiloh and Cornish found their land between both armies, who looted or helped themselves to food, horses, wagons and anything else they wanted—including Sam's boots. Sam had left his boots on the porch while doing chores, and when he found them gone, he promptly rode to the nearby union encampment, aimed his pistol at the soldier who wore them and proudly wore his new boots home.

Perhaps this angered him so much, that he felt that the South needed him to help fight the "damn Yankees," although he was now over 35 years old and had a large family. His year-old son, Cal, begged to be allowed to go to serve as a drummer boy, so they went off to battle.

As a medic in the war, great-grandfather learned the rudiments of the medical profession, and after the war ended, he set up his medical practice in the sparsely populated hills. No license to practice was required. He set up his practice delivering babies and treating malaria, typhoid, yellow fever, and sewing up wounds, while he simultaneously raised cattle and fast horses and cleared fields for his crops. Doc seldom treated a patient without first purging them with castor oil.

He believed firmly and made sure his sons believed that the bowels should be emptied several times daily for the body to remain healthy. Apparently, it worked, for his sons and daughters grew sturdy, strong, and healthy. My grandfather Cal, the drummer boy, had returned to the area and established his own farm nearby.

Sam's other children spread into the northeastern Mississippi countryside with their wives and many robust children. So many men had been killed in the war that mates were hard to find in the sparsely settled area, so they often intermarried. His land grazed his cattle and horses, and his sons worked his crops side by side.

Then, a new law was enacted that required a license to practice medicine. But the law did not always stop Doctor Sam since he was the only one in the area available for medical services. Finally, the authorities issued a writ demanding that he either complete his education or cease practicing medicine. Although Doc was not intimidated by the law, he recognized that a medical degree could only help him and the friends and neighbors he treated, so he committed to his studies until the authorities recognized him as a country doctor and finally, at the age of thirty-nine, he received his license to practice.

Unfortunately, when the war finally ended, Sam's farm had fallen into ruin. His slaves had been freed, and with all available labor forces away, fighting, there was no one to work his land. He was forced into bankruptcy shortly afterward. Now a pauper without his lands, he turned to what was left of his medical practice until his death.

When Doc's sons and grandsons were unable to survive from their farming because of drought or pestilence or flooding, or lack of rain—some of them used the corn they grew to make corn mash whiskey in the hills and hollows, away from prying eyes. Although most of the family rarely drank the product they made, they felt that somebody had to do it. God-fearing neighbors and their Methodist church congregation accepted it, as long as they attended church regularly and continued to lend their deep bass voices and musical instruments to the body.

Nothing made my grandfather Cal happier than plowing, planting, and harvesting cotton and corn on his farm than raising cattle and horses and making good use of the timber from the tall trees that grew there. After Doc passed away, Cal, now known as Cap (a title earned from his adventure in the civil war), was determined to find the most productive land possible and to make his living as a farmer. His brothers' tradition of distilling spirits was not for him. But like Doc before him, he sometimes treated injured horses or bloated cows that had eaten too much clover, when his friends or neighbors requested help.

So, Cap devoted his efforts to farming. Wasted effort, he said, to be forced to clear the hill land before he could plant corn and cotton or pastures for his herds. He was tired of the heavy rains that washed the thin soil into gullies deeper than the giant oaks that covered the forested hillsides. Like his father, he dreamed of the delta. So, Cap set out on his favorite mare, seeking affordable land in the delta, only to learn that he had not saved enough to buy the rich delta land he wanted.

Finally, he had to give up and purchased acres with soil like blackstrap molasses adjoining the Tippah River, not far from his father's bankrupted old farm in the hill country. It would have to do. He bought it, then cut oak and maple trees and built his log house and barn. He loaded the chickens and pigs and horses and moved them there. In a matter of a few short years, he had added ten children to his family, several new rooms to accommodate them in the cabin, and a dozen horses and two dozen cattle. The family prospered. Cap and Mary's sons and daughters were strong, hearty, handsome, and mischievous. Each tried to tell a more barbaric, implausible tale than the other when they weren't playing tricks on each other.

My father, Mason, outdid them all. He made every event in his life sound like an adventure out of Arabian Nights. The runt in a family of giants who grew to well over six feet tall, he only reached a height of five feet and six inches, which led his brothers to make him the brunt of their pranks. Being the youngest, he wore his size like a badge—boastfully and with dignity. He was tough, with a barrel chest and broad shoulders acquired by following his father's strenuous activities in the fields and in the woods. He always said he could "whip anyone in the family"—and he could, although the boys seldom fought seriously. He was quick and firm and could handle a horse better than any of the others. When the boys created contests to see which of them fell a tree quicker or plowed a field better, he was often the victor. After the older boys and girls married and took their families into adjacent hills to farm, he was his father's constant companion and together, they plowed the fields, harvested the crops, and took care of the animals. As they worked, Cal tutored Mason in the medical knowledge he had learned from Doctor Sam.

It was no secret to anyone that the runt of the family was also the favorite. Mason and his father shared many of the same interests. They might have been writers or politicians in another era. Cal (Cap) insisted that his children learn to "read, write and figger," but most of the rural schools in the area were non-existent in the early 1900s. The only school still open after the Civil War was the one room school that Mason's father had built before he died. Before he died, Sam's wife became a part-time teacher to give his brood and the neighboring children the rudiments of an education after the crops were harvested, or as time permitted.

In this little 8x10 log cabin, Mason received the equivalent of an eighth-grade education. The big family entertained each other with comical tales about the most ordinary of events, leaving everyone in stitches. As often as possible, they rode into town to get the latest news of national and local events.

Although they had no telephone or radio, they always knew who was elected to local offices, and they made a point of getting to know them personally.

They also managed to keep up with what was going on in Washington, D. C., and were enraged when their favorite candidate failed to win the election. In the meantime, Cap developed a good farm, a number of cattle and horses, and six children. He was content. Each morning he got up, had breakfast, hitched the mule to the bottom plow, and headed for his good bottomland next to Tippah River. At nightfall, he returned home, had dinner and went to bed. On Sundays, the family attended church or "all-day singing," with "dinner on the ground." When his sons were old enough to work with him, they frequently sang hymns as they worked. The mortgage on his 300 acres did not worry him—he grew good crops of cotton, corn, hay, and peas on his rich Tippah River bottomland. He had horses, mules, cows, and plenty of the necessities of life. When the older children left home, Cap and Mason worked and sang together, with Mason taking the bass part to his father's tenor.

Then, disaster hit in 1905. Mason was fourteen years old. Torrents of rain fell and the river began to rise. Within a few days, water had spilled over the banks into Cap's cotton and cornfields. His animals, unfenced except for a black mare that he kept for riding into town for provisions, strayed into adjacent fields. Cap rode his mare into the hills to search for lost animals, but most of his cattle and horses were gone or washed down the raging river. The flood had barely settled back into river banks when the greatest freeze ever known in that part of the country hit. Eight out of ten of Cap's mules froze to death; the rest had been swept away by the flood. The crop was gone. Cap was ruined. Unable to pay his mortgage, he found nothing left to do except share-crop for someone else. He and his family moved from place to place, working for farmers who advanced the price of seeds in return for a share of the crop at harvesting time.

Mason worshiped his mother and had great admiration and respect for his father, but by 1907, they were both gone, and he was on his own. He worked with, or for his brothers after the death of his parents until he was old enough to start a farm of his own.

As a young man, he played baseball in a minor league in Memphis, where he won accolades and promise of a career as one of the best catchers and hitters the team had. But his love of farming—the beautiful hills of northeast Mississippi and his nine brothers and sisters who lived nearby—was more important to him than a baseball career. The money he would earn was not important.

He needed the smell of the soil that he plowed and planted, the gold of the hills at sunset, and the trees that towered over hills bordering the fields

After a few years, he gave up his promising baseball career in pursuit of the striking young 19-year-old who lived on an adjacent farm. He simply didn't want to be far away from his passion for the young lady and his beloved Mississippi hills. It never occurred to him to make his living any other way. All of his ancestors had been farmers from the time they left the old country to first establish farms in Virginia, then migrated to farms in the Carolinas. Finally, many of them settled on farms in Tennessee, where many of them continue to live and work to this day.

Dora (my mother) was a tall, slim, somewhat dainty brunette, who wore her hair knotted at the nape of her neck or hidden under a hand-made sunbonnet to protect her ivory complexion. Although she felt slightly uneasy with Mason's reputation as a lady killer and wild horsemanship, she succumbed to his charm and agreed to marry him. Mason's concerns, however, had more to do with whether his delicate young bride could withstand the rigors of a farmer's life, which was anything but easy. He has spurned Dora's hearty older sister after years of friendship that could be considered courting. Dora's shy, but take-charge attitude and sweet smile had won over practicalities. There was no doubt that she loved the land, gardening, sewing, and cooking. Her family worked a farm not far away, where he had seen all members of the family in the fields and orchards at one time or another. Dora knew how to work. She milked the cows, made the butter, planted and harvested the gardens.

Yes, she would do well as the wife of a farmer, my father must have believed, in spite of her sometimes-imperfect health and nervous energy. Her family came from a long line of farmers, all the way back to their English ancestors. Unfortunately, they had not improved their lot by escaping England in favor of freedom and rich farmland that they were led to believe could be found in the new country. Her parents found farming the clay hills of northern Mississippi tenuous at best but had managed to build a suitable home and plant orchards and crops that yielded a decent living most of the time.

Mason thought if he and Dora could find the right piece of land, they would have everything they needed, but neither wanted to wait for the good land to present itself before getting married. So, on January 25, 1919, they climbed into the buggy and drove to Chewalla Church where a visiting minister married them. They didn't bother to go into the church. They said their vows from the seat of the buggy with the minister delivering the ceremony as he held the restless horse's harness in one hand and the Bible in the other. They took Mason had saved and bargained their way into their immediate household needs—a bed, a rocking chair, a dining table and chairs, and a few pots and pans. It was enough. Mason needed little to make him content with what they had. Then, the young couple rented a small primitive farmhouse on a few acres that they would share-crop until they could realize their dream of buying their own land.

Mason cleared and planted small parcels of land as a tenant farmer, but as his forefathers Doc and Cap, Mason dreamed of farming the "black gold" of the delta.

A year later, their first daughter, Patricia (Pat) was born, and another daughter, Melanie (Mel), followed in 1921. Mason was disappointed that his first children were girls, but his disappointment turned to joy when a beautiful, healthy son was born in 1924. They called him Truman after a Missouri politician they admired. They adored Baby Truman as he grew and thrived

into an image of his father, with broad shoulders, short legs, and happy dis-
position.

Unfortunately, the little cabin they lived in was little more than a shack,
where the cold wind penetrated through thin walls and kept the unheated,
interior walls cold and damp. Their only heat, the roaring fire in the fireplace,
scarcely warmed the crib they kept nearby and little Truman soon developed
a cold that almost overnight burned hot with fever, a runny nose, and cough.
Dora applied hot mustard compresses to his tiny chest and tried to lower his
fever by sponging his little body with cool water day and night, but nothing
seemed to help.

After several days, they had no alternative but to find a doctor in the little
town some five miles away. Because Mason's father and grandfather had
tutored him in the miracles of medicine, he believed that he was as adept at
doctoring as any licensed doctor, and he resisted Dora's demand to visit a
practicing physician so far away, but Dora's pleas prevailed. Mason finally
cranked the old 1918 Ford and they started for town. They were halfway
there when little Truman passed away at the age of nine months.

Soon afterward, Dad moved his young family to the banks of the Mississippi River in the heart of the delta, where the soil was rich and crops grew so
fast that "you plant a seed and step back." Again, he cleared land and planted
cotton, corn, and peas. Cotton was in great demand, although no one knew
what cotton would sell for in the 1920s. He planted cotton that grew shoulder
high. It promised a bountiful cash crop that would sustain the family well
through the winter months. He was unable to see over the tall corn he had
grown to provide feed for his cow and mule and cornbread for his family. As
usual, Mason was optimistic. My parents had a good crop of cotton and corn
and field peas. In spite of ill health and poor diet, Dad was full of optimism
for the future despite their loss of the baby.

But in August 1926, the Mississippi started rising, passing flood stage at
Cairo, Illinois on New Year's Day, 1927 and remained in flood for 153 con-
secutive days. The flood shattered levees from Illinois to the Gulf of Mexico,
inundating 27,000 square miles of land—including the land they farmed.

The city of New Orleans was spared but at the cost of dynamiting levees
and intentionally flooding the poor and politically disenfranchised parishes
downstream and especially poor farmers to the north. The 1927 flood was so
disastrous that the government was forced to step in, ushering in the subsequent era of growing Federal involvement in disaster relief and recovery. The
relief effort was massive but uneven, with inequities largely falling along
racial and "sharecrop" lines. As sharecroppers, the Laytons were not helped

by Federal disaster relief and lost their bountiful crops as well as almost everything else they owned.

Life in the delta had always been far from perfect. The mosquitoes swarmed around the family and tortured the animals they raised. Malaria was rampant. The family subsisted on vegetables and fruit they grew and lived on black-eyed peas, turnip greens, sweet potatoes, and an occasional butchered pig. In winter, they often had to depend on fish they caught or wild animals like squirrels and rabbits that Mason trapped or shot for food.

It was during the great flood that I was born. Dad was again disappointed that he did not have a son to help with the farm work, but he reasoned that daughters could also fulfill that need when they were old enough.

Dad was not earning enough as a tenant farmer to meet the family's growing needs. It was difficult to earn a good living at farming even when farmers owned the land, but tenants who shared half of their crops with the landowner met nearly impossible odds, but at least they could eat on the vegetables and fruit they grew. For a while, he found a job as a road grader for the county that paid 50 cents a day in the winter season between planting and working the land, but the Great Depression left the county penniless for such services, and he was laid off. He did not mourn because he preferred farming and fervently believed that living off the land was the only way to prosper.

After he was laid off the county job, we moved again to a three-room shanty house on some good land near the future site of Sardis Dam. However, like their prior home, it was too close to the river and the streams feeding the Mississippi River had no respect for hard-working farmers when it rushed over its banks and inundated the crops, laying waste to everything.

There were many bayous filled with fish left by the river, so they cut cane poles from the banks, fitted them with lines, hooks, and bobbers, and went fishing. The river deposited not only bass, catfish, crappie, and perch, it also deposited Lamprey eels. Deadly water moccasins were common. Everyone was deathly afraid of snakes and eels, and the children received constant warnings to watch for them. When we caught a water moccasin, we dragged it all the way home so Mom could cut it open and retrieve the hook.

"Waste not, waste not!" she admonished. Hooks, like almost everything else, were scarce, and there was no money to buy more. The next year, they had a crop of cotton and corn and field peas on their new farm. In spite of bouts of chilling and shivering with malaria fever from the hordes of mosquitoes that hounded them, and their poor diets, they felt hopeful.

Unfortunately, it was another year that the great river again overflowed its banks and washed away nearly everything they grew.

The children took great delight in watching the swirling brown waters rise all the way to the top of the road bank in front of the house. Despite Mom's warnings to be careful, we stood on the bank watching, pretending to fish with cane poles lowered above the water. But Mom had said that she had seen enough water to last her a lifetime and wanted to get away from the overflowing waters of the giant Mississippi, and its swarms of mosquitoes that caused malaria fever. She insisted that Dad find another place to live, demanding that they go back to the "old home place," in the hill country, or at least near where her mother and sisters and brothers lived.

The ocher water was lapping at the road bank in front of their house before the rains finally stopped, and it was weeks before the muddy roads became passable enough for anything besides a sturdy horse or mule. Ill with malaria, anxiety, and fatigue, Mom insisted that her husband search for a better way of life. She missed her family, but even more compelling was her hope that they would not lose another crop to floodwaters, or worry about her children drowning in the ever-overflowing river.

So, Mason reluctantly headed back to the hill country where the family hoped to escape the flooding, mosquitoes, poverty in the delta, and all too often sick children. A week later, he returned to tell the family that he'd rented the "Higdon cabin" and a few acres of land in the hills of northern Mississippi.

A by-product of the constant flooding of the river was the swarms of malaria-infected mosquitoes. They were everywhere. There were no screens, and we slept under a sheet for protection. The mosquitoes would bite and the children would scratch the bits and become infected. Mom applied coal oil to the bites, which reduced the infections, but it did not protect from malaria fevers. First one, then another of the family would come down for weeks with sweating and fevers. One or another of the family members seemed to be well one day and sick the following day with measles, mumps, whooping cough, scarlet fever, or yellow fever.

A fifth child, Bubba, was born in 1930, but he failed to thrive and grow. He was nearly always sick. Mom failed to have enough milk for the baby, and he was forced to drink cow's milk. Finally, they learned that he was allergic to it and they had to find goat milk as a substitute. Then, malaria hit and he lay under a blanket day after day to sweat the fever away. When they could afford it, each member of the family took quinine to combat malaria but it was never enough.

When Dad was down with the fever, he couldn't work, but when Mom was sick, she was forced to care for the four children, do the laundry and prepare meals, plant or weed the garden, and all the other duties of a farmer's wife.

Finally, malaria, Bubba's failure to thrive, and the frequent drowning of their crops by the river had taken their toll. Our parents had to make a decision. Another dream of the black soil in the delta had died for them as it had for their forefathers.

It was weeks before the floods receded enough to dry out the red clay roads enough to travel. Dad set out to find a tenant farm and when he returned, they packed their meager belongings on an old T model truck and left during the Christmas holidays for the hill country where flooding was less likely.

The depression was in full swing. There was food and shelter, even if it wasn't always adequate. "Sometimes, you just have to count your blessings and hope for the best. The Lord will provide!" Mom announced.

"God won't do it by himself, younguns," Dad said.

# Chapter 2

In the twilight, a light drizzle glinted on the little truck as it labored up the mud-slick hill. Occasionally it slipped from side to side or dropped into deep ruts. The motor raced with effort as it climbed out of one rut, only to end in another. Finally reaching the crest of the hill, the lights of the town could be seen.

It had taken most of the day to drive from the Delta to reach our destination just 35 miles away. Driving through deep ruts, mudflats, and laboring up steep hills meant Mom and my older sisters often had to unload to push the truck out of the mud when its tires mired to the axle. Once we had to stop to fix a flat tire.

From our perch on top of beds, chairs, damp boxes, and animal pens filed with nervous chickens, a goat and a pig, Pat, Mel, and I pulled our light coats tighter around our shoulders. In our excitement over moving, we had not noticed the December chill until the drizzle started to form ice crystals in our hair. Covered only with a thin scarf, it was stiff and matted with ice and we shivered both from the cold and anticipation as we approached the lights ahead.

The sight of the little town wrapped in glistening Christmas lights was enchanting. We had never seen anything like it before. Freezing crystals gleamed on thousands of Christmas trees' lights and colorful decorations that hung from every light post. It was the first time we had seen an entire town lit up with electric Christmas lights before and we stared until our eyes burned, occasionally letting out a "Wow—look at that." A few figures huddled in front of storefronts, lights changing their faces from green to red and red to green. Then, the loaded truck slipped through the town and entered a world that was dreary and gray and cold. Except for the truck's headlights on the road ahead, only the outline of giant oaks and maples beside the road were visible. We nestled together for warmth until we arrived nearly two hours later at a small unpainted, weathered structure sitting in the edge of a grove of giant oaks, elms, and maples. Inside, it was a shell with no interior walls or ceiling.

Unpainted pine boards, with a single-window and door, framed the building. The same kind of simple boards partitioned the little house into two square rooms about 12 feet in size with an adjacent lean-to kitchen. A door stoop consisting of a board mounted on cut-off logs stood beneath the door. Dark shadows beneath the house attested to the lack of a foundation. Icicles, hanging like stalactites from the metal roof, glinted in the truck's headlights.

Pat and Mel climbed from the top of the load and helped me down from my perch. Mom held three-year-old Bubba in her arms. He was whimpering softly from the rough ride, the cold, or hunger.

The kitchen held an old wood cook stove; otherwise, the house was empty and cold. Bare plank floors met bare walls from which fading light could be seen through the cracks. The middle room held a fireplace and the lean-to kitchen offered only a small window from which stark outlines of trees could be seen through the freezing drizzle. The floors were of rough planks carelessly nailed almost—but not quite—parallel to each other and were raised off the ground so that the earth and daylight were clear through the cracks. There was a small platform nailed outside the kitchen lean-to held an old cracked grey enamel pan for washing and an extra bucket of water containing a blue enameled dipper.

Adjacent to the weathered house was a small barn with a crib to hold corn and a lean-to shelter for animals. There was no outhouse to be seen, but next to the barn was another small building for our chickens. Dad lit the lantern and unloaded the pigpen and chickens so he could reach the household goods on top. He had brought the old milk cow and installed it in the lean-to the previous day so Mom had to milk the cow before we unloaded the truck.

By the time I found a pile of stove wood by the back door and stacked it beside the cook stove, the others had unloaded the truck. Pat started a fire in the fireplace which brought the little house little warmth, but some cheer. The fire made it feel like home even though everyone still shivered from cold. I helped drag two shuck mattresses into the middle room next to the fireplace and an additional one into the third room for our parents. They set up the table in the kitchen beside the cook stove and unloaded pots and pans and dishes into the old "safe." Boxes filled with clothing were stacked in corners of the bedrooms. Tonight, the beds could be slept in with only quilts and pillows. Tomorrow would be soon enough for sheets and pillowcases. Mom had brought a jug of milk and a pan of cornbread—there was no energy for cooking tonight. She placed the cornbread on the table, poured milk for each of the children, and we ate hungrily, too tired from the journey to care.

Nearly everyone was in the same poverty-ridden condition during the depression. There were no jobs and farmers could not sell their crops for the price of seed money. Mom and Dad reasoned that we were luckier than most. The woods were filled with wild game, nuts, and fruit: Muscatine's, grapes, wild plums, chestnuts, hickory nuts, huckleberries, hazelnuts, and in the meadows were wild salad greens or (salet greens) picked from the poke plant in the woods. We had a few sweet potatoes, turnips, dried butter beans, canned green beans, and tomatoes. The cow provided milk and butter and occasionally there was a hog or young steer to butcher for a winter supply of smoked ham, (sowbelly) bacon, roasts, and ribs.

"Pity the poor people who lived in cities with no access to the fruits of the land," Dad told us. We came from a long line of hunters and gatherers of the bountiful wild fruits, nuts, and vegetables found in the hills and hollows surrounding the little farm.

Dad told us, "We'll clear the land during the winter months, and plant crops in the spring. We will find a way to get through the winter. I'll find out if the railroad is buying cross-ties for the cash we needed for coal oil, flour, and cornmeal. We'll get by with the cash Mom gets from selling eggs and butter."

Christmas morning brought bright sunlight streaming through the window, and there was a fire glowing in the fireplace. Light fog hovered over the meadow where the sun started to melt the frozen red earth. Pat and Mel broke the ice in the water bucket and poured it into the stove's reservoir for bathwater, then put a large pan with water on the stove to heat. When it started steaming, the children took turns washing before getting dressed in our overalls and warmest shirts and shoes, shivering in the cold. Mom brought in a steaming bucket of milk and poured one into the churn to make butter and the other into a jug for the family to drink. Then, she made breakfast and woke the children. I was shaking with cold in my wet clothes. "What am I going to do with you? Will you ever stop wetting the bed?"

I hung my head but said nothing. Mom helped me take off wet clothes, wrapped me in a towel, and washed me off in the left-over bath water used by my sisters. Pat and Mel looked at me in disgust and anger, calling me "pea-tail, pea-tail." Since we shared the bed, they were both damp and smelled of urine also.

Mom said, "Stop it. Now go put up a line and you two take the mattress out to dry."

"Whew. It stinks," Pat said, "Why do we have to do it? She's the one who wet the bed!" Acrid aroma of the wet bed waived through the house, as

Mel and Pat obediently the mattress full of corn shucks and carried it outside and draped it across a line, where it steamed in the sunlight.

"Can't we just replace the shucks, Mom?" Mel asked.

"No, we'll just have to make do. There are no more shucks to stuff the mattress. It'll be better when it dries out."

She turned to me, "Don't you see all the trouble you've caused, young lady? Now we're going to have to do a washing—when we have so much else to do." I vowed to run away and then she would be sorry. The older girls spent the rest of the day calling me "pea-tail." I said nothing until I could stand it no longer and then started flailing my arms at them. But they were larger than me and my small fists made little impression.

Although we were barely aware of it, Mississippi was virtually bankrupt. Banks throughout American either had closed or were preparing to close. Nation-wide, there were from 15 to 17 million people without work. Millions of young men hopped freight trains from city to city to search for work, but there was no work. Long bread lines wrapped around city blocks to soup kitchens that had been sat up in most towns, often to find nothing left by the time they reached it.

Everyone was in the same situation; no money, no jobs, little food. Medical care was almost unknown and depended upon a charitable doctor who agreed to accept chickens, eggs, or butter for his services. No one had money. People subsisted from produce they raised, salet greens and wild fruits from the meadows, black-eyed peas and cornbread. Rural families traded eggs, butter, IOUs, labor, or a portion of the pig after it was butchered in the fall for staples such as flour, sugar, and coffee. Since the crash, farmers were unable to sell their crops for any amount of cash; even those who had cash often could not spend it until the merchant took their bills to the nearest church to exchange for coins.

After breakfast, Mom started unpacking the boxes. There was no place to hang clothes, so she drove nails into the studs and hung coats and shirts from them, leaving underwear and socks in boxes which she arranged next to walls for easy access. In the kitchen, she placed jars filled with shelled peas and beans on two by four cross beams. Tin cans holding flour and meal were placed on the floor around the room, and pots and pans were hung from nails. Mom noted that there was little flour and meal left and wondered if the chickens would produce enough eggs to exchange for staples.

When she caught up with the laundry and getting the clothes, she had made so the girls could start school after the holidays, perhaps she could get acquainted with her neighbors. She had noticed several lights on in scattered houses along the way. How she longed to have friends and neighbors to talk with and to see all her brothers, sisters and their children again. She sighed.

It was a luxury that rural families seldom had, except for church activities in rural Mississippi in the '30s. It served as social life as well as a place for the women to trade something they had for something they needed, or for the men to trade horses or cattle or services. The church was the center of family life, dear to all for the spiritual comfort received in spite of preachers who tortured his frock with hellfire and brimstone messages—a message Mom believed in wholeheartedly. It did not occur to her how a loving God could allow His children to burn forever in fire and brimstone—the Bible was the truth, the whole truth and nothing but the truth. There was no way she allowed her children to disregard the scriptures, even if they wanted to. The message was embedded too deeply. God was good, but He was a jealous and vengeful God. He would provide, but man must supply the labor. She knew how to work from "sun up until sundown," and never get it all done. Her back was aching already from packing and unpacking, cooking, milking the cows, and feeding the animals. Soon, the laundry must be done and she dreaded packing the big, black tub down to the spring to boil the clothes. It would take several trips with the washtub and rub-board, clothes, and soap, and then hang them to dry. She hoped it wouldn't be so cold and her hands would not get so chapped and raw, and that the clothes didn't freeze on the line.

The next fall, Dad took our meager corn crop to grist mills to be ground for corn meal—a staple that no one could do without. Most of our breakfasts consisted of salt pork, biscuits, sorghum molasses, and milk. There were jams and jellies that Mom made from wild Muscatine's, grapes, plums, or whatever else she was able to find. Dinner, the mid-day meal, consisted of soups made from dried beans or peas, dried or canned tomatoes, potatoes, corn, green beans, and any other vegetables we had grown. It was seasoned heavily with salt pork and was delicious. The evening meal was leftovers, cornbread and milk, or a big pot of wild salet (Poke Plant) greens which we searched for in adjacent hills almost every day in the spring. Although meager, it was satisfying and tasty.

# Chapter 3

Once again, they headed into the setting sun
Once again, they headed West out of
The Great Plains and hit the highways
For the Pacific Coast, the last border
Blown out—baked out—and broke
Nothing to stay for… nothing to hope for
Homeless, penniless and bewildered they joined
The great army of the highways**
**Bob Dylon

Mel and Pat brought The Weekly Reader home from school. It told of the great migration west with stories and photographs of the exodus. The Weekly Reader was the only source of news we had and the family read it hungrily. It told of farmland ravaged by erosion, baking in the sun; homesteads buried in dust, dead corn with dried out stems poking out of the shallow soil, dust storms boiling up in black clouds over lonely little towns, black children stooped to pick half-dead cotton, dragging their cotton sacks behind them in the big fields of the Delta, and Hispanic children making adobe bricks. It showed factory stacks silhouetted against empty skies, guns and labor violence in major cities, and homeless men gazing with empty eyes on park benches, waiting, always waiting; women old at 30 and 40 with loose teeth in their mouths. It showed lonely caravans of cars held together with baling wire and hope.

Cities were running out of relief money and there was rioting for food, while others were suffering from malnutrition—or starving to death. People were living in culverts, under bridges or on park benches. Thousands of jobs disappeared daily. None of this seemed to affect my family a great deal. We had rented land to farm, had a roof over our head, and an old mule to pull the plow. We lived on the game Dad killed and the food we dried, canned or gathered to eat and somehow managed to do with inadequate clothes, gasoline for the little truck and coal oil for our lamps.

If my family took any of those words and images in the *Weekly Reader* seriously, we were not aware of it. Dad ridiculed those who escaped the Dust Bowl and left the land with the only household goods they had piled high on their cars and trucks to search for a better life. "They need to stay with the land," he said, "Land will always take care of you."

"Well, we don't have four feet of dust. We will stay here and plow and plant and grow and we will carry on better than those poor people."

Dad had the idealism, while Mom had the fear, anger, and despair. Her anger erupted when the children had no shoes and only one item of clothing each to wear to school. She despaired when the supply of coal oil for our lamps ran out and there was no money for more. She endured in the face of fear when the cornmeal and flour supplies dwindled. She hoarded eggs and butter to sell or trade for necessities, bitter and angry that it deprived the family of eating our own eggs for breakfast, and because she had to serve biscuits and gravy for breakfast instead.

There was never any discussion of our family leaving for greater opportunities at the time. Without money for gasoline for our little truck, we couldn't have left even if we wanted to. If my parents saw the failure to meet our basic needs for money and food and clothing, they held continual hope. Perhaps Dad's constant optimism and trust sustained us when he kept telling us, "We're the lucky ones. We have everything we need."

As children, we were immune from worry and barely noticed that we had little to eat besides the milk and butter our cow provided and the foods we gathered from the forest and hills surrounding our little lean-to cabin. The worst suffering we endured was when we shivered from the cold that penetrated through our thin coats and sweaters in winter or when we had to break ice for water to drink or bathe in.

The stock market crash of 1929 and thousands of bank failures affected a few of the southern tenant farmers who lived from one day to the next with virtually no money. We felt fortunate that our landlord—the owner of the farm we rented—had not lost his land to foreclosure. But the people would nurture a permanent distrust of banks, trust companies, and financial institutions, seeing them as brokers of speculation for many years in the future. We had no money to lose, but our faith in the virtues of thrift and responsibility was shattered. The world of money had not simply failed but had betrayed an implicit trust.

Rollin Kirby's most effective editorial drawing of 1931 depicted an unemployed man (victim of bank failure) sitting disconsolately on a park bench.

He had no feed for the squirrel on the ground in front of him, begging for peanuts. "But why didn't you save some money for the future when times were good?" the squirrel asks. "I did," the man replied.

The rest of the business world was seen in the same sense of betrayal. The corporate world, as a result of the Great Depression, found itself restricted with regulations intended to protect the American people from capitalist excesses for the many of the following years. The people found hope in the New Deal—those who swarmed to Washington during the bitter winter of 1932 and '33 would bring their own hope.

Playwright Sherwood Anderson wrote in 1932 of the new expectations of government. "If there is to be a new world, we want it to be an American world. Many of us are looking forward to a new time of restlessness. There is much hidden just under the surface. There may well come soon now a time of protest, of wide discussion, of seeking. There will be new literature, a new romantic movement, new religious impulses. If the machine has really made for us a new world, we may at any time now begin the movement of trying to go into the new world. God grant it may be a better world."

Dad lived on hope, Mom on faith, and I lived in my dreams. 11-year-old Pat and nine-year-old Mel were beginning to develop a sense of purpose. In their future, they were determined to overcome the distressing events of The Great Depression and find a way to secure economic security and better life than we had in the depression era. My own hopes and dreams for a better life soon developed as I matured and grew. Americans today are a result of collective ambitions to reshape their own futures after the depression.

# Chapter 4

It was Christmas morning. The children huddled around the fire, wondering if Santa would find us in this strange new place. As a five-and-a-half-year-old who believed in Santa Claus, I had a hard time getting to sleep the night before, dreaming of the hard candies, juicy red apples, nuts, and oranges that I hoped would be in our stockings the next morning. Would there be a toy or pencils and paper to draw with? I had lain in bed for what seemed like hours, hoping to catch Santa in the act of delivering gifts, but fell asleep before Mom hung the stockings on the fireplace.

In his chair beside the fireplace, Dad rolled a cigarette and smoked alone until Mom joined him. His face glowed red from the flames, as he stared feverishly into the fire. Suddenly, his body began to shake and shiver uncontrollably, his heavy shoulders jerking from side to side violently. "Get some blankets, Hildred. Ple–a–ase. I'm freezing," he shivered.

Mom felt his forehead, "You're burning up, Mason. We'll have to sweat it out of you. There's no more quinine." She rustled in the boxes to find several quilts. "Get in bed now, it's just the fever—we'll get it under control." After helping him to bed, fully clothed, she packed quilts around him until perspiration dripped from his flushed face. His body continued to shake for a long while, until he finally fell asleep, as Mom sat beside him to wipe the sweat away.

Malaria fever came and went for each of us, almost from one day to the next. Mosquitoes tortured us from morning to night. In the winter, we slept under sheets to discourage them from biting but in summer, it was much too hot for that, so we endured as well as possible. Our parents tried to keep quinine on hand; there was never enough money for all our needs. *Malaria. Christmas—what will we eat? Stockings for the kids. Oh yes, better take care of that first.* There were one apple and an orange and a few nuts and hard candy for each child. Wearily, Mom found the stockings, filled them, and placed them on the hearth. *Food—flour, cornmeal. Water, milk, clean clothes, gasoline, kerosene, wood. Milk the cow. Feed the animals... How will we possibly manage? Bubba? Is he going to be all right?* Her mind filled with questions with few answers, and she wearily dropped into bed beside Dad's burning body. For a while, she tossed and turned, her mind reliving the past. Bad crops, washed away by the overflowing river after Mason was laid off his job as a grader operator on the highway, and all the crops washed away. On top of all that, losing Truman.

Then, Bubba was born—another mouth to feed, when they could hardly care for the others. Bubba's illness lasted for all those months until they learned he was allergic to cow's milk. Well, at least Bubba seemed to be slowly regaining his health. He could never replace Billy. Such a pleasant child before he died of pneumonia… while Bubba seemed to always be sick. And now, back to hill country in this house—in which most people wouldn't place their animals. It can't be helped. The depression can't last forever, though it had already been three years since the banks failed. Well, at least they hadn't lost any money—there had been none to lose. Finally, she told herself that God would provide. He always did—then she slept to the sound of sleet on the metal roof. Somehow, the sound comforted her instead of filling her with fear that their house would wash away during the night. In a few days, the New Year would arrive, and she hoped it would be better.

The winter of 1932 was one of the coldest on record. Even the roaring fire Dad started when he got up hardly numbed the cold. The rain had stopped. Outside, the sun rose over trees glistening with a silver thaw, and the ground was covered with sleet that hid the red soil beneath the frozen land. The beauty of it took his breath away. He piled more wood on the fire and found an old sweater to cover his back where the heat from the flames did not reach. Life on Christmas morning required a good cup of coffee and some hot oatmeal for the still sleeping family.

He found a bucket and filled it from the spring down the hill. The water was already freezing before he reached the house, but the wind didn't cut through him as it had in the delta when it whipped across the mighty river. Ice crystals had formed on the ground which had swollen with blue-white shining ice crystals. It covered every straggled leaf hanging from the giant trees. Brush along the ground hung thick and heavy with it. Even the sky was a grey-blue silver color.

The children stared, committed it to a photographic memory and never forgot that it was prettier even than the Christmas lights and decorations as they drove through the little town yesterday. I hugged my quilts around me, dragging them in front of the fire where I could both see through the window and stay warm, but I was absorbed in the stuffed stockings on the hearth. The others joined me to inspect the contents of the stockings. I poured mine out on the floor to see the contents. Mel and Pat both began nibbling on the apples, while little Bubba did not seem to know what to do. Mom, who had been busy making coffee in the kitchen, came in and watched, smiling. "I'm glad Santa found us," she said, "But I guess his load was a little empty by the time he found us. Maybe next year he'll find us a little sooner." She turned to Mason. "How're you feeling today?"

"Better. Maybe I can get some quinine before it hits again," he stated, "In case you or the kids need it. It seems to hit you all a lot harder than me."

# Chapter 5

Appalachia in Mississippi's 1930s was a land of contrasts and extremes—thickly wooded hills and impassable swamps surrounded by red clay soil that grew cotton like no other place on earth. Its people were divided between the fiercely proud rich and the poor—black and white, old aristocracy, and new immigrants. Mississippi, the utmost of all southern states, held passionate emotions about their church, their relatives, and especially their independence. Although a few of the old aristocrats considered the poor white farmer "white trash," others delegated them to a slightly higher cast. Most were clean even if they often had to break the ice in their bucket of spring water in winter to wash, and most were hard and honest workers. "Sharecroppers," who worked tenant farms, had a lower social worth, but stuck together, helped each other, and established their own pecking order. Blacks and "trash," on the other hand, were simply ignored by the old families—the aristocracy—but sharecroppers found a way to help them, often when they could not help themselves. They reasoned that someone had to take pity on the "poor white trash"—families who were starving because they were too shiftless too ignorant to work. There was no one else to help. But no tenant farmer considered that he was a member of the "poor white" class.

Sharecroppers paid the rent on the land they farmed with a share of the crops they made, but after supplies provided by the owners were paid, there was often little left to share if in fact the crops could be sold at all in those hard times. Most owned only a mule, or at best a couple of them, to pull the plows that sometimes the owner provided. All "croppers" as tenant farmers were known, coveted the land, dreaming of the time they would own some of their own. Nothing was as important as the land. Land meant a chance for future prosperity, own a respectable home, and graze fat, healthy cattle and sleek horses and be, if not landed gentry, at least reasonably secure.

Occasionally, Old Classie, a black woman of uncertain years would appear, walking only God only knows how far, to take care of Mom's sisters and brothers' families. She was the nearest thing to God to all of us. A daughter of one of the family's former slaves who was born there and served the family during the Civil War, she was kind and gentle and loving. Everyone considered her an important part of the family, yet she never sat down at the table to eat with any of them. She'd wait for them to finish their meals and then she would eat her food. It was an unspoken way of showing respect, but the family expected it. It was the way of the Old South. Everyone loved and revered her for her devotion, but had no way to pay for her help. Each family gave her what they had to give—canned goods, a piece of salt pork, milk and butter, or perhaps a bit of coffee or sugar, or some old clothes.

Classie was an integral part of the family as long as anyone could remember. She walked from one of Mom's sisters and brothers to another, delivering babies, doing the laundry, cooking and caring for the sick, asking for little except their love. If God is in His heaven, Classie is probably sitting next to Him informing him of His subject's needs.

In depression years, Classie was already old, but she lived to well over 90 and as long as she could manage, she made the rounds of the aunts and uncles to fill whatever need there happened to be. She took care of babies and the ill, washed dishes and did the laundry. She drew the line at picking cotton but could be induced to help in case bad weather was expected to ruin the crop—although she grumbled about doing it. She hated it almost as much as we did—dragging a heavy bag of cotton behind her, bending in half or crawling on her knees to grasp soft cotton from the sharp hulls that held it. When she became too old to fill her appointed rounds the family took care of her needs as well as they could. If she ever saw a doctor or a dentist in her life, no one was aware of it but she appeared to be healthy. Sometimes, she sang old Negro spirituals as she worked.

Classie gave her services cheerfully and always seemed more concerned for others than herself. She was not the only visitor. Almost daily some unkempt stranger would appear at a farmer's door to ask for a piece of bread and a place to sleep for the night in return for cutting firewood or doing other chores. Mr. Man was a frequent visitor to the Layton home who had asked to sleep in the hayloft many times. Like many who had fallen on hard times during the depression, he rode the rails or hitch-hiked to search for a handout in return for his services. Unlike some others, Mr. Mann expected to pay for what he received. He shared the food, joshed with the children, cut firewood and weeded the garden or repaired roofs or fences. The children were fascinated with him and grew to love him. He captured us with stories of people and places he had experienced in his travels and told us about the "bulls" that guarded the rail cars he rode and how he out-witted them.

The youngsters learned something of the character of our countrymen from him—the kindness, disappointments, fears, and emotions of his fellow travelers. He told of facing shotgun threats from those who were afraid of him to kindness from others who accepted him as a member of the unfortunate in those trying times. Either Mr. Mann had few bad experiences in the hobo jungles he frequented or refused to talk about them to the children. But he would grin and tell us about the mulligan stews he and his fellow travelers made under the railroad tresses. Each person contributed something—a rabbit or squirrel, bread, wild garlic they had picked, or fruits and vegetables pilfered from a farmer during the night. But all farmers knew when they found rows of corn with missing ears or empty spaces in the cabbage or sweet potato patch. Sometimes a chicken disappeared, and when watermelons were in season, there were empty rinds thrown into the brush beside the field.

The farm families grumbled about the losses, but mostly because things were taken without permission. No farmer had any use for thieves, and most would give freely whatever they could spare to the less fortunate. It was a major loss to farm families when their chickens were stolen because it was often the only meat we had. So, when Classie or the derelict from the rail yards showed up, it was the only help the Laytons had when family members were ill or unable to complete the necessary chores for survival on a Mississippi poor dirt farm.

Pegleg Pete showed up once and ended up staying to help with the plowing, hopping the rows strangely on his one good leg and his wooden peg in return for a place to sleep and the food we shared with him. He cut and stacked firewood, cleared land, burned brush, helped butcher the pigs when we had them, brought water from the spring, and fed the animals. Ultimately, "Pegleg" Pete apparently did something to displease Dad. If he knew what happened, he never disclosed it to the rest of the family, but suddenly he was gone with no explanation. Several months later he reappeared. It is still a mystery, but our gentle, loving shepherd—mix dog, who seldom met a stranger, suddenly went after Pegleg Pete. He tried to hop and run from the dog before he did real damage to Pete's good leg. No one saw him again.

The New Year arrived in a white world; six inches of snow lay heavy on the trees, bending their limbs nearly to the ground. Occasionally, there was the loud cracking sound as limbs broke beneath their weight.

The new school year began for Mel and Pat, who usually enjoyed it, but now they preferred to stay home and play in the snow. Mom would not allow that; she was determined that her children get an education. After breakfasting on oatmeal, Mel and Pat hurriedly dressed in their warmest clothes and started the long trek to meet the school bus that would take them to their new school. I cried to be allowed to go with my sisters to school. Mom told me that I was too young, but I had hovered over my sister's books so long that I felt I knew the words. Sadly, I watched them hike through the snow in their thin shoes and light coats.

By the time they returned from school at nearly 5:00 pm, they were drenched to the skin and their shoes were so heavy with red clay mud they could hardly lift their feet. The snow had melted, turning the clay into a thick paste that attached to their shoes like a magnet. They scraped their shoes off as well as possible and started their chores. I drove the cows from the pasture to the barn while Mel helped Mom milk them, while Pat started supper in the big old iron wood stove in the kitchen. Then, I slipped and slid down the bill to bring several buckets of water from the spring to finish my chores for the day.

After homework was done, Pat read aloud from her Weekly Reader. The candidate for president, Franklin Roosevelt, it reported, wanted to pass bills to help the small farmer by lending them money for seeds (later horses or mules) to pull the plows, and many other programs to help tenant farmers buy their own land. From that day on, Roosevelt became the next thing to God to our household. There was no radio, but Mom and Dad tried to keep up with current events through the subscription to a farmer's magazine, what they could learn in town when they did the weekly marketing and talking with neighborhood farmers.

I remember clinging to my mother's skirt one day when a man came to our door peddling magazines. Reluctantly, she allowed the salesman into the house, but when he showed her the Farmer's Almanac he was selling, she looked miserable and exasperated. She told him, "We have no money for magazines. It is all we can do to buy necessities."

"What if I agreed to take something in trade?" he insisted.

"Do you have any old jewelry—anything?" he asked.

"I don't have any jewelry except an old cameo my mother gave me, and it's one of my most sentimental possessions now that she is gone. It isn't worth much and even if it were valuable, I wouldn't want to trade it."

The salesman persisted, "Can I see it? Maybe we can do business."

Reluctantly, Mom looked into a little box she kept of her treasurers and produced the little cameo brooch for his inspection.

Mom's eyes were brimming with tears as she handed over her little treasure. I found her later in the kitchen crying her eyes out. Mom never could resist a sad story, and she grieved over the incident for a long time. Her hunger for reading material apparently was stronger than her sentimentality. The entire family poured over the little publication for an entire year.

There was no doubt who would be the next president of the United States in rural Mississippi. Everyone was sick of President Hoover, whom everyone believed was the cause of all the homeless who gathered in camps called Hooverville.

In Washington, D. C., WWI veterans gathered to demand that Congress pass the promised bonus, but General Douglas McCarthy and his young aid, Major Dwight D. Eisenhower, fired upon them, then overturned and burned their make-shift shelters. Two inhabitants and some policemen were killed. There was no one to blame for the hard times but Herbert Hoover.

When Hoover announced that he could solve the nation's problems by asking the Senate to pass a national sales tax to balance the budget, no one cared about the national government—people only wanted jobs so they could feed their families. There were no jobs, no money, and food was scarce. Children had inadequate clothes or shoes. People asked how the government could get money out of turnips. Farmers wanted to be able to sell their crops. Everyone blasted Hoover's attempt to pass the National Reconstruction Finance Corporation as a "steal from the poor to give to the rich" proposal.

People applauded Huey Long for his filibuster against a banking bill that would only make things worse—if things could get any worse. It was too much for the average population when Hoover made the statement that selling applies on the street was the way to get a better price for them when no one could sell their crops anyway. In cities and towns, thousands lined up at soup kitchens, often to find that the soup was gone by the time they wound through the long lines.

Hungry marchers invaded Washington, D. C., and riot police barricaded in the Capitol. Farms all across the country were being repossessed and some owners guarded their farms with rifles and shotguns. Roosevelt was the only hope anyone had. Banks were falling like rotten apples all across America. 21 states had declared partial or total bank holidays, and others teetered on the brink. Gold reserves were below the amount needed to back the currency and the treasury could not meet the government payroll. The United States was bankrupt. Our family had no money to lose, but every farmer knew no one could buy crops until the banks became healthy. There was a sense of doom, lost hopes and dreams. People gathered after church each week to discuss their problems. Someone had to do something, and the Laytons believed that no one could be worse than Hoover.

Both Mom and Dad supported the young Roosevelt, while others thoroughly hated him, saying that he wanted to discard the U. S. Constitution and was a tool of Communists—or wanted to be a dictator. His ideas were new and radical, but my family believed, "The ox is in the ditch and someone has to get him out." Many who supported him were also afraid of what he would do. Even Mom and Dad, who never questioned America's capitalist system, worried that he might turn the country Socialist, or at worse Communist. Even Dad was apprehensive when he predicted that someday we would have to fight Soviet Communists. I remember feeling horrified at the thought.

When Roosevelt made his inaugural address, the family crowded around a radio at a neighbor's house to hear him speak.

"This great nation will endure as it has endured, will revive and will prosper... the only thing we have to fear is fear itself." His powerful voice was smooth and confident. It was a call to battle—a challenge to those who had lost hope. "This Nation asks for action, and action now." He asked the Congress for broad Executive power to wage a war against the emergency, as great as the power that would be given if we were, in fact, invaded by a foreign foe.

# Chapter 6

Fear again reigned across the country when Roosevelt declared a national bank holiday, with gold hoarding a violation punishable by a fine of $10,000 or ten years.

Will Rogers quipped, "This is the happiest day in three years. We have no jobs, we have no money, we have no banks; and if Roosevelt had burned down the Capitol, we would have said, 'Thank God, he started a fire under something.'"

While I longed to join her sisters in school, I spent my time hovered in a corner with one of my sister's old books, sketched on used school papers with the stub of a pencil, or helped Mom with the laundry or my usual chores: gathering the eggs, feeding the chickens and pig, bringing in wood for the kitchen stove and fireplace, then driving the cow from the pasture to the barn for milking.

During those forays, I studied cloud formations, made note of the shape, color, and texture of trees, brush, water, rocks, and grass. In my mind's eye, I painted these scenes on a canvas with bold, brilliant colors, and shadows of grey and blue and lavender. I would be an artist and writer and would travel the world in search of adventure, and as I walked, I invented great stories about Indian tribes kidnapping me in exotic countries and allowing me the freedom to go my way because of my bravery or skills. I would be a ballerina as I danced across the pastures either mimicking steps I could only imagine, or do cartwheels and back flips that I had seen my sisters trying.

Sometimes, I climbed the huge old maple in the middle of the pasture and dreamed of flying into the sky and back down to the ground. While there, I once had a dream so vivid that I was certain I had risen from the earth high into the sky before lowering gently to the ground. It was only at night that I dreamed of falling deep into a well for an indeterminable time, waking to see myself lying flat at the bottom. Sometimes, there was water in the well, and I awakened, cold and thoroughly disgusted for wetting the bed again. It con-sumed me with self-hatred, anger, and humiliation. That humiliation was with me afterward for many years. Every night before going to bed, I told myself repeatedly, "I will not wet the bed tonight. I will not wet the bed tonight. I will wake up in time." But nothing helped. Each day, I was confronted by a despairing mother and sisters who teased, cajoled, and nagged.

One day, I awakened to find Mom sitting at the kitchen table, holding her ashen face in her hands. It wasn't like her, who never stopped working from five in the morning until nine at night when she sewed for the kids. She told me that she was ill and that I must take care of my little brother. She was often not well, so I paid little attention. Living in my own little dream world, I had learned little about compassion for others. Mom groaned a little for a while, and then went back slowly and painfully to her usual tasks.

Several days later, Mom and I loaded the dirty laundry into a sheet and carried it to the spring to do the laundry. Sometimes, she entertained me by singing a funny little ditty as we worked together, but there was no song this time. She worked slowly and painfully as she bent over the washboard with grim determination. We washed sheets and pillowcases first on a rub board and then boiled them in the big black tub over a fire. My job was to fill two tubs with water, one for washing and the other for rinsing, and then transfer the clothes into boiling water. After the clothes boiled for a while, I lifted the clothes from the boiler with a broomstick for a final rinse. Then, we wrung out the heavy pieces together—on each side of the sheets or towels—twisting the fabric opposite directions to remove the water.

There was a smaller bucket where old flour sacks were soaked in pale red water. "What is this, Mom?" I asked.

"Well, you're too young to worry about things like that," she answered. Years later, I learned that she had suffered a miscarriage and had used the flour sacks for pads, as was the custom in that era. No one spoke of such things. The pads were washed and re-used as long as the fabric held together. The fetus was buried in a box in the oak grove behind the little home. There was never another word spoken on the subject until after Mom died at the age of 86 when Dad finally told me about it.

Now Mom had two children to grieve for—the child they lost at nine months old of pneumonia before I was born, and now this little one. Perhaps she was glad there wasn't another mouth to feed when there was so little for the rest of the family.

Dad worked at cutting cross ties all winter, earning a little when the railroads were buying. He would cut trees from the hill behind our house, remove the bark, and hew them almost square with a crude, sharp hand tool. I watched the muscles in his broad shoulders ripple as he worked, and thought he must be the strongest man in the world. Mom sold eggs, milk, and butter, or traded them for staples in town. Sometimes, I helped Dad clear land when he wasn't cutting firewood, looking for a job, or cutting and shaping cross ties to sell to the railroads. I delighted in setting fire to the huge piles of brush he had cut from small hillsides for a small plot to grow something on. Dad showed me how to gather small twigs to start the fire, and how to light the matches without burning my small fingers, trusting me to carry on without further supervision. It was much more fun to work with Dad. I enjoyed the woodsy setting, cold wind in my hair and the skill as I broke smaller branches and added them to the pile to burn. It wasn't women's work, which I did not like. Dad sang or told entertaining stories as we worked, and did not complain that his back hurt.

Mom's strange behavior began in 1933. The children often heard her crying or screaming at Dad. She was short and impatient with us or nagged that we wouldn't help her do anything; she was worn out and couldn't do it all herself while we wasted time reading. She started yelling that we would never amount to anything with our heads in a book all the time or wasting time climbing trees.

# Chapter 7

Mel snapped, "Who wants to help an old nag?" which only increased her screaming. Her arguments with Dad worsened, and she would accuse him of not trying to provide the flour and coal oil they needed so badly. She was sick of the sawmill gravy she made with meals instead of flour to go with our biscuits. The supply of molasses was nearly gone and the cornmeal would run out soon. There was no more "fatback" bacon, and the children had nothing to take to school for their lunches.

At first, we tried to get out of her way while she was having a tantrum, but the tension grew until everyone was yelling at everyone. The children started talking back disrespectfully to her, and she would kneel in the middle of the floor and pray hysterically at the top of her lungs, "God, forgive them for they know not what they do." No one, least of all Dad, understood that she was exhausted and often hungry, or perhaps the miscarriage and death of her son had brought on her insane behavior. Still, she persisted in keeping the milking, ironing, cooking, laundry, and sewing, sometimes crying as she worked. She demanded that Dad butcher the old goat we had bought to milk for Bubba since he no longer needed the milk. The children protested. That goat was a pet, and we had no intention of eating it. But Mom cooked it and we ate it even if it did have a strong odor and the meat was stringy.

Then, one day, we found our old mule, "Old Blue," mired up to his head in the pond. It had wandered in to get a drink and the mud had sucked him deeper and deeper. Dad grabbed halters and rope and tried to lead the poor animal out, but it was no use. Dad also soon became mired in the mud so deep that it was difficult to extradite him. He couldn't afford to lose the only mule he had to pull the plows—there had to be a way to get it out. Finally, he struggled out of the mud, went to get the old truck and drove it as close to the pond as he could. He then attached a rope to the truck and tied the other end to the animal, and started to try to pull Old Blue out of the muck.

The little truck grunted, groaned and roared, moving only a few inches at a time. Mom stood on the bank screaming that he was going to choke the animal. "Well, what do you suggest?" Dad answered angrily, "He'll choke from the mud if we don't get him out."

Mom sighed, "We have to do what we have to do."

There was no choice. The truck labored an inch at a time. The mule's piercing neighs hurt our ears, and his eyes rolled with fear, but inch by inch he was pulled from the pond. He was so weak that he lay on the ground quivering for a long time, while we struggled to get him to stand up. When we finally got him to his feet he wobbled painfully home to the barn. He was unhealthy for weeks, and Dad realized that he had developed distemper. He treated him with everything he knew about distemper. In time the animal recovered some of his strength but was never strong again.

Big storms, with lightning and thunder, were common in the area. We were used to them and only slightly afraid of them. Then one day we were all terrified when the sky lit up, black clouds gathered and vociferous thunder and wind howled outside the little house. The wind whipped tree limbs as we watched them lose their attachment to their roots and tossed them through the air like broom straws. The sky was full of uprooted debris that slammed into the house, threatening to overturn it. Suddenly, the house rocked from pier post to pier post, first on one and then the other side of the house, only to settle back down like a sledgehammer.

I felt sure we would fly through the air like the debris. Mom was hysterical with fear. Bubba dove under a bed. Finally, it stopped as quickly as it had started, and we were safe. We had caught only a small part of the Tornado of 1936 that struck Tupelo, Mississippi that still ranks at number four in America in terms of the number of people killed.

The massive funnel had moved east-northeast across central Lee County, passing through residential areas in the northern half of Tupelo, over 35 miles from our house. The tornado leveled over 200 homes, many of good construction on the west side of town. It completely swept away poorly constructed homes several miles to the west of town and on the northeast side of town. Entire families were killed, up to 13 in a single home. When the official death toll of 216 was set, there were still over 100 people in hospitals in three states. Many were in serious or critical condition. The Mississippi State Geologist estimated the final death toll at 233. Since only the names of the white injured were published in newspapers, it is not possible to know the fate of the black injured. This racial aspect of tornado documentation was common until the late-1940s, and occasionally present in some form, for many years afterward.

About 150 box cars were brought to town as temporary housing. A movie theater was turned into a hospital and the popcorn machine used to sterilize instruments. This tornado had an estimated cost of $3,000,000 in the little town of Tupelo. The Laytons were spared, but many homes closer to Tupelo were damaged.

Mom's periodic insanity continued and she and Dad quarreled more and more. No one wanted to risk her wrath so everyone tried to stay out of her way and do their chores without prompting from her. It didn't occur to us to think it strange when one of her relatives visited, or that when we went to church, she was calmer and more content, happily singing the hymns and greeting neighbors. It never occurred to us that few visitors arrived except on Sunday, or that Sunday was a day of rest in which no one in our family worked except for the most essential chores. Mom always dressed immaculately on the Sabbath, brushing her hair until it shone, and her mood seemed to change as if by magic.

Sundays were a day to attend church or sometimes to visit relatives when weather and muddy roads permitted. If the roads were too muddy, we would take the wagon to the church about a mile or so away. Occasionally, one of Mom or Dad's sisters or brothers visited us. Those visits with our little cousins and beloved aunts and uncles, who bragged on our looks and told us how smart we were, created never forgotten memories. Mom could usually find enough food to load the table down with biscuits and gravy, fried chicken, canned green beans or turnip greens or last year's dried black-eyed peas.

If she had nothing for dessert, she would make her fried sugar pies made from dough filled with sugar and butter, or sometimes chocolate or cinnamon. The dough was rolled into a thin, round circle, then filled with the mixture and folded into a crescent shape. She would crimp the edges of the dough and drop it into a frying pan. The filling would leak out and melt in the butter it was fried in, turning it a deep caramel color, which she'd spread over the dough. It was crisp, sweet and filling. For years, this was the main desert the children took in lunch boxes to school, but we were ashamed of it, while other children ate their "loaf bread" sandwiches and store-bought cookies. None of us appreciated how good our "sugar pies" were until the other children started asking to trade them for their sandwiches or cookies.

If the weather was good, sometimes we piled into the old truck and braved the deep ruts in the clay dirt roads to visit relatives. We loved visiting Dad's brother, Uncle Mint and Aunt Ollie, about ten miles away, which could take almost half the day on the muddy roads in winter. In summer when the roads were dry, we choked on the cloud of dust that billowed behind our little 1927 Chevrolet as we coasted down the steep roads and struggled up the next hill. We had to go down a steep hill to Chewalla Creek Bottom, then up another long, steep, treacherous hill that required all the horse-power the little truck had.

There were always some spots along the way where rain washed deep pockets of heavy sand and we invariably became stuck in it. Dad would have to back the truck up repeatedly to get enough speed to make it through the sand-traps. Often, the entire family got behind the truck to push it before making it up the hill. Mom would invariably become hysterical as the truck threatened to slip into the side ditches, where there was deep quicksand that was nearly impossible to get out of. But the children loved Aunt Ollie and her "sodie" (soda) biscuits and thick slabs of smoked ham and homegrown butter beans.

Aunt Ollie was the most serene person I've ever known. She went about her household duties with a pleasant look on her face, wearing a shapeless cotton dress made from flour sacks and when she stood in a doorway, it was plain that she wore no underwear or bra. Nothing seemed to faze her, even when her four children misbehaved or one of the aggressive geese she raised for eggs and feathers for her thick, spongy beds threatened her.

Occasionally, I spent the night there in a thick bed that Aunt Ollie had constructed from her supply of goose feathers. I sunk into it, dreaming of sleeping on a cloud. It was wonderful, until the next day I awoke with numerous bites from bedbugs that also inhabited the bed.

The only time I ever saw Aunt Ollie disturbed was when she asked me to watch her baby while she did the laundry by the spring that supplied their source of water. She placed a blanket and baby on the ground a few feet above the spring and told me to take care of it while she rubbed the clothes on a rub board. I must have fallen asleep because the next thing, I knew both the baby and me were upside down in the spring. I was soaked, but apparently held the baby high enough above the water that she didn't get wet.

Aunt Ollie snorted, "I'm just about to say poot!" That was the nearest I ever heard an expletive from her. Many years later before she died of cancer in her '80s, she stoically announced with a smile that she had some "female problems."

Our cousins always had fireworks on the Fourth of July and the children spent the day setting off giant firecrackers under tin cans or buckets or sometimes throwing them at each other. Aunt Ollie would mildly admonish us to be careful, but we never were. Often, we went home with burns from explosions, and once, I nearly blew my thumb off.

Sometimes we would have shooting contests with our cousin's 22 caliber rifle. Someone would set up a tin can on a fence, but that was too easy. I demanded they put a shotgun shell there, and I would show them how to hit it.

Russell wedged the shell firmly in a tree branch and said, "Bet you can't hit the firing pin!" I did, developing a reputation as the best shot in the family. At home, when they butchered hogs, Dad allowed me to shoot them. It gagged me but no one knew that. I was proud of my skill and thought shooting was great fun. Each of the children had been taught how to use a rifle, but none of us knew much about using Dad's heavy 12-gauge shotgun that he used for hunting squirrels.

# Chapter 8

My assignment was to bring water from the spring, which was down a long, steep hill that I always ran down, then struggle slowly back up with two gallons of water. As I filled the buckets with water, I noticed something chattering and moving leaves in a huge nearby tree. It was a couple of big grey squirrels—the kind that Dad killed and Mom fried to a delicious golden brown. The family was always short of food that winter, and my only thought was that I had to kill at least one of those squirrels.

I tiptoed quietly away from the spring, leaving buckets where they were, and ran back to the house to get Dad's old double-barreled shotgun, which I had never shot before. But I knew I could do it. I sneaked back as quietly as possible not to frighten them away. I had accompanied Dad on several hunting trips and watched him kill game. You cock the gun, aim it, and then fire. You settle the stock firmly into your shoulder, aim, and fire. I knew the gun kicked—Dad had explained that but it didn't worry me. Nothing to it. So, I stood at the base of that big tree, cocked the heavy long-barreled gun, set the sight firmly on one of the squirrels high in the tree, and fired. The squirrel didn't fall, but I did. The percussion knocked me down, and I went tumbling down the hill with the gun falling behind me.

Mom and Dad were so relieved that I wasn't hurt that they forgot to spank me, but I got a lecture to last the rest of my life.

Spankings were common in our house. If the children failed to obey a command, behaved irresponsibly, or disrespected Mom or Dad, we were spanked. Mom would gather a slender switch from the peach tree. The blows stung our legs and left thin red stripes but the marks disappeared quickly. We told each other, "It won't last long," and endured, though it was doubtful that it improved our behavior for long.

It was worse for Pat and Mel; perhaps Mom became more tolerant toward the younger children or expected less from them. Mel especially resented the punishments, and they only made her more stubborn and disobedient. She and Mom (and sometimes Dad) were always at loggerheads. They always said she was the most stubborn child alive, but the punishments only made it worse. Mel was her own person, and no one would change her or make her do anything that she refused to do.

On several occasions, Dad beat her unmercifully, repeatedly, but she just endured it, screaming, *"You can beat me to death before I'll give in."* After such incidents, Dad was determined to break her spirit or die trying. Pat was more compliant except when she felt that the punishment exceeded the misdeed. Then, she would find devious ways to make our parents sorry they had punished her unjustly.

Dad only spanked us when our behavior was completely out of line, but when he did we knew we had been spanked. He used his razor strap, a long black piece of leather that he used to sharpen his straight razor. Sometimes he only hit us lightly a few times, but if we angered him, he could leave purple bruises from the strap on our legs.

No one in that era considered spankings to be a form of violence against children even when done inexcusably in anger, but my anger was beginning to develop over the cruelty I perceived when we were spanked. As a result, we towed the disciplined line established for us. You respect your elders; you do what you're told to do. We had firm boundaries to guide us and if there were any drugs, rock and roll, or sex to worry about, we were totally unaware of it. If our parents' values weren't strong enough, we always had the God-fearing church that made us afraid of wrongdoing or thinking. We were told that erroneous thinking was no different than wrongdoing.

# Chapter 9

1933 was the height of the depression. Black Thursday and the crash of 1929 had not affected the rural south—most never had enough money for food and shelter, much less investing in the stock market. Roosevelt had seen the tragedy suffered by the poor in Warm Springs, Georgia—the tenant shacks, the lack of food and clothes and the hollow-eyed children who clung to their mother's coattails, shivering in the cold. From the back of his campaign trail, he had heard the pleas from dirt poor farmers, the homeless, and the hordes of unemployed throughout the country. While many of the poor wondered how a man born with a silver spoon in his mouth could possibly understand the plight of the poor, somehow, he seemed to have empathy for poverty-stricken citizens and was determined to do something about it.

In his first 100 days, Roosevelt called a special session and battered Congress to pass multiple measures that he hoped would bring the country back to normalcy. The Agricultural Adjustment Act was an allotment plan which gave farmers subsidies for reducing acreage for some crops. He believed this would increase the price of commodities. While some farmers agreed with the act, many consumers knew that the cost of food would increase. FDR assured them that their prices would not go up.

Another bill created the Civilian Conservation Corp, which would give 250,000 jobs to young men who would plant trees, improve roads, and build or remodel buildings, among other things.

Roosevelt's Federal Emergency Relief Act provided $500 million for food and shelter for the homeless and dispossessed. It was a drop in a bucket, but more money was later appropriated. The Farm Credit Administration established low-interest loans to farmers who were facing foreclosure.

This bill alone saved thousands of farms throughout the country. The Home Owners Loan Act established a revolving $2 billion fund for homeowners who faced foreclosure. Most of his programs did little or nothing for us. When we finally allowed our pride to accept food subsidies, there was oatmeal, dried fruit, flour, and a few items that we used, but we needed cash for oil for the lamps, and shoes and coats to keep us warm. After all, we lived on a farm, where we dried or canned our own fruit, but the flour and oatmeal allowed us to sell the eggs that we usually had for breakfast.

The Emergency Railroad Transportation Act was enacted on May 4. The bill intended to coordinate the rail transportation system, consolidate lines and institute regulatory reform.

[2]On April 19, Congress passed a bill allowing the United States to go off the gold standard. Roosevelt was concerned about the deflationary pressures of his economic measures and believed that the dollar would find its own level and give international trade a boost. It provided fines for hoarding gold and annulled clauses in both public and private contracts that required debts to be repaid with a specific content of gold. On May 17, the National Industrial Recovery Act was passed, authorizing a $3.3 billion public works program to provide jobs and increase buying power. It suspended antitrust laws, set maximum hours of labor and minimum wages, and guaranteed collective bargaining rights. When Roosevelt signed the bill, he stated, "The law I have just signed was passed to put people back to work." History will probably record the NIRA as the most important and far-reaching legislation ever created by the American Congress. In his first 100 days, Roosevelt had sent 15 messages to Congress demanding immediate action and all 15 had been enacted. His promise of "bold, persistent experimentation," was fulfilled.

By the middle of June, the stock market reached the highest level in two years. Factories were beginning to hire again, and relief programs were feeding the hungry hoards. CCC camps were hiring young men—some for the first jobs they had ever held. Crops came to market that fall, instead of being burned.

Mom and Dad credited FDR because they were able to sell their bale of cotton that fall, but most of the other measures changed our lives very little. It was a constant struggle to provide clothes and shoes and put food on the table.

Mom sadly said, "Maybe next year will be better with the good Lord's help." That winter, we were notified that a program to use surplus cotton for bedding would be taught in the local church. Mom immediately signed up, along with most of our neighbors. They were taught to construct to compress the thick cotton into the ticking for mattresses. Our shuck mattresses were exchanged for cotton, and I no longer had to sleep with my two sisters. They were ecstatic that they would no longer be awakened in a bed that I had flooded. My brother and I now shared a bed, Pat and Mel had one, and Mom and Dad had another. Unfortunately, it exasperated my bedwetting problem; the cotton didn't dry as quickly as shucks and wet cotton could not be removed. But we dragged the heavy mattress out into the sun or propped it up in front of the fire to dry. The odor just got worse. I tried to retreat into my dream world, but the problem refused to go away.

Dad signed up for WPA for work that fall, when he wasn't farming, cutting firewood, or hewing cross ties for the railroad. There were hundreds of men ahead of him, but occasionally, he would get work for a day or two for 50 cents a day.

Mom seemed pleased. "It keeps the wolf away from the door," she declared. This cash was used mostly to buy "half-soles" for our worn-out shoes. Dad glued or tacked the half soles on by stretching shoes over metal last. I called them my holy soles…

Cutting trees for cross ties, hewing them by hand, then hauling them to town was slow, tedious work but better than traveling four miles to town only to find no work available was even worse. When the railroad stopped buying, he made the rounds of adjacent farms, searching for trades. Sometimes Mom, Bubba, and I went with him, taking her eggs or butter to exchange. It was the only social life she had except for church and visits to or from relatives.

One day, Dad returned from a bartering trip with a tiny black puppy and several screeching piglets. "Meat for next fall!" he explained of the piglets.

"What are we going to feed that puppy with?" Mom asked angrily, "Don't we have enough mouths to feed?" But Dad usually had his way. The puppy delighted the children, but Mom nagged about him for years until he proved his worth. Both animals were fed with milk and table scraps. When there was little food for the pig, the children gathered pigweed, corn cobs, beet tops or vines to add to leftover dishwater.

I wondered how that soapy dishwater nourished the little pigs, but by the next fall, it was ready to butcher for delicious smoked hams, bacon, and chops. We celebrated the occasion by roasting portions of the loin on a stick over a fire. Nothing ever tasted quite as wonderful as that roasted loin.

Memorial Day was one of the highlights of every year when all the inter-related families gathered from miles around with their smoked hams, pies, cakes, homemade bread, canned fruits and produce for the annual tribute to their dead in the old family cemetery. Cars and trucks were load with baskets and boxes of iris, peonies, roses of every color, crepe myrtle, honeysuckle, and every other imaginable flower as the families weathered miles of old rutted, muddy or dusty roads, labored through swamps, thickly wooded hillsides and shaky old bridges to the site of the ancient dilapidated church to clean the graves of their ancestors.

The old cemetery was located in a sun-dappled dell of oaks, maples, and saplings, with wild grapevines intertwined with honeysuckle, which saturated the air with perfume. Grave markers from weathered boards to huge concrete statues marched across the area, with an occasional fenced-in area of family plots.

While the adults racked foot-high piles of leaves and pulled wild grape-vines from the graves and markers, the children chased each other or played hide and seek among the trees. The odor and smoke of wood smoke filled the air as they burned piles of leaves, broken tree limbs and debris from the graves. After clearing the graves, everyone pulled weeds and grass and rounded the graves into row after row of mounds. They worked until dinner (lunch) and then spread their huge baskets of food on long, heavy planks nailed between huge old oaks or maple trees. One of the elders offered an interminably long prayer while everyone waited for the feast to begin.

"That is the best cake I ever ate," one relative would say, while others bragged that another sister or brother's home-cured ham was mouthwatering.

"My cake was so light that it fell apart," complained one of the aunts, while another one apologized that her cucumbers or lettuce were slightly bit-ter that year.

"It's been too hot," another relative complained, wiping the sweat from his brow.

It was the occasion of the year for everyone to catch up with news of their relatives' activities, brag about their beautiful children and meet old rel-atives they had not seen for years.

"Mel is the prettiest," one aunt would say, while another would reply that my other sister was the prettiest. "My, how they've grown," was heard over and over.

Everyone piled their plates high and ate until they could eat no more. "Good gracious alive," they would say. "This is so good." Or, "I can't eat another bite." They visited for hours while their food settled and then re-turned to complete the work. When they were finished, the old cemetery gleamed with rows of fresh dirt mounds and markers dating back to the pre-vious century or earlier. Fragrant peonies, roses, and other flowers that had been piled on the mounds had changed the forested setting into a beautiful multihued aromatic garden that filled the senses with delight.

The yearly tradition continued for many years until the old church finally collapsed and the wooded gravesites filled in with young saplings and broken tree limbs after the families of the dead became too old or feeble to continue raking leaves and pulling vines and dead limbs from the graves.

We struggled home reluctantly with bulging stomachs, trailing an odor of wood smoke, smoked ham, and potato salad in our clothes, waving goodbye to all our cousins and aunts and uncles, "See you next year."

"Yawl come see us, now."

"It's your time. We came to see you last." We yelled goodbyes at each other as we roared down the dusty roads in an effort to be first in line to avoid the clouds of dust that overpowered the cars and coated the line of cars behind us with a thick paste of dust that all but obliterated our features. We tried to hold our breath or covered our nose with the hem of our dresses to avoid choking on the dust.

Before we reached Chewalla Creek an hour later, my sisters and I started pestering Mom and Dad to stop and let us clean up in the cool, clear waters of the stream. It was one of our favorite places in the world. The older girls often went there to splash and swim to cool off on hot summer days. I loved the surrounding trees and the primordial odor of swamp grasses and mud. The temperature could be 90 degrees in the shade, but you could feel the coolness of the creek bottom long before you arrived there. The atmosphere completely changed from nearly unbearable heat to an almost air-conditioned comfort as we approached. Occasionally, Mom took us there to fish for bass and crappie in the creek's cool depths, where I later learned to swim. Sometimes, our pleas were heard and we were allowed to remove our shoes to wade knee-deep into the water and splash away the dust from our faces, arms, and legs.

It was a contemplative, pleasant time despite our blistered hands from handling hoes, shovels, and rakes until our parents pointed sadly to the dilapidated marker on our little brother's grave. Although I was born after his death, sadly, he still seemed to be a part of the family that I somehow grieved over.

# Chapter 10

Our small fields of cotton yielded only one bale that year. By the time the cotton was ginned, and the landowner took their share, there was nothing left except the seed for next year's planting. At least, Dad said, we were able to sell it for something, as little as it was.

There would be no new shoes or dresses except the ones Mom made from flour sacks for us. Now that picking cotton was finished, Mom's little peddle sewing machine hummed as she bent over it to make our school clothes. She washed and bleached the rough cotton muslin, then cut out dresses from the pattern of an older dress. Sometimes she bought a box of Rit dye and dipped the material in it for variations. At other times, she cut saved scraps into attractive decorations or purchased a bit of rick-rack to apply to collars or pockets. Some manufacturers in the 1930s began to sell flour in attractive flowered or patterned sacks which made much more attractive dresses that she made for us, and she used the white sacks for undergarments like panties and slips.

School began after the harvest was in. I was full of excitement and anticipation because I would be allowed to attend school this year. But it was not to be a good beginning.

The children on the bus started teasing me about my flour sack dresses. They found that I didn't take kindly to teasing and it only made things worse. They were insulting me and I was not going to take it, so I fought them. Soon they started calling me "little Banta rooster." Because I fought back, I became the brunt of their cruel jokes. A sixth-grade bully named Russell made my life hell on the bus for most of my young years.

Nearly every day, I came home from school with purple bruises or black eyes. The bus driver never attempted to stop him from beating me up, and I refused to accept that I couldn't hold my own against the older, larger kid. By the time I reached school, I was trying desperately to keep from crying but I never complained to anyone else. I knew it wouldn't do any good.

Between the almost daily beatings on the school bus, Mom and Dad's constant fighting and my humiliation from awakening every day wet, cold and miserable from wetting the bed, I became more and more angry and shy. At school, I avoided recess activities and played alone on the swing set gym, or stood forlornly away from groups. I didn't need them—they were snobs, and I was better than they were.

Classmates often called upon me to recite just to hear the children's jeers at my embarrassment and fear. One teacher especially seemed to enjoy my humiliation. She would call on me to go to the board and write out answers to questions while other children answered from their desks. It angered me that she picked on me, but shaken and red-faced, I managed to get through the recitation. They all laughed when I shuffled to the front wearing the only dress I owned, with the soles of my shoes flopping. I felt ignorant and stupid, even though I could read as well as any of them. It was like waving a red flag in my face. The children seldom invited me to join their games and I was grateful for that. I didn't want anything to do with them. I would show them. I was determined to go to school and learn to read and write and no one would stop me. One tortuous day followed another and I withdrew into my shell of dreams, mental images, and imaginations. Words and images formed in my mind as Mel, Pat, and I walked the long mile to meet the school bus, and during the hour it took to get there, and I was almost oblivious to the cold, rain, sleet, or snow we struggled through. There was an old building where we huddled together for warmth while we waited for the bus to arrive. Sometimes, we built a fire to warm our frozen feet and hands if we arrived too early.

My anger built at the cruelty of the bully who picked and prodded me into a fight almost daily. I would learn to fight so the sixth-grader would not dare to bother me again. Even if it took the rest of my life, I would show them who and what I was made of. If the snobbish Daughters of the American Revolution, prosperous bank owner's kids, and goody-goody little monsters wanted to taunt me, I would never let them win. At home, I started training to be the fighter I wanted to be to protect myself. I shadow-boxed with my dad and little brother or sisters and with the few friends I had. If I got hurt, as I often did, I would not allow them to know it. I became immune to pain as my anger built.

Pat and Mel had their own battle with the daughters of the owner of the land we farmed. The two Higdon girls claimed certain seats on the bus and would allow no one else to sit there, so they decided to change that. After they got off the bus one evening, there was a knock-down, drag-out fight between my sisters and the Higdon sisters. My sisters lost and the Higdon girls retained the seats they claimed to be theirs. My bully tortured me until I finally moved away from the school three years later.

I loved to work with my Dad because he allowed me to help pull stumps from the ground as he cleared land for planting, then roll or drag them to a burn pile. He let me use the ax to cut branches from trees that he had fallen and to help pull the old crosscut saw when he cut trees or branches into firewood. I repeatedly carried huge armloads of firewood and dumped them into the wagon. Dad encouraged me by challenging me with "bet you can't lift that big log." I was his boy, and he wanted me to become tough as much as I wanted it. If he invited me to ride the mule to a field, I would usually refuse because it would make me stronger if I ran beside them. When I asked him to teach me to box, he taught me to move quickly and agilely, feign moves and ambush with a surprise left. He believed that everyone should know how to protect themselves, even little girls. He told me, "Never start a fight, but always be sure that you finish it if you are forced to fight." I wondered how a six-year-old girl could ever be strong enough to finish a fight with a 14-year-old boy, double my weight, but I would try to take his advice.

# Chapter 11

The malaria attacks continued. First one member of the family or another was sent to bed with chills and a high fever where we were alternately cold then burning with fever. Mom would pile on layers of quilts when we were chilled, and when they subsided, she made us endure the resulting heat until we sweated out the fever. Periodically, each of the children came down with the measles, chickenpox, or scarlet fever or mumps—one after the other. At other times, we suffered from constant boils that Mom called impetigo; even Mom and Dad often had huge painful pustules with thick yellow crusts that she opened with a needle to drain. If the abscess refused to drain, often she was forced to open it with Dad's straight razor and apply hot compresses until it drained.

Coal oil (turpentine) was our miracle drug. Mom wet a soft cloth in it and dabbed it on our sores each day until they dried up or drained. Even our animals were given a spoon full of coal oil for their illnesses. It seemed to work. It was the only medical treatment we had during our young lives. We were taught to clean our teeth with twigs that we chewed to soften the ends for brushes.

None of us connected our health problems to the spring water we drank and washed in or for use of the bushes and trees for a toilet. Our new President spoke of unsanitary living conditions in the rural south, but it would be many years before anything changed much. A new program began, however, for inoculations for smallpox, diphtheria, typhoid, and mumps—no doubt too late for some of us who had already suffered from the diseases, but undoubtedly saved some of the younger children.

The school instructed us that shots for smallpox would be given after school at Chewalla Church, en route home from school. Dutifully, we stopped at the church and received our shots. I walked the rest of the way home so ill that I didn't think I would make it. My head started pounding and I had a raging fever which kept me in bed for several days. When the sore on our arms healed, our scars were nearly as large as a silver dollar. Mom thought the nurses who administered the shots were ignorant of the correct dosage and had given us too much of the antitoxin. Still, she was grateful that at least we wouldn't have smallpox. "A dose of preventative is worth a pound of cure," she declared.

The school year gradually came to a close in time for the new growing season, and we returned to the fields, the garden and gathering of wild fruits for canning or making jellies. We gathered "salet" greens from a Poke plant almost daily from the hills and picked may apples and persimmons when they were ripe, between planting and weeding the seedlings we had planted.

I turned seven in June and was proud that I could now read and write. I practiced my new skills by trying to read my sisters' books. Next year, I would be allowed to bring books home from school and I could hardly wait.

Soon, it was watermelon season. Sometimes on Sunday, Dad would pick a large melon and take us to the creek for swimming. The water, coming from gushing hillside springs, was like ice, swift and clear. I asked Dad to teach me to swim. He showed me how to extend my arms over my head and grab the water ahead of me. After numerous failed attempts, he told me impatiently, "There's only one way to learn to swim. If I throw you in, you'll learn very quickly."

"I can't do it!" I screamed.

"There ain't no such thing as can't," Mom told me.

I protested, but when he threw me in, I knew it was either swim or drown. I swam. You do what you have to do.

"See what I mean?" Dad praised, as I returned to the shore. "You do what you have to do!"

It was a lesson that I would never forget but apparently, one that my Dad never learned. He was a farmer and didn't believe in working for anyone but himself and never would accept defeat. Those who owned their own land seldom made more than a few hundred dollars a year while we were sharecroppers who shared our crop with the owners. This fact did not compute in my father's mind. He was defeated before he ever began.

Summer passed quickly and it was harvest time. We gathered corn and stacked it into the little barn, then cut the stalks for fodder for the cow. Then, it was time for picking the cotton, and we gathered in the fields with our heavy sacks dragging behind us. It was hard, back-breaking work but had to be done. When we finally finished, the little barn was full, so we unloaded the wagon full of cotton and after rearranging the beds, piled it in the corner of our bedroom until we could take it to the gin. My brother Bubba and I begged to be allowed to sleep in it. It was so dusty that we could hardly breathe, but it was so soft and warm that we cuddled down in it and slept heavily.

But again, with our small acreage, the crop was too small to yield much more than a few dollars after we shared it with our landlord. Our one bale of cotton yielded enough to half-sole our shoes and buy a few yards of material for our school dresses. The cottonseed that remained would be retained for next year's crop.

Mom's discontent and unhappiness was growing. Another winter with inadequate clothing, insufficient food, and a house that leaked so badly that we had to place all our cooking utensils out to catch the drips was more than she could take. She announced, "This is the last year I am going to live in this place!"

Dad pleaded with her, "I'll clear more land this winter and we'll have a bigger crop next year," but Mom would not be swayed. For once, she replaced her nagging and complaining, with a firm position.

"If you don't find another place, I will. We've been here two years now and will never make a living here!" she announced. Soon, they were shouting and yelling at each other, but Dad saw that she was determined. While Mom seldom took so firm a stand, Dad knew that he would not change her mind. The search for a new home began.

Dad seemed to be happy with whatever situation we were in, while Mom would never be satisfied with poverty and deprivation.

# Chapter 12

Our new home had two bedrooms, a parlor, a kitchen, and a dining room. There was a third bedroom but it was locked, and the owner agreed to rent the house and 100 acres of land to us as long as her furniture could remain stored in the room. Both the large bedroom and parlor had a big fireplace, and we later sat around a roaring fire in the evening. An inviting porch stretched across the front of the house for a swing and perhaps a rocker or two, and there was a large barn, a dilapidated chicken house, and a well house in addition to a bubbling spring beneath the hill.

The well house contained a cistern where water from the barn roof was collected. It had a primeval, mysterious odor of milk that had been stored there to cool. There was a pasture for the animals, a garden spot, and a large orchard. Unlike our present home where we had to sweep the hard-red clay in our yard, the house was surrounded by a grassy but poorly kept lawn.

Mom and Dad would occupy one bed in the combination bedroom/living room, Bubba and I the other, and Pat and Mel would have a room of their own. There was even a small tenant house that we could rent to a sub-tenant to help farm the land. We thought it was going to be a fine place to live. But Mom had her doubts when she learned that the previous occupant had died of tuberculosis in the house. She was deathly afraid of the illness since one of her brothers and a niece suffered from it and she had watched their deterioration.

Before we moved in, we cleaned, disinfected, and fumigated every wall, floor, and ceiling in the house with sulfanilamide and home-made soap until it sparkled. We worked for weeks to get it ready. We scrubbed with mops, brooms, brushes, and disinfectants until every surface was spotless except the locked room. Barrels under the roof collected rainwater for cleaning, so we saved multiple trips to bring water from the cistern or spring. We were delighted that the owner had left a heavy leather oak divan, two matching rockers and a big oak library table in the parlor. The divan folded down to made an extra bed. We thought it was the most beautiful room we had ever seen. It was finally finished, and we moved our meager belongings in.

The piglets had grown into huge, fat sows and a litter of ten piglets. Our cow had freshened and produced a baby steer. Dad told us, with a humorous glint in his eyes, that if we lifted the baby each day, we'd be able to carry it anywhere when it was grown. We believed him. Mom scoffed at his foolishness, but she was happy there would be meat for the winter.

The dog (we named him Doggie) was our constant delight, both as a "tool" to drive the cattle home from the pasture and for hunting and guard duty. Dad found ingenious ways to use him. A very wealthy inventor (Lunati) bought a large piece of undeveloped property a few miles away and began to plant orchards and raise herds of cattle and pigs. He built a dam from an uncontrolled creek to form a lake and installed a generator to supply electricity to an area that had never had electricity. The occasional work Lunati provided our family that winter kept our family afloat.

That winter, Mr. Lunati hired Dad to build a bridge over the creek to allow farm machinery access to one of the apple orchards to weed and cultivate the land. Dad assembled the wood decking and heavy beams for the bridge, and hauled them to the site in his old T Model truck, and then assembled a six-man crew from among our neighbors.

Verdi Brown was a bony bachelor neighbor of uncertain age who frequently walked or hung around our farm, hoping for day wages. We considered him something of a nuisance because he apparently was attracted to my older sisters. They laughed at him and would have nothing to do with him. But he sometimes came in handy when odd jobs were available.

Other neighbors were the Johnson Negro family, whose brawny 18-year-old son James was, Dad thought, one of the most dependable workers in the area, so he was hired. We had great respect for this diligent, responsible family whose adjacent farm was one of the finest in the area. I thought James was the brightest, most impressive black man I had ever met and I admired him and his family. They were always respectable, well dressed, and honest and friendly. When the additional crew members were hired, the work began.

A few weeks later, Dad came home from the Lunati farm with a saddened expression on his face. I knew something terrible had happened from the way he looked. He explained that the crew was having lunch on a nearby hill overlooking the bridge when James asked Verdi Brown to teach him to swim while the others cooled off from the suffocating heat. After repeated requests, Verdi finally agreed and the two entered the narrow little creek that was only about 12 feet wide and less than seven feet deep. "The next thing I knew," Dad reported, "Verdi and James were in the middle of the stream struggling."

He told us that James panicked and Verdi was afraid of being pulled under by the strong young man so he kicked him loose and he went under and drowned.

"Why didn't the crew jump in?" Mom asked. "There were six of you—surely he couldn't pull all of you under!"

"Well, everyone was afraid. I thought about my family that I am responsible for and didn't think I could take a chance of drowning too. He was a big man."

"Why couldn't you throw him a rope or some of the bridge lumber into the creek?" I asked. "What about the other men who stood around and did nothing?"

I don't remember ever being as furious and disturbed in my young life. My Dad and a six-man crew had allowed a man to drown without trying everything possible to help. It was the first time that I lost respect for my father and for the self-aggrandizement stories that he was always telling us—especially about his baseball expertise. It was also an awakening that Negroes were expendable in the southern culture. I hated my Dad for that. There was simply no excuse for the loss of this young man. I have always grieved about it and the kind of culture that produced such thinking.

The Lunati family arrived in Mississippi during early depression years after he received a large sum of money for an invention that we understood to be an early version of the hydraulic lift, although we were never certain. They settled in a nearby swampy area on several hundred acres where meandering streams inundated the surrounding land into a Brazilian-like jungle so thick with gooseberries, blackberries, and filbert bushes that it was nearly impossible to penetrate, and set about controlling the streams to empty into a beautiful lake. Then, they installed a dam to control the flow and, to generate electricity for the farm and to irrigate the apple, pear, and peach orchards they planted over a period of time.

Apparently, their motive was to escape the rat race of the big cities and to establish a rural church where they could preach the gospel and enjoy the peace and quiet of gentleman farmers. Once the streams were deepened and controlled, they converted one of the farm dwellings into a church and invited everyone to attend. We attended the church faithfully for several years and became close to the family.

Dad was always bragging about ole "Doggie." When Lunati's pigs escaped from their pen into the untamed underbrush and turned wild, Dad told the owner that he and "Doggie" could retrieve them.

Lunati's farm manager laughed at him. "Some of those pigs are well over 300 pounds," he said, "No dog could get them out of brushy wetlands so thick that you can't crawl through it." Dad challenged him to a bet that he could retrieve those animals with the help of our dog. Word had gotten out that "Doggie" was special. He had been stolen twice, but somehow escaped to return with a chain dragging from his neck.

Dad was promised a big bonus if he could rescue the wild hogs. Dad and "Doggie" came home muddy and exhausted from the farm day after day, telling us that they had rescued more of the wild animals. He was determined to win that bet—it would mean much-needed cash for the family and he did not intend to quit until he had them all. He told us, "I sent Doggie into the brush after a hog and he'd grab him by the back leg and hold him until I attached a rope to drag him out." Finally, he caught them all, but the manager refused to pay off the bet he had made. Dad argued. He had to accept less than he'd been promised for three or four weeks of backbreaking labor.

Dad seemed to be able to do anything. He was adept at making the grist mill and the old truck run efficiently, build bridges and roads with no training, and once, he bought an old Packard engine which he used to run a little sawmill that he built. His greatest talent, other than storytelling that kept everyone's rapt attention, was trading. Sometimes, he would start out to visit neighbors with some little thing he wanted to trade and come home with an item far more valuable. I always felt he could have been successful at almost anything if he ever gave up his love of farming, but farming was in his blood and would not be denied.

Dad went to town and negotiated for a loan to buy two mules and more cotton seed for planting in the spring, but the Agricultural Agent insisted that we vary our crops to include growing peanuts in addition to our usual cotton, corn, and beans on some of the 100 acres we rented. Dad grumbled that the government always knew what was best, but they gave him no choice if he wanted the loan. He knew the price cotton would bring, but the market for peanuts was a much larger question.

Then, Dad started searching for a sub-tenant to occupy the little tenant house in return for part of the crops. He finally located Othar Buford, a huge black man with muscles like stone, his energetic wife, and two active young boys. They had a reputation for honesty and diligence. An agreement was made and they moved in. Their two boys became our favorite playmates who constantly came up with unique games to occupy our time. We found an old truck tire, and one of us would curl up inside, and roll the tire with the youngster inside down the steepest hill we could find. If we rolled the tire straight and fast enough, whoever was in the tire would end up at the bottom of the hill, but if it wobbled too much, we were shaken out. The results were often bad spills and scrapes and bruises.

Dad installed a rope swing from a huge old oak tree, where we played for hours on end. Then, he came up with the idea of making a merry-go-round. It consisted of a thick, 16 feet-long 2x8" plank with a hole in the middle. The big plank had a hole in the middle between each end in which a metal peg was inserted to allow the board to be pushed around and around into a circle. One of us would sit on each end of the plank, and another would start pushing the plank round and round until it revolved so fast that we had to cling to the board with all of our strength to prevent the centrifugal force from throwing us off the end. Often, we were thrown off. Once, Mel was thrown off the end and slammed against the big oak tree with a huge goose egg bump on her head. Mom decided that was warning enough, and made Dad remove the dangerous game.

Bubba and I were constant play companions when we were not busy hoeing, planting, or weeding—sometimes along with our tenant's two boys. I would rush through my chores: ironing, churning the butter, helping mom in the garden to rush outdoors to explore the world with my brother and our two little Negro friends. We explored the woods, examined frogs and bugs in the little pond, climbed giant oak and maple trees, and built dams in the little creek beyond the pasture.

At the end of the day after playing in the woods, we came home, scratching the chiggers we'd picked up from the trees and bushes. Chiggers are an almost microscopic spider-like insect that thrived in the southern woods. It was nearly impossible to wash them off our skin. Sometimes, the chigger bits became infected into boils that Mom rubbed with turpentine to kill the bugs and disinfect our skin. We were happy and free, and if we encountered boredom, one of us would think of another activity to relieve it.

Pat was seven years older than me, and Mel was five and a half years older. For the most part, the two were good companions who enjoyed each other, except when Mel decided to wear Pat's clothes. In their spare time, they visited one of their friends who lived only a mile or so away, searched for Indian relics around the area, or found other ways to amuse themselves. I pestered them to take me with them on their forays, but most of the time they ignored me and Bubba. Clearly, we were the pesky little sister and brother who was in their way.

Pat thought I was "cute" and wanted to "mother" me by managing my behavior, the way I looked, and making sure that I dressed appropriately—she was always ordering me around and giving me advice. My sisters were my role models who I followed blindly without question. Only on rare occasions did they condescend to actually play with Bubba and me.

Once on a beautiful summer weekend, they decided to do a theatrical production and charge five cents admission to raise some money. They hung quilts and sheets from a long rope for curtains, announced to the family that the "play" would be at 5:00 pm the following weekend, and began to tutor Bubba and me on our acts. I would do cartwheels, backbends, and other feats of athleticism along with Pat as my assistant. Bubba would put Doggie through his tricks—lie down, beg, roll over, etc. while Mel would quote some Shakespeare she studied in school.

They recruited their neighbor and friend, Sybil, to play the guitar and sing. Each of us practiced our art every day and by the end of the week felt that we were ready. Invitations to the play went out to our tenant, their boys, Mom and Dad, and our nearest neighbors; chairs were spread on the grass and the play began. Perhaps that was the beginning of my sister Pat becoming the "Director" in my life, but she was to play that role to some extent for the rest of my life. Mel, on the other hand, would be my friend, mentor, and confidant.

Churning the butter was one of my favorite chores. I read hundreds of books I'd brought home from the library as I churned, getting lost in another world. I discovered a new world each week when I checked out so many heavy books that it was a chore to carry them home. I read all the Tarzan, Nancy Drew, Jane Austin, Augusta J. Evans, and was the first in our family to read *Gone with the Wind* when it came out around 1939. Mom objected if I read instead of doing my chores, but when I tried to read while I ironed the sheets it brought on her ire.

I loved searching the big pastures for our cows in the evening and Doggie helped drive them home for Mom or my sisters to milk. I knew where all the persimmons trees, wild blackberries, and wild plums grew and ate them until my stomach ached. The odor of wild garlic in the pasture was like perfume to me—although I hated it when our milk tasted like the wild garlic. The real world escaped me and I was full of joy. Only the distraction of Mom and Dad's discord or my sister's occasional quarrels could affect my happiness.

# Chapter 13

Our little brother started school that year and soon was reading what we called the Dick and Jane books. When he started reciting the book word for word without looking at it, we realized that he had somehow memorized the words. Suddenly his name changed from Bubba to Dick. Dick could do no wrong in our house and became the pet of the family. He also became my constant companion and co-mischief maker. We roamed the woods, dug forts in sand ditches, paddled in creeks, climbed trees and tried to ride the young steer. He was the baby, or sometimes father when we built playhouses with old boards for tables, scraps of dishes in which to cook mud pies and made beds out of boughs to sleep in. While I once had cried to accompany my sisters on their forays to visit neighbors or scout for wild fruits or Indian relics, I stopped pestering them with my demands as often.

Pat and Mel, despite often bickering and fighting between themselves, became a united front against our parents' bickering and fighting. Dick and I formed our own refuge. We united against the injustice we felt when we were punished or when bullies teased or excluded us from recess activities. We would protect each other against the world. And now each of us had mounds of heavy books that we had checked out from the library in which to escape. During my grade school years, I read nearly every book in our local library, including scanning some of the encyclopedias, while Mom and Dad complained that my eyes were always glued to the page of a book. My search for knowledge only distressed my parents.

Our new farm had numerous heavily wooded areas with huge trees, creeks, springs, pastures, and fields to roam in and fireflies to capture in a jar in the evenings. I loved watching the bats chase each other in the twilight and listening to nightingale songs, or bobwhites and doves calling to each other in the evening. I was lost and satiated in the vivid fluffy clouds lit by the sunset's carmine, orange, and maroon. When the sky turned dark with storm clouds, lightning lit everything in sight, and rain fell in torrents.

The land, trees, wildflowers, birds and sky, and I became one. Here, I felt the hand of God—of profound grandeur, peace, and tranquility. This God spoke to me, unlike the words of the scriptures being represented in our little church, but of eloquent gentleness, love, splendor, and joy. My mind recorded the beauty of it in a mental file as I tried to apply words to my impressions. Someday I would be able to communicate it all in words and paintings. My ambition was born: to grow up, go to college, and become a writer and painter. I developed a strong sense of future destiny and saw the materialization of my dream of writing books and painting masterpieces, along with future fame and fortune.

In the meantime, family survival depended upon each of the children taking a share of the responsibility to grow the crops, help with the animals, do the laundry, the cooking, and supplying the water. As Mom and Dad's parents before them, children were the labor force necessary for farm life and it never occurred to them that anything had changed. It was the way it was. Without our help, farming would be impossible, even now that he had Othar to help with plowing and planting.

While Mom usually nagged for help with her duties, Dad used charm and challenges to induce us to help. Dad told endless stories as we worked about the time he had hit the baseball so far out of the ballpark that it was never found. He told about being drafted in World War I, after contracting measles, and riding to the train station on his favorite horse for several hours in a snowstorm, only to learn that Armistice was signed that day, so he didn't have to go.

It was much more fun to accompany Dad to the fields; sometimes he let us handle the mules and plow long, straight furrows in which the seed would be planted. We were allowed to ride the mules to the fields, but only occasionally the mare for personal pleasure. So, we plowed, planted, thinned and chopped around the young seedlings until the fields grew tall and green with strong stalks of cotton, corn, beans, and rows of squat peanuts. As we worked, the sun beat unmercifully down on us until our clothes were wet with sweat and steamed into our eyes. At the end of the day, I had driven the cows home from the pasture and Pat and Mel helped Mom with the milking. Later, Bubba and I brought water from the spring, fed chickens and hogs, and brought in eggs from the henhouse.

After dinner of leftover food from the noon meal, which Mom had stored in the little oven over the wood stove, we had time to read and do our homework. Occasionally, if they weren't too tired, Mom would set up a little table and we would play pitch, or "high, low, jack and game" cards. With a more functional family and less poverty, our lives could have been idyllic.

In the evening, Mom would settle wearily into one of the rocking chairs and read the Bible. She often read it aloud, insisting that we put aside the book we were reading, to listen to "the word of the Lord." There were always Dad's improbable stories that we were forced to listen to. Fascinating, but improbable!

4-H Club was started for children of rural families when I was ten or 11, offering my first real socialization outside of school and church when I had a chance to attend the summer 4-H club camp at a nearby lake. There was no money for the camp but my sisters stepped up to help with their pennies and left-over shorts, swimsuits and other necessities to help me attend.

My parents saw that I was determined to go to the camp, so they bargained to exchange garden produce in exchange for the tuition, and I was off for two weeks in the sun, and more fun than I'd ever had. There, I was to meet kids who, like me, were the children of tenant farmers who were not prejudged against that social structure. I made many friends and felt accepted and even sought after during the following summers. We were given the chance to learn other skills such as personal hygiene, good nutrition, the dangers of contaminated water and we were taught how to sew our own clothes, croquet, quilt, or other skills. I chose sewing and made my first dress when I was 12, which won an opportunity to attend and model the dress at Mississippi State College. I will always remember how frightened I was when I shyly paraded in front of a big audience in my white dotted Swiss dress, but I credit the pride I received for winning a prize for increasing my confidence and self-assurance. I began to "come out of my shell."

Saturday was marketing day, and we loaded into the little 1928 Chevrolet for the five-mile trip to town. While Mom visited with relatives and shopped, the children walked around the square to search for friends or browsed the isles of the dime store for things that we only wished we could buy.

Sometimes, if there was any money, we were given a quarter for a hamburger and coke or a dime for the new talking movies with Tom Mix, or later Roy and Dale Rogers and Trigger. It was a great adventure. Pat and Mel were beginning to attract admirers—usually, some of the boys who were working in CCC camps—and they would gather on the courthouse square under huge old magnolia trees to visit with them. Mom and Dad were aghast when the boys asked them for dates. They were too young and there would be no way they'd be allowed to go out with them.

Pat was 15, then 16 and 17, but she was not allowed to date until she was almost 18. My sisters thought this was terribly unjust and invariably brought a raging argument after we returned home. Between Mom and the church, we were thoroughly taught that dating was fraught with the dangers of pregnancies, sexual diseases, and marriage before maturity. Pat argued that Mom was married at 19 and she had no intention of getting married, even if she was allowed to start dating. Mel was obstinate and less controlled and delighted in finding ways to make our parents believe that she was immoral. There was little danger of immorality—our parents had brainwashed us too well.

My older sisters were often at odds. Pat took great pains sewing and taking care of her clothes, which Mel would borrow and strew around their bedroom after wearing them. They frequently quarreled when Pat wanted to wear a garment only to find it piled and dirty, on a chair where her sister had left it. She confronted Mel angrily until they tore into each other with fists flailing.

Before anyone could stop them, Pat pushed Mel through a window, landing in broken glass in the yard. Fortunately, except for her pride, she was unhurt but unrepentant. Dad decided Mel needed to be punished when she refused to be contrite.

She said that she would do what she wanted to do and no one would stop her. This resulted in the worse spanking any of us ever had. Dad applied his razor strap repeatedly but she refused to give in. In the end, Mom stood by, screaming and praying hysterically for him to stop. The next thing I knew, Mom tried to stop him and Dad slapped her across the face to stop her hysteria. It only got worse. Mel's angry bellows and Mom's piercing screams and prayers lasted a long time.

It was one of the few occasions that I found no solace in my books. I was horrified at the violence and injustice and scared to death that the next time someone would be badly hurt—or worse. I thought Pat was fastidious, Mel too stubborn, my Dad too brutal and my mother too hysterical. I became very depressed, wondering why I was born into such a family. All I wanted was to get away from this poverty, hard work, anger, and hate. I couldn't understand the anger, hate, and humiliation, or the frequent family disagreements.

Finally, everyone calmed down and went about their chores. I was left alone in the house. The 22-caliber rifle was hanging over the dresser and I grasped it, checked the chamber for bullets, and faced the mirror to aim it at my chest for a long time, waiting for the courage to pull the trigger. Perhaps the thought of my little brother losing his playmate or my love for my two sisters finally brought rationale back.

The incident also changed my perception of my parents. Mom, despite the frequent bouts of hysteria, was our protector and my father, whom I had worshiped, bullied Mom as well as Mel. I still did not comprehend that Mom's hysteria was caused by fatigue, worry, overwork, and poverty. I also knew Dad's determination to tame Mel's stubborn streak would never work.

The incident was a milestone. Family traits seemed less etched in stone. Pat and Mel soon became best friends again. My little brother was my special friend who may have saved my life. Mom's hysterical streaks subsided for a while as the family began to gain slightly more security on the new farm, although Mom never learned to control her hysterical fears completely.

The cattle had reproduced until we had several milk cows and a few heifers. Dad had traded for a grist mill, where we began to grind our neighbor's corn into meal. The two mules we had acquired were healthy and Mom and Dad started to haul our milk and butter to sell or trade in the town. We had a huge garden and a large orchard, where we picked baskets of fruit and vegetables to can hundreds of quarts of food for winter. We had a hog that was butchered for our winter supply of meat. Only money for staples, shoes, and clothes was in short supply.

My sisters obtained part-time work at school under one of Roosevelt's programs, which helped them buy material for dresses and an occasional pair of shoes. But little of this penetrated my mind, absorbed as it was in the books I brought home from the town library. When the fanciful world of books failed to relieve my depression, I wandered through the hills and valleys of the farm to remove myself from family bickering and found temporary peace in the wonder at the color and patterns of the land and sky. My turmoil changed from a dream-like state one minute to love of the land the next, then to anger, as I faced day-to-day family discord and the daily trip to school and back, where teasing was daily torture that ended in black eyes and bruises.

It never occurred to me not to fight back, but I wouldn't give in and the daily beatings only ended when I arrived at school or upon returning to the final bus stop back from school. My anger built. I shadowboxed with everyone—sometimes playfully, but often to prove that I was tough enough to take whatever that person wanted to dish out. It became a way of life that lasted most of my youth and ended many years later when I understood the rage and humiliation that caused me to want to hit something or someone. I didn't realize the stupidity of fighting with no chance of winning. Perhaps it was a way to exercise my anger, although it was years before it went away.

# **Chapter 14**

Holly Springs was a pretty little town, surrounded by rolling hills covered by huge Oak, Maple, Pine, Cottonwood, Sweet gum, Pecan, Hickory, Walnut, Chestnut, and spring-fed hollows filled with giant Holly trees, from which its name was derived. In the fall, the children shuffled through three feet depth of multicolored, dusty leaves in our bare feet—or later, water-soaked foliage permeated with a primordial odor of mold and decay.

Surrounding the little town in the rolling hills were cotton and cornfields, impenetrable swamps in the bottomland and occasionally a huge 100-foot deep sand-filled gully that was the result of erosion from "gully washing" torrential rainstorms that hit the area periodically. Black threatening clouds would gather in the sky, deafening thunder would crash and lightning would flash across the earth. An ear-splitting bang announced that a strike had hit a tree. It left huge black scars running down the trunks on the ones that had been hit. Sometimes, a tree caught on fire. The odor of sulfur filled the air in those storms and steam rose from the earth from the heat and humidity. We watched somewhat anxiously for the storm to lose its wrath and when it subsided, we begged our parents to let us stand outside in the gentle rains that followed. I can still feel the refreshment we felt as the rain fell on our young bodies.

Bubba and I loved to play in the dry sand of the huge eroded ditches near our house. We dug caves into the banks of those cavernous ditches, buried each other in the sand and piled it in huge piles to jump into from the hill above. Mom worried that our caves would entrap and smother us, warning that children had been known to die in cave-ins.

Sometimes in the bottom of those sand ditches, we found evidence of the fierce warriors of the Chickasaw Indian tribe who had migrated from the main tribe in Huntsville, Alabama in the 1700s to occupy northeast Mississippi. We dug for, or our bare feet sometimes were cut on chards of their pottery or on their spear and arrow points in those ditches. They were great finds and we took them home proudly to add to our sisters' collection of artifacts that they had gathered.

Little remains of the hunters and the farmer culture of the Chickasaw tribe, a part of the Choctaw nation that still exists today. By the beginning of the 18th century, their population was down to about 10,000 and by the end of the 19th century; they had been relocated to Indian Territory in Oklahoma, where they number about 35,000 at present.

After Roosevelt started the Civilian Conservation Corp, the Corp planted the sand ditches with the Kudzu vine. It stopped or slowed the erosion, but overwhelmed adjacent foliage and killed the trees it climbed into and choked the life from them. Nothing will stop the Kudzu vine. Defoliants failed and cutting the vines was hopeless. At the same time, the CCC planted huge Pine forests all over the South to replenish the hardwoods that had been harvested.

Our marketing trips into Holly Springs on Saturdays were one of our favorite pursuits. Nearly all of the farm families arrived in town in their wagons (or cars later) to buy their coal oil, coffee, and cornmeal and to visit with relatives and friends.

In the town square was the County Courthouse, a three-story structure built of brick made by slaves before the Civil War. It was centered on a few acres of tree-studded land filled with dozens of giant magnolia trees whose blossoms perfumed the air with their fragrance in the spring and summer. A block of stores surrounded the courthouse on four sides with broad sidewalks, canopies, and picture windows advertising their wares.

We walked around those blocks repeatedly, greeting our numerous relatives to catch up on their activities. Some of them, like Mom's brother, parked their wagon in the early days, or their car later, in the same place year after year to sell their Watkins products. His children followed the tradition for years afterward. We always knew where to find Uncle Will and his family. Mom bought the vanilla she used to flavor her cakes, or other products from them. It was an "old home week" when we found our cousins.

Unlike at school, where we felt humiliated and degraded by the merchants' and city leaders' children, we felt love from our aunts, uncles, and cousins, who were mostly farmers like us. It embarrassed us when they hugged or kissed us and bragged about how pretty we were because our parents never did.

Dad bragged about his children and Mom showed concern for us by sewing our clothes and seeing that we were carefully groomed and as well-fed as possible, but neither of them were "touchy-feely" parents who demonstrated physical affection. Our numerous relatives in the area showed the caring that we lacked at home. I had never seen my parents kiss or hug each other, and found myself wondering later how they ever produced five children.

Current residents live on the battlefields which were lost and retaken many times during the War. Their ancestors produced 11 Confederate generals and nine members of the Confederate Congress. General Grant established his headquarters in the old Van Dorn hotel, which still exists.

The prosperous settlers built elaborate antebellum houses that have been opened to tourists since 1936 during the annual spring "pilgrimage." 60 of the homes attest to the unique architecture of the beautiful little town. Tour guides, dressed in colorful costumes of the Civil War era, guide the visitors, who arrive by horse-drawn buggies, through homes that often contain antique furniture of that era. Some of them still have a statue of a little black boy waiting to hold the horses' reins in front of their gates.

Class consciousness was alive and well. The residents took great pride in their status as Daughters of the American Revolution and looked down on anyone who failed to occupy that high status. "Old Money" and elite status was their claim to fame. They were the elite who snubbed the poor white farmers or anyone they considered "beneath" them in social position, especially the children. By the time we were in high school, class distinctions became less prevalent—or perhaps we gained a better sense of self-worth that allowed us to overcome our feelings of inadequacy.

# Chapter 15

We lived on that 100-acre farm for four years until I knew and loved every tree and meadow and plant. When the crop of corn and peanuts filled the big barn and the cotton was sold, my parents discussed buying the place. My siblings and I crossed our fingers that it would happen. In 1938, the owner wanted to sell the home, outbuildings, and land for $1,200. Dad and all the children thought it was a good price and that we could easily make the payments under the terms offered, but Mom argued against it, fearing we couldn't make the payments.

In spite of on-going hardships, we had achieved progress. There were hundreds of quarts of fruits and vegetables stored from the orchard and garden, the grist mill Dad installed in the barn provided a few dollars cash from the corn our neighbors brought to be ground, and there were several milk cows for milk and calves to grow for our winter meals. The barn was filled with peanut vines for animal feed, plus a stored supply of peanuts to nibble on during the cold winter months. We were doing well compared to other neighbors and relatives who continued to suffer from the unfortunate economic conditions that all small rural farmers and sharecroppers endured.

When the cotton was picked and sold, Dad had $400 cash left after paying the landowner. The big fall circus had come to town and he decided to take the family there to celebrate the harvest. It was a rare treat for the children, whose only usual recreation consisted of an occasional movie or a swim in the creek or a church function. We had never been to a circus before. We wandered the grounds to gawk at the colorful games and exotic shows promising unbelievable feats of accomplishment, exotic dancers, bearded ladies, and "The Wild Man of Borneo." Dad agreed to give each of us enough money to see one or two of the shows.

The famous Sally Rand appeared at one show. I had to see her. If my parents saw me going into a so-called nudity show, they would have been aghast, but I had to see her dance with that beautiful fan. Looking around furtively for my parents, I paid the fee and slipped into the theater. She pranced across the platform, weaving a huge brilliantly colored fan over and around her tiny body, her golden curls gleaming around her pretty face. I was mesmerized. She had the grace and beauty of the swan as she mimicked its movements as she fluttered the fan over, under, and around her petite body in time with the music.

Miss Rand became famous for her performance at the World's Fair, but she commonly made appearances at state and other local fairs. I will never forget her performance. Sally was still strutting with her fans as late as 1963, when she would be about 63 years of age, and had some small movie roles before then. No one could call her performance in any way offensive, even in the '30s when nearly everything was considered immoral or indecent in the southern Bible belt. Apparently, she wore a bodysuit that hid all but small glimpses of her body. I loved her show and decided I must learn to dance as she did.

Then, roars from the "Wild Man of Borneo" show fascinated me. Where in the world were those strange, unnatural, sounds coming from? I had to find out. Again, I sneaked into the theater where roars, grunts, groans, and the thuds of some objects being thrown came to my attention. A wild-looking, heavily bearded creature with untamed hair, eyed the audience and tormentors around him with ferocious eyes, snarls, and piercing growls. He hardly appeared human, but it was clear that he was violent and untamed. The creature was crawling on his knees in the bottom of a metal cage when his keeper produced a fierce racket that grated on my ears like a fingernail assaulting a caulk board. He rose up in anger and terror and let out a hoarse scream as he tore at the cage, rattling and shaking it until the tent shook. His keeper kept up a running commentary as he threw a live chicken into the pen for his prisoner. The creature grabbed it and proceeded to tear it into little pieces and crammed them into his mouth. Feathers flew in every direction, as blood coated the floor of the cage as the creature tore at the chicken's flesh. The odor of excrement, blood, and feathers overwhelmed the room.

My stomach turned inside out and I felt faint. I had to get out of there before I added my vomit to the scene. I wanted to run and shout that some poor creature was being used and abused, but I didn't know where to go or what to do.

It was clear that the person, or thing, was half-human and most likely an escapee from a mental institution. It took all my effort to control my anger and distress. What kind of person would treat anything or anyone in this manner? It was beyond comprehension. I was revolted that I had been a part of the audience who witnessed this sub-human behavior. The fair was no longer fun. I wanted to physically hurt those who were responsible for this debacle, while I hated myself for seeing it.

All the gaiety and color of the games and shows were too much for Mom. She wondered around for a while but the only thing that held her interest was a quilt show, where she gathered with other like-minded women in awe and admiration. Dad, on the other hand, was attracted to a game where for a few dollars you could try to outwit the carnie and win some money. When he walked up to the game, the vendor reached down to whisper in his ear. "If you will put up $2.00, I will let you win $4.00 just to get the show started." Sure enough, the vendor gave him $4.00, and then $8.00 and then $16.00. Dad was hooked. Before he left, he had squandered the $400.00 cotton money. It was a con, but Dad was naive enough to believe him. He agreed to "invest" a small amount, then a larger amount on the basis of his promises, but ended up losing it all. He brought the matter up with the Sheriff, who only laughed at him. "How could you fall for that old trick?" he asked. The family was staggered with the loss.

Both Mom and Dad were inconsolable, but the money was gone with no way of getting it back. Perhaps Mom visualized the same kind of thing would happen if we bought the farm. I doubt she trusted Dad much after that. Dad didn't have the courage of his convictions and gave in to Mom's usual timidity. Our lives might have taken an entirely new course if they had taken this small chance because property would never be available again at those prices again. So, sadly, we were forced to move from the place we had learned to cherish. Pat and Mel had their first teen romances, and I, my first successful friendships and challenges in 4-H Club.

# Chapter 16

Mom's passion for fishing was only exceeded by her passion for God and duty. Her mother and sisters' claim to fame was the big bass they caught in their little farm pond, or the weighty catfish they caught from the brown waters of the Tippah (or other) Rivers. Mom caught the spirit and nothing pleased her more than finding the time away from her duties to look for a stream, lake, pond or river in which to fish. But first, she demanded that all the responsibilities be taken care of, before allowing the luxury of taking a few hours away from her duties. Mom's passion for fishing was only exceeded by her passion for God and duty. Her mother and sisters' claim to fame was the big bass they caught in their little farm pond, or the weighty catfish they caught from the brown waters of the Tippah (or other) Rivers. Mom caught the spirit and nothing pleased her more than finding the time away from her duties to look for a stream, lake, pond or river in which to fish. But first, she demanded that all the responsibilities be taken care of, before allowing the luxury of taking a few hours away from her duties.

Any body of water would do. She insisted that there was fish anywhere there was water. Chewalla Creek was a free-flowing creek near our house where the water was cold and clear. She gathered a long cane from the adjacent woods, fitted it with line and a baited hook and waited patiently for the bobber to go down. When it did, she squealed in delight. It mattered little if the fish was a small bream or a big bass. It was a testament to her skill—and it was supper. If the children became restless and suggested going somewhere else, which was seldom because we loved to fish as much as she did, she said, "Not yet. I'm fixing to get a bite."

Occasionally, we accompanied Dad when he received a few days' work on the Lunati farm after the crops were laid-by, or after the cotton was picked. The children gathered beneath the dam spillway and collected buckets full of minnows to use for bait to fish for big bass in one of Lunati's lakes. Mom taught us how to bait the big hooks through the back of the minnow, and cast our bamboo rods as far into the lake as possible.

We concentrated on placing our lines into dying wild gooseberry bushes or debris from dying trees where it was an ideal place for big bass and crappie to school and waited for the bobbers to signal that a fish was going after our minnows. When the bobber disappeared beneath the surface, we jerked the line to set the hook and then pulled a big bass to the bank. During those times, Mom's smile lighted her face, her worry lines retreated, and she became animated with pleasure.

Mom demanded that we attend first to our farm duties before any pleasure and devotion to fishing. "Get the work done first and then go," she said when we wanted to go fishing. While we often balked at doing our chores, we rushed through them quickly when fishing was mentioned.

The brown water of the Tippah River was a favorite for the huge mud and blue catfish lurking beneath its muddy waters. Again, Mom cut cane poles from the adjacent forests and we jammed the poles tightly into the banks to leave overnight for a big "cat" to bite during the night. Then we would return in the early morning to heave the heavy fish ashore. Some of the fish we caught were in excess of 25 pounds, and we shared them with neighbors and feasted on fried catfish and "corn puppies" (fried cornbread) until we were "stuffed to the gills."

By the time Bubba and I reached the age of nine and 12, we were allowed to spend our spare time to romp in the woods and explore streams, ponds, and lakes at our leisure. The Lunati Farm was our favorite destination, despite a tortuously long walk through woods and streams to get there. We reduced the seven-mile trip by road to four or five miles by cutting through the woods, crossing streams, and laboring over hills and valleys. There were streams to explore, lakes to fish and swim in, and swamps where endless snakes and turtles were present to shoot at with our 22-caliber rifle. We had great respect, but little fear of the poisonous snakes we encountered everywhere. Turtles sunned on dead logs in the swamp, and water moccasins slithered through the murky waters with their heads above water. If we aimed carefully at their heads, we could kill them with a well-placed shot.

We found that the quickest and easiest route to reach the lake to go swimming was to wade down the shallow stream that fed the lake. Heavy underbrush grew on the steep bank of the stream and we encountered water moccasins all along the way, but they skittered away at the sound of our splashing through the water.

"They're more afraid of us than we are of them. They won't hurt us if we don't hurt them," I told my little brother. God must protect innocent little children, because we were never bitten in an era when people often died or became ill from snake bites in that region. Rattlesnakes were also common in that area, but we never encountered one, although we heard them warn of their presence occasionally. Unfortunately, when we dived into the lake, sometimes we encountered wild gooseberry bushes that struck thorns into our flesh and threatened to imprison our bodies. It didn't take long to learn to avoid such traps and find more open water in which to swim.

After swimming, fishing, and shooting snakes, a day of stumbling around in water, muck, thorns, and underbrush left us exhausted and hungry, so we started the long way back home. Once, we stopped to rest beside a little stream, digging our bare feet into the warm brown sandy bank. Suddenly an angry, startled hive of bees rose from the damp earth close by. We had unwittingly disturbed a giant hive of bees that flooded around us, over us and into our clothes and hair. Before we could escape, we were stung repeatedly and painfully over most of our bodies. Live and learn!

As we continued, the sky filled with huge black clouds that threatened a thunderstorm. Rain was not a problem, but we were afraid of lightning as we hurried our steps toward home. It was so hot that walking in a gentle rain was welcome and pleasant.

We often begged Mom to let us walk, run, and play in the rain, but if lightning or thunder accompanied it, we were not allowed outside.

Suddenly, the sky lit up with lightning and the loud claps of thunder threatened our eardrums. I became frightened. The heavy rain that followed relieved the painful bee stings on our bodies. It began to pound us in torrents, heavier than I had ever seen in an area where intense rainfalls were common. Cloudbursts after cloudbursts followed—one after another.

The thick red clay clung heavily to our feet as we struggled through the storm for what seemed like hours until our legs became almost too heavy to move. I wondered how I would ever manage to get my little brother home when I was having such a struggle with my aching muscles, but in time, we finally reached a sand ditch that bordered one of our fields. I knew that we were within a mile of home.

The sand ditch, normally nearly empty except during heavy rain falls, was a roaring, cascading torrent of water carrying brush and all kinds of debris. There was no choice—you do what you have to do. We would have to cross this runaway stream someway—and I had no idea how to do it.

Shaking with fear, I watched the roaring stream for what seemed like hours before I had an idea. We had left some hoes and rakes in the field when we were chopping weeds a few days before. Perhaps they would still be here. I retraced my steps to look for them, warning Bubba to stay exactly where he was without moving an inch. At least a hoe or rake would be something to hold on to, in order to cross the raging water.

When I found a hoe, I told Bubba to grab hold to the end of it for dear life and I would tow him across the turbulent water. Taking one tentative step after another, I slowly made my way through the two- or three-feet depth of the powerful current. The water threatened to take my body downstream each time I moved my legs. I planted my feet as firmly as possible in the muddy bottom, wandering if each step would be my last, afraid that my little brother would be washed away.

Slowly, gradually, we made our way across as Bubba bravely clung to the end of the hoe. We were finally on the other side and I could control my struggling breathing again. By the time we reached home, Bubba and I made an agreement. We wouldn't tell Mom and Dad about our misadventures, although we did tell them about getting stung by the bees.

# Chapter 17

The family ate a hearty breakfast of oatmeal, biscuits, and molasses by six o'clock in the morning. Pat or Mel milked the cows and led them into the pastures while Mom made breakfast, then we left for the fields to weed or plant or harvest, depending on the time of the year. After working all morning, we stopped for the mid-day meal, which was often food that was left over from the prior day that Mom stored in the warming oven above the woodstove. The milk was taken to the spring for the cream to rise for making butter, and to avoid spoiling in the heat. We had no icebox and only a small hand-dug cellar that kept potatoes and other root vegetables fresh.

When we returned from the fields at noon, Mom heated the leftover food or sometimes made cornbread, biscuits, or a vegetable for our mid-day dinner—the main meal of the day. In the evening, we often subsisted on cornbread and milk to avoid Mom having to cook another meal.

On a hot mid-July day in 1935, we returned home for our mid-day meal and a short rest before returning to the fields in the afternoon. After Pat and Mel finished ironing the sheets, and I churned milk to make butter, Mom sliced the pork roast in the warming oven above the stove for our mid-day meal. Engrossed in a book as I churned, I didn't stop to eat, and Pat and Mel told Mom and Dad that they wanted to finish their chores before they would eat. In a few minutes, Dad finished eating some of the pork roast and prepared to return to the fields for his farming duties. Shortly afterward, he began groaning in pain. He was doubled up in agony in the back yard, vomiting his heart out. Minutes later, he had diarrhea and vomiting at the same time as he groaned in pain from stomach cramps.

"You've got to get me to the hospital. I feel like I'm dying," he gasped between bouts of vomiting and diarrhea.

All of the children were taught to drive the old farm truck in low gear in the fields when we harvested corn or cotton, but none of us knew how to drive on the old country roads in high gear. Mom had never learned to drive at all, so she screamed for Pat. "Do you think you can drive him to the doctor?" she asked.

Pat said that there was no alternative. She had seen Dad start it many times. The old truck had a hand crank and she knew it required strength and enough spark to start the motor. We watched nervously as she spun the crank several times before the motor roared to life.

We half-dragged, half-carried Dad to the truck, loaded him in it and Pat nervously got it into gear and drove away with Mom having hysterics beside Dad in the front seat.

When they arrived at the hospital, the doctor immediately recognized that Dad was a victim of food poisoning from the left-over pork roast when they told him what he had eaten for lunch. He said, "You'll have to sign a waiver. The only medicine I have for food poisoning will either kill you or cure you."

"What are the odds?" Dad gasped between bouts of vomiting and diarrhea.

"50-50," he answered. Dad nodded weakly and Mom and Pat concurred. There was no other choice. "You do what you have to do."

Our lives were guided by that principle. When presented with a dilemma, we did what we had to do. Within a few days, Dad had recovered his strength, but the ten lost pounds showed on his diminutive frame. Our forefathers believed that family members were responsible to and for each other. Farm families needed each other to plant, weed, feed the animals, and harvest the crops they produced to benefit each member to ensure mutual survival. It was the only way most southern farmers could survive. Unlike the present, where parents smother children with every want and need, children of that era were taught to be responsible for their parents.

My siblings and I subconsciously (if not consciously) grew up in that tradition. We grew up with the belief that we must overcome all obstacles to supply not only our future children with more abundance than we had as children but to provide security for our parents as well. While we had issues with the way our parents reared us, we loved them in spite of their antiquated methods of rearing children and yearned for adult-hood when we could secure our own prosperity as well as that of our parents. Despite our young age, it would be one of the guiding principles in the life of my siblings and me in the coming years.

# Chapter 18

The next farm they chose had an old unpainted house with two rooms divided by a dog trot hallway, a large kitchen lean-to, a small barn and a few acres of mostly unclaimed bottomland next to a creek lined with giant hardwoods. Even though the house was a disappointment, at least we would stay in the same school, where my sisters would soon graduate. We had a shorter walk to meet the school bus on a road that had been lightly graveled so it was less muddy in bad weather. The land had not been worked for some time, which meant much harder work for all of us when we weeded the new crops after they were planted. It was a borderline farm with less acreage, which made me wonder why they rented it at all.

Verdi Brown was a frequent visitor, a nuisance that we had learned to endure for years. He flitted from chore to chore that we gave him to keep him out of the way, sometimes picking peaches for Mom to can, and leering at Pat, Mel or me in a lewd manner. We knew what Verdi Brown wanted. Pat and Mel had more experience in handling his pitiful efforts to engage them in a romantic liaison and thought he was laughable. But at 12 years of age, I had not learned how to handle his suggestive remarks and innuendoes as well, so I found ways to keep away from him. Mom, on the other hand, was often left to deal with his lechery when he helped pick and peel peaches, tote water for canning, or other duties he was assigned to do.

His frequent habit of just showing up to help was disconcerting to all of us, but Dad began to think that something was going on between Verdi and Mom.

Dad, Dick, and I were working in the bottom field the day Verdi came to pick peaches. Dad seemed distracted and more uncommunicative that day. After working awhile, he called me over to a shade tree to tell me, "I don't like having Verdi Brown there when we're all away. I want you to go to the house and see what's going on."

I wanted to laugh at the thought of our strait-laced, religious mother having an affair with anyone—much less with the ubiquitous Verdi Brown. She undoubtedly may have suffered from a lack of attention and affection from my father, who had never learned anything about showing romance, but it was inconceivable to me that she would be interested in Verdi. Dad was jealous of that nincompoop Verdi Brown.

He told me, "I want you to go to the house and check up on what they are doing. There's a big hole in the fireplace. Look through it without being Our new farm seen, and come back and tell me what is going on."

Alright! It was a good way to get out of the back-breaking work I was doing, so I ran the half-mile home to comply with his irrational wishes. It occurred to me that he had lost his mind.

I sneaked quietly up to the house and looked through the hole in the fireplace. I could hear them talking in the kitchen, but couldn't see anything. I sneaked around the house to the edge of the back porch, where I could see them busy at work, peeling peaches. So much for my father's suspicions! Mom would never have looked at her helper with anything but pity! *At least*, I thought, *maybe Dad does care for her more than he pretends*.

Still, my Dad, always the optimist, thought he could make a living on this farm after he learned he could obtain a farm loan for a pair of huge, stout, Percheon horses with feet like dinner plates. He bought the horses, put them in the corral and warned my brother Bubba and me to stay away from them, explaining that they were young and untested. Five minutes after he left, my brother and I climbed on the horses from the top of the corral fence, the only way we were able to mount their great height. The gentle horses carried us, feet outstretched over their broad backs, around the corral a few times. They were beautiful and we fell in love with those gentle beasts even after we learned they were very uncomfortable for riding. Plowing untrained draft horses was not easy, as my Dad soon learned. Their big bodies moved too fast to keep up with and despite their gentility, required a lot of training before they were comfortable with pulling plows.

Pat graduated from high school in 1938 and found a job in Memphis and the rest of the family got by on a little money from the crops and the food we raised. She came home as often as possible, bearing gifts of cast-off clothes for me, small toys for my brother and a little money from time to time for Mom and Dad that she had saved from her meager salary. Mel followed her the next year when she graduated, and soon found a job as a cigarette girl so she could add her pennies to benefit the family when she could spare the money. Dad had indoctrinated us well. It was our responsibility to take care of our parents and we accepted it without question.

It took my family only two years before they learned that there was no way to make this untamed land a viable farm.

We moved into a little house near town, where Dad took work where and when he could find it for another year or two. Nevertheless, Dad wasn't ready to give up farming. After a while, disillusioned with working for wages, he searched for another farm. The Waterford place, which they next rented, consisted of few acres of red clay hills for cotton and a few acres of bottomland where we grew sorghum and corn. It had the usual three-room shack, plus a similar rental shack on the hillside above.

That winter, Dad traded something for a small used sawmill to use for milling the surrounding hardwoods timber into lumber. I became his assistant logger. After he dragged the timber into the mill site with the big Percheon, my job was to roll it onto the carriage for cutting. He taught me how to "set block"—cutting the lumber into one, two or more inches thick. When the old Packard motor needed repairing, my small fingers were used to adjust or clean the carburetor or other parts.

When the sorghum was mature, I helped cut and harvest it and feed it into the mill for molasses, which was one of our staples for hot buttered biscuits, morning and evening. We piled the sorghum into wagons and hauled it to the spring beneath the hill. The mill consisted of a rusting iron frame holding grinding wheels to crush the sorghum. The wheels were turned by a long pole attached to the top of the iron frame. A mule pulled the pole in a circle, round and round, to activate the grinding wheels, which squashed the sorghum stalks that we fed through the wheels.

We built a fire pit nearby for the big metal trays to cook the juice into molasses. The exact amount of heat for cooking the juice was critical. If the fire was too hot, the juice would scorch, making the molasses too dark and strong. The ideal was a clear, dark mahogany colored liquid with just a touch of thickness. The liquid must be sweet without becoming sugary. Making molasses was an art. There was a long-handled mall used for scraping the trays repeatedly to avoid the juice from sticking and becoming scorched, and we cooked and scraped and tasted repeatedly until the molasses was perfect. Dad took great pride in his annual preparation, and most of us enjoyed it for breakfast with our biscuits all our young life.

It was men's work, but I loved being outdoors, using my developing muscles, and being "one of the boys." I hated picking cotton and often found some way to avoid it, which would get me into more trouble than I was ready for.

Here, Dad started a "pick-up" baseball team where neighborhood men and boys gathered in the pasture to play ball on Sundays after church. I was the only girl and the butt of all their jokes, but in time they accepted me as part of the team with equal skills. I loved it when they'd say, "Bet you can't catch this ball," and threw it with all their strength. Our equipment was home-made bats that Dad had cut, whittled, and sanded from hickory trees, and worn out (or no) baseball gloves. I tried to catch whatever they threw at me even when my hands became black and blue with bruises and never lost my love of the game.

Sometimes, the same group of neighbors gathered at someone's home for a "country dance." One neighbor had sons and daughters who played guitars or fiddles and sang all the popular songs like "Begin the Beguine," and war songs like "When the lights go on again," to dance half the night away. Sometimes, the boys took time out to visit their pickups to drink the "white lightning" they'd brought with them. Occasionally, the dances had to be stopped when drinking got out of hand but usually, the group was orderly. It was great fun as I became aware that many of the young men were attracted to me and started asking me out at 14 and 15.

Our current farm was even further from Holly Springs School. It required walking a mile to meet the bus to take the rural children to town. I started running the distance each day to build my stamina and endurance. At least the bully who teased and pounded me at our last home was no longer on the bus to torment me, and I was free to read or visit with the neighboring children as we traveled.

# Chapter 19

In the ninth grade, I started making friends with some of the students who rode the school bus with me to and from school for nearly an hour each day. Mary Frances was stiff and unfriendly at first, but she warmed as we started discussing books that each of us read en route to school each day. Soon, we were recommending books to each other, or comparing notes about the books we checked out from the library. Before long, when one of us returned a book we liked, we started going to the library together to check out the one that the other one turned in. We had a lot to discuss after reading the same books again and again.

When Gone with the Wind came out in 1939, we would spend the entire time traveling to and from school talking about Scarlett and Rhett or the characters in the book that intrigued us. We started screaming, "Frankly, my dear, I don't give a damn," to each other at any relevant time, or using any excuse to say the word "damn." Both of us loved the book so much that we checked it out of the library at the same time to read it again. It was the most sought-after book that year and for years to come. Our little library had stocked up on them.

Mary Frances was a tall, slightly overweight girl who walked in a stiff, rolling gait that started from her tiptoes as if she was stepping over rows of cotton. This fascinated me, and I started mimicking her high stepping gait. We spent most of our lunch hour at school walking to the library together. Afterward, we grabbed an RC Cola and a moon pie at the local drug store for our noon meal.

Another girl in our class was an avid reader who shared our love for books. Bertie May Buffington was, to me at least, the most inspiring girl in our class, and was rapidly becoming famous for the exciting stories she wrote and read out loud to her classmates. Her stories were somewhat gruesome and frightening—reminiscent of Stephen King—but our classmates loved them.

Our English teacher took every opportunity she could to get Bertie May to read one of her compositions to the class. Her macabre style had some of the students clinging to each other in horror as she read her stories of capture, torture, and blood and guts. Despite her penchant for horror, which I didn't like, her writing style was brilliant and her imagination beyond belief, and Mary Frances and I admired her talent as a storyteller.

Bertie May was something of a loner, but Mary Frances and I cultivated her friendship until she finally warmed to us. After that, the three of us trekked to the library every few days to check out loads of books. Soon, we became the three musketeers who spent our time together, talking books, drinking RC Colas and eating moon pies for lunch.

Our English teacher was a stern German woman named Miss Bernrutter who glared at us from the front of the class and accepted no nonsense or excuses. She grilled us for hours and if someone couldn't answer her questions, she was furious. Nearly all her students hated her except her "pets," who could do no wrong in her eyes. To those of us who detested her, she became Miss "Derntutter." The class clown was a son of one of the "city fathers" who could do no wrong and received good grades even when he neglected to turn in his papers. Clearly a class snob, she was skilled in humiliating students who were shabbily dressed or poor. The sons and daughters of bankers and lawyers were openly favored. Bertie May Buffington was the only exception, who she called upon often to read her creepy stories to the class.

One day, she asked the class to write an essay describing someone or something to bring to class the next day. I chose to write about a classically pretty girl I admired in the senior class.

Miss Bernrutter started the class the next day with the class clown's essay, which she read aloud, followed by one written by another one of her class pets. After reading several essays aloud, she picked up mine and began to read it aloud. She read the first few sentences in a normal voice and then started reading it sarcastically with her voice rising in ever-increasing rage. Suddenly, she stopped reading abruptly, pointed her skinny finger at me angrily, screaming, "Where did you copy this from, young lady?" She was furious, glaring at me as if I were some cornered animal. "You didn't write this. Where did you get it?"

"I wrote it. I didn't copy it from anywhere."

She kept arguing that I didn't write the essay for a full ten minutes, asking me to stand while she berated me by calling me a liar. Nothing I could say convinced her that she was wrong. I was so humiliated that I wanted to melt through the floor. Only long afterward did I understand that perhaps the essay was superior to one that the average ninth-grader could be expected to write. It took years before that humiliation finally went away and I could believe that perhaps I could become a writer someday.

# Chapter 20

FDR's second term as President slowly drew to a close. His administration was a mixed blessing—but a blessing—in our household. We credited him with a few jobs Dad had been able to get under the Works Progress Administration, with the loans he had been able to get for the horses we bought and with putting thousands of young men to work in the CCCs. The hard times had called for intervention in the affairs of the poor and middle class, but Dad resented that the government insisted that he plant certain crops and that income taxes were increasing. We had never had to pay taxes but every farmer dreamed of prosperous times in which we might be called upon to pay some of our hard-earned dollars to the government. We wanted the government to stay out of our lives. At the same time, we realized the necessity of government interference when people were out of work and hungry. Roosevelt's military buildup from 1938 to 1940 finally increased employment opportunities in large cities all over the country, although it did little for small rural towns in the South. We supported him when he began to re-arm and re-equip the country to support Britain, France, China, and the Soviet Union, while Charles Lindbergh and other isolationists attacked him as an irresponsible war-monger.

When Roosevelt sent a message to the Democratic National Convention that he would not run unless he was drafted, the delegates started screaming, "We want Roosevelt." He won an unprecedented third term as President with 55% of the popular voted in 38 of the 48 states.

On December 7, 1941, the students in my class had a radio blasting away in the room. At first, I thought the teacher must be absent to allow such behavior, but she was there, listening as intently as the students. I heard the sound of bombs exploding behind the voice of an outraged announcer shouting, "We're at war! We're at War! The Japanese have bombed Pearl Harbor."

All the kids were hushed and attentive at first and then started babbling, all at once. The anger and shock in that room was beyond description, especially among the older boys, who couldn't wait to enlist in the army to get the "Dirty Japs."

Few in that room even knew where Pearl Harbor was—or that it even existed. Finally, order was restored, and our teacher tried to put some perspective to the horrendous event. Gradually, the details that were known were disclosed to us and there was talk of nothing else among the students for the following weeks and months as details became known. Our youthful innocence disappeared in the following years as we watched the older boys in our school enlist to go to war.

The family counted on my brother and me to help weed, plant and pick the few hillside acres of poor cotton we had grown, and I hated it. Many of the disagreements my sisters and I had with Dad concerned the ways we found to avoid picking cotton. Any excuse would do. We were sick. Mom had given us chores to do. We had to do homework. The great fight with my Dad started when he stated, "You don't care about helping make a living!" He had brainwashed us to believe it was our duty to help the family earn a living, but he was right—I never completely believed that it was the children's duty to help parents make a living. I answered, "That's a lie." No one calls my Dad a liar and gets away with it. He demanded that I take it back but I refused. Finally, I said, "Well, you are a liar," and that did it. He went into the house, grabbed his razor strap and began beating me on the back until it was almost raw. I was 15 years old, determined never to allow that to happen again.

At school the next day, I learned that one of my school mates had a ride into a nearby town where she planned to get a job for the summer vacation. The nation was preparing for a potential war in Europe and jobs were plentiful. I asked if I could go with her. She agreed, saying that I could live with her until I found a job.

When I returned home from school, I told Mom and Dad that I was leaving. They didn't try to discourage me, but Dad finally offered to give me the few cents he had—a whopping 75 cents, and I left with my classmate. I did not intend to return, but I was touched that Dad offered me the only money he had. I believe he understood that I would never allow him to beat me again. I would never forget the beating, nor completely forgive him, although I knew it was a combination of his forefathers' traditions and ignorance.

The place my friend took me to was an old battered house with rough floors, a leaking roof, and little furniture. There were no beds. I slept on the cold floor for several days with little food to eat until I found a job in a Greek restaurant next to the railroad tracks, where soldiers by the hundreds embarked daily from the local military camp. When the trains came in, the restaurant was so full of servicemen; it had to be closed periodically. The young men told me how beautiful I looked and asked for dates, which gave me confidence. But I was still bitter, angry, and full of distrust. I had been betrayed by too many people in my young life. After a while, I found a small apartment to rent and began to accept dates with some of the young soldiers. After a month, the landlord thought the soldiers deserved a place to live more than I did so they asked me to move. I was still a naive young girl but those young servicemen always treated me gently and with respect. They were also young and vulnerable, though sometimes a little wild.

The major problem was housing. With so many soldiers and their families in the small town, there was nothing available to rent. When I couldn't find a place to live, a young mother invited me to sleep with her and her newborn baby in the rooming house where she lived. I slept little that night for fear of rolling over the baby.

There was no recreation all summer. Even if I had more time, I couldn't go swimming because my back still bore the marks from the razor strap. Finally, I found a landlady who agreed to rent a tiny garage efficiency apartment where I could at least cook a meal on my day off. When I finally started dating a young soldier, Jerry, I invited him over for a Sunday dinner, only to find the landlady peering into the window to see what we were up to. Apparently, she thought I was immoral because suddenly she and a policeman appeared at the door and told me I had to move immediately. I was so humiliated and furious at the injustice that I could hardly bear it. Jerry was almost as young and naïve as I was. Although we had raging hormones, neither of us knew much about sex; we hardly knew how to kiss.

There was little money, constant housing problems, and I learned that my Greek employer expected special favors from his waitress staff, which was the shock in my young life. I went along with his invitation to take a ride in his big Cadillac and watched in horror as he started pawing one of the girls. Needless to say, I never joined my fellow workers when he invited them again.

Still, when school started, I enrolled in the local high school from 8:30 am to 3:30 pm, walked a mile or two to work until 11:30 pm and then walked home again, bone tired. Six weeks of this schedule made me realize it was impossible to keep up so I had no alternative than to return home and finish my last two years at the new school. I needed the credits because I hoped to find a way to attend college after graduation. After missing the first six weeks of my hardest subject (algebra), I had a near failing grade on the first report card. Teachers told me that I had to make up all the lessons I'd missed if I wanted to understand algebra. It was torture but somehow, I managed to catch up with my classmates by the midterm and earn good grades again.

Mom and Dad's new farm meant that I would have to change schools from the one I'd attended for more than ten grades, and go to a small school an hour bus ride. I was relieved to get away from the "Daughters of the American Revolution" students with whom I had been attending school. The bullies who teased me and the teachers who humiliated me in my old school would be left to torture someone else.

# Chapter 21

But alas, this move only lasted two years before my parents decided to move to another small town near my new school where I could, at last, participate in the basketball program I wanted. I had never before been able to be an athlete because sports programs were after school hours and I had to take the bus home. It was a good move for me. I was immediately accepted on the basketball team and felt more accepted among my fellow students.

By the time I was 15 years old, my family had moved at least every year or two from one unpainted 2-3 room shack after another. Dad, who had never been lazy, had tried making cross ties for the railroad, tenant farming, logging, and sawmilling lumber, growing sorghum, corn, cotton, beans, and peanuts. He had raised pigs and cattle, plowed with sick old mules and big-footed Percheron horses, and started a small diary. He had even operated the small mill that ground corn for cornmeal.

The closest to security we realized was when we rented the 100-acre farm where we had plenty of food from the garden, orchard, and a few dollars from the cotton, peanuts, and corn we grew. All of us worked our hands to the bones and had nothing to show for it. Dad was still robust and strong and still believed in farming, but the grass was always greener over the next hill. It appeared to me that he moved each time he got close to success. On the other hand, Mom was worn out. She was thin and unhealthy. Her beauty disappeared and she had gained a hunched back from overwork and osteoporosis.

Although Dad was never ready to give up farming, his "labor force" was mostly gone now that Pat and Mel were working away from home, and I had left before I turned 15 to work as a waitress during school vacation. Mom was no longer able to do the milking, ironing, cooking, and other chores plus work in the fields, so Dad was left with my brother and me to help with farming. He tried supervising a forestry crew who cut logs for the pulp mills and the job showed great promise, but the venture also failed.

He seemed to have programmed himself to fail. Mom told him that he paid his men too well. Both of my parents must have been tormented with doubt, fatigue, loss of hope and frustration. I subconsciously understood that the beating I had endured had more to do with his state of mind and poverty than the disrespect I'd shown him. Whippings were the customary punishment for misbehavior by most Southerners for previous generations. No one questioned the practice, and somehow, I believed he felt sorry for having lost control, but it was never spoken of after I returned home. But it got worse.

A similar incident occurred after I returned to finish school. Mom and I had a disagreement about something. I made a vow never to accept another beating from either of them. Perhaps I was disrespectful or disobedient, but Mom broke a small branch off the little cedar tree in the yard and slashed me across my bottom with it. I reacted by covering my buttocks with my hands. The branch cut through the flesh of my hand, laying a wide, jagged cut all the way to the bone. Both of us went into shock when we saw the open profusely bleeding wound. She screamed, crying hysterically for Dad, who ran for our little truck to take me to the doctor in town about 12 miles away. The doctor made numerous stitches in the jagged wound. Mom kept saying repeatedly, "I'm so sorry. I didn't mean to hurt you!" I knew that was true. Like Dad, she had taken her frustration out on me. It took over a year before the wound completely healed and much longer before the ligaments healed enough to close my hand. I carried resentments and almost a love/hate relationship with my parents for some time after that summer, mixed with pity for them. They were a product of their forefathers, just as I would be someday—although I hoped I would overcome the mistakes of my parents.

But my need to finish school was more important to me than a chaotic dysfunctional family.

I had to struggle to catch up on the six weeks I'd missed in Algebra. It took until midterm to change my first term grade from a D to an A by studying harder than ever.

Then, I started to look for ways to earn my own money. My sisters often came home on weekends and Mel—who worked as a hostess and cigarette girl at a large Memphis hotel—suggested that I get a job there during the two-week Christmas holiday. America was now at war and all kinds of jobs could be had for the asking. I only had to fill out an application to be accepted as a waitress in the taproom at the same hotel, even though I was 15 instead of the required 18. Like the restaurant I'd worked for the previous summer, the taproom was crowded with soldiers, sailors, and marines from morning until closing time. I had no knowledge whatsoever about the different brands of beer they served, or even how to pronounce the word "Budweiser" for instance—but I learned. Surprisingly, the young military men treated me with respect, other than an occasional pinch on the bottom that earned the perpetuator a nasty retort. My fighting instincts were still in evidence. I would take nothing from anyone that degraded my dignity.

Within the first few days on the job, I was offered dozens of dates and offers to take me home after my shift was over. I accepted the offer to walk me home to Mel's place, where I shared a room—an offer than entailed riding a bus from downtown to the outskirts, a place I had only visited after arriving in Memphis the day before. I had the address, but little knowledge about how to get there.

My soldier and I chose a bus I thought would take us there but I had forgotten all the landmarks and we got off before crossing a long bridge, only to learn the street we sought was on the other side. We walked across that bridge two or three times before I finally recognized the correct street.

When I told him I was only 15, he didn't believe me. He said I looked to be in my twenties. The courtesy and patience of that poor soldier was amazing, but I felt humiliated that I didn't even know where I lived. Later, I went out with a young sailor named J. G. LeSieur, who sang one song after another to me beautifully as he accompanied me home after work. After I quit the two-week job to return home and back to school, J. G. came to visit me from Memphis several times. I met him at the bus station, a couple of miles from my house, and we walked the rest of the way. I will always remember those songs and wonder if he was ever able to use his talent as a professional singer. I also wondered if he became the famous news anchor by that name.

The following summer, when I was 16, I got a job in Memphis again, working as a telephone operator for a large hardware company. It was a strange choice since I had never even used a telephone before.

# Chapter 22

I returned to school on December 7, 1941. All the talk among my friends was about the tragedy in Hawaii. Before long, we would see parades of military jeeps and heavily laden trucks filled with rowdy soldiers go by our house to some bivouac camp in the hills and hollows nearby.

When I was in viewing distance, they hooted, hollered, and whistled wolf calls at me. I smiled and waved, grateful for the attention. Those poor young boys had no inkling of the tragedy, death, and destruction of war, nor did I. Camping out and playing with guns in camouflaged uniforms was a big game they were enjoying to the hilt, and a pretty country girl who waved at them added to the romance of it all. I was grateful that they weren't judging me by the dilapidated shack nearby: they must have known I lived there.

A few days later, they returned from camp in a cloud of dust. I was waiting for the school bus with my books and sack lunch beside the road when a truck full of young men careened around the corner and smashed my lunch beneath their tires as they wolf-whistled at me. Too startled to react, I picked up my books and entered the school bus. About a month afterward when my teacher told me I was wanted at the principal's office, I was scared, wondering what I could have done wrong. What the…? My grades were good, and the only trouble I had gotten into was when the boys called me "new grape bottle," and I reacted angrily. I didn't understand they were referring to my shape—similar to the shape of the New Grape bottle.

The secretary handed me a letter, scrawled in pencil across a paper from a cheap pencil tablet. It was addressed to "to whom it may concern," to an address on the rural road where I lived. The school had picked my name from the students who lived on that road. She asked, "Are you the person whose lunch was smashed by a military vehicle recently?" When I replied that, yes, the bivouacking soldiers had smashed my lunch, she gave me a letter.

It was from a soldier who was full of apologies because his jeep had run over my lunch and then went on to say that he would love to meet the pretty young girl he had treated so poorly, if accidentally. He asked if the young lady would reply to him in the future. He signed the letter with an address of a nearby military base. What a wonderfully thoughtful gesture it was, that left me feeling there were good men in the world to take the time to apologize for such a minor incident. I glowed from his use of the word pretty. He asked me to answer his letter.

He hadn't judged me, as my classmates often did about my well-worn dress or the poverty in the area. At 15 years of age, Mom and Dad might have consented to my answering the letter, but meeting the young man would have been a whole different story. I thought I would never see the young man again, and I was right.

Shortly afterward, we moved again to another small farm near another town not far away, where I had to change school. It was much smaller, with more rural farm students, and I was happy to be leaving Holly Springs, where I was so often by the children of the old and wealthy families who had lived there since the Civil War—or before.

When we moved to the town of Potts Camp, it made it possible to join the high school basketball team. Although I had never played the game before and didn't know the rules, I quickly "made the team" because some of the 11 girls in my class didn't play. Now that I had made up all the points, I needed for my sophomore year, I had only morning classes and could devote the entire afternoon to practicing basketball and reading.

I had a wonderful English class teacher who recognized my thirst for knowledge and recommended a reading list that no doubt furthered my education more than any other method could have. Fortunately, she had a good library, which our school did not, and kept me supplied with many beloved old classics.

I never heard "you'll never amount to a hill of beans" from her as I had from my parents for having "my nose stuck in a book" all the time. She became my mentor and good friend long after I had graduated and encouraged me as I poured out my dreams of going to college and becoming a writer and painter. If there were grants and loans available in those years, neither of us was aware of it. No one ever even suggested it was possible for me to go to college. But basketball was my school's claim to fame. Our boys' team always was in the state finals, and soon the girls' team became almost as popular when we got into the finals as well. Unfortunately, we lost the final game, coming in second in the State playoffs.

I graduated in 1945, one out of 11 senior girls and one boy who hadn't joined the military with other classmates. Exhilarated and blissful after the graduating ceremony, I felt ready to meet any challenges that life had to offer. I wish I had saved the long poem I wrote that day in which I asked that life present me with all kinds of diverse experiences from which I could learn. I wanted to read every book, know everything there was to know and to achieve great wisdom by confronting countless kinds of experiences and challenges. The old saw, "Beware of what you wish for," did not occur to me at the time, but my requests would be rewarded more than I ever dreamed of being possible.

I again headed for Memphis for a job, hopefully to save money for college. My dad's sister, Aunt Carrie, and her daughter owned a big house divided into one and two-room apartments and each of my siblings lived in one or another of the apartments off and on during our early working years. They treated us as adults but worked with us if we were short of cash for the rent, though we were careful never to take advantage of them. Sometimes, food was scarce and Aunt Carrie seemed to know when to supply us with a plate of cornbread and greens, a bowl of soup or something. Mel and Pat sometimes helped me through rough times.

The war continued and clerical jobs were easy to find. Pat worked at Memphis Army Supply Depot and suggested that I apply for a civil service job there. A few months later I was hired only to face a reduction in force only six months later. Pat and I went to work together, had lunch together and often used the base recreational facilities and swimming pool. There, we met handsome young soldiers who wanted to take us out to movies or dancing. Pat and I occasionally accepted casual dates, but neither of us found anyone that interested us for very long.

Soon, I found employment at a nearby airline, where I performed routine office duties. I had only worked there a couple of months when I was called into the Personnel Office, where I was offered the chance to train to be an airline stewardess—until they learned that I was only 17. It was a huge disappointment when I was told I was too young

But I was having a great life; working during the day and going to skating rinks and dating the young men I met at the rink or at work.

Johnny, an army corporal, was the first young man I dated on a regular basis that summer. He was more serious than many of the boys I dated but he knew how to enjoy life. We went to the best restaurants and dances, including the rooftop of the Memphis Peabody where famous bands like Tommy Dorsey played. Usually, one or more couples accompanied us to lakes for swimming, movies, dances, nightclubs, restaurants, and skating rinks in his little convertible, laughing and sometimes singing en route. He bought tickets to the famous Memphis paddle wheeler, The Memphis Bell, where we danced and drank champagne as we watched the muddy Mississippi flow by.

Money seemed to be no object and he entertained me lavishly. Only when he lightheartedly told me that he had lost $800 in a poker game did it occur to me to wonder where he got all that carelessly spent money on a soldier's pay. It shocked me when he said that the money he lost could have been a down payment on an engagement ring—which neither of us had ever discussed before. I liked him, but marriage was the farthest thing from my mind, as I thought it was from his. But it did not matter. We went everywhere together and had a wonderful time.

One very hot day that summer, I asked Johnny to drive me to Mississippi to visit my parents on Sunday and he thought it was a great idea. Off we went. Mom loaded the table with homegrown vegetables and fried chicken. Despite the flies that hovered over the table and the almost unbearable heat and humidity, Johnny ate as if starved. We always frequented the best restaurants in Memphis, but I had never seen him enjoy a meal so much. He told mom it was the best food he had ever eaten, leaving her beaming with pleasure. Afterward, we sat out in the "dog trot" to visit with Mom, Dad, and my brother Dick as we swatted flies and fanned ourselves to cool off.

Johnny was strangely silent as we returned to Memphis. I repeatedly asked him what was wrong. He didn't reply until he dropped me off at Aunt Carrie's little apartment. We had a date the following day, August 15, 1945, and as we waved goodbye, he said, "I'll see you tomorrow."

The next day, one of Johnny's friends phoned me from the base. He told me that Johnny had been shipped out and would be unable to keep our date, but he would write later. Shortly afterward, I heard Aunt Carrie yelling, "The war is over! The war is over! Thank God!" Car horns and fire stations sirens were blasting all over the city. My roommate and I joined the crowd on a nearby street corner to catch a bus downtown to join the festivities. As we waited for the crowded bus, a little convertible full of noisy soldiers passed by, screaming and waving like maniacs. It was Johnny and his friends. "Shipped out, eh?" I said to my roommate.

Suddenly, I understood his attitude and silence the previous day. The bus came and we continued downtown, to streets so crowded that no one could move. Everyone was kissing everyone else. I vowed that nothing was going to spoil this occasion—but Johnny's lie left me reeling. Again, I was faced with discrimination because of family's poverty.

I had never spoken to Johnny about my parents' poverty or mentioned the little three-room, un-ceiled house where they lived. It had never occurred to me that my parents or their poverty had anything to do with my relationships. I was devastated, not because I'd lost my friendship as much as to discover his prejudice and lack of character. Later, one of Johnny's friends called me and explained that Johnny was from a very socially prominent, wealthy New Orleans family. So what, I thought? My family is not good enough for them? That is just too damn bad! Johnny's lie was one of the most humiliating experiences I had as a young woman. I would be myself whether elitists thought I was good enough or rich enough for them. I had enough of these superior attitudes from socially conscious classmates as a child.

In spite of the anger I felt, I put the experience into perspective. My parents were intelligent, but they were uneducated, unsophisticated, and indoctrinated by the religious fervor of The Southern Baptist and Methodist Churches.

While I felt comfortable in most social situations, I could not imagine my parents fitting into the social circle that Johnny apparently occupied any more than I felt I belonged in the three-room shacks, with flies buzzing on the food in the little house. How could I blame Johnny, when my parents were full of their own prejudices? Not only the Negro race was beneath them, but Mom was critical and judgmental about our friends and relatives and even her own children. We invited sexual exploitation if we wore shorts, we would go to hell if we used an expletive, and our hair and clothes were never well-groomed enough to satisfy her. She made us feel that our friends and even many of our relatives were never quite good enough for us. Even my beloved sister, Pat, often criticized me and told me what to do. Feeling superior to others seemed to run in the family

# Chapter 23

It was unpopular for married women to work at all because they were taking jobs that husbands need. The war was over and employment opportunities were changing as young men returned from the war. We were relieved when we could buy nylons and gasoline again when civilians no longer were expected to plant victory gardens. When men returned from their war adventures, Pat and Mel could stop spending all their time writing letters to their men as they drifted home from far shores, and the few who had cars from the early '40s could buy tires for them. Returning servicemen began to claim the jobs that young women had held in defense factories. Employment for women was harder to find and we were expected to accept only support jobs such as office work and let our returning heroes take the better-paying jobs. The baby boom began when the young men drifted back from the war and started families.

It was a brave new world for returning servicemen who were rewarded for their service by The Servicemen's Readjustment Act (G.I. Bill of Rights). Three times as many college degrees were conferred in 1949 as compared to 1940. College became available to the capable rather than the privileged few. This act no doubt raised the intellectual level of thousands of Americans, and I only wished that the country would authorize programs for the rest of the nation's citizens.

Although television came out at the 1939 World Fair, the war interrupted further development, but by 1947, 13 commercial television stations were available to the public. And although the first computers were developed during the early forties, by 1945 they weighed 30 tons and stood two stories high. Few of us could envision a use for those monstrosities.

The United States emerged from World War II as a world superpower, challenged only by the USSR. While the USSR subjugated the defeated countries, the US implemented the Marshall Plan to help war-torn countries rebuild and rejoin the world economy. Disputes over ideology and control led to the Cold War. Communism was considered worse than a contagious disease, and anyone who had contact with it was under suspicion. A former hero of the New Deal, Alger Hiss was indicted as a traitor and his infamous hearings began.

After graduation from high school, I managed to find office work to fill in while I waited for better civil service jobs to become available. One was in the payroll department of a Memphis newspaper, where I hoped to work my way into the news department as a writer or reporter. I didn't have the credentials, of course, but at least I could try. After a year without meeting my goal, I decided to try something else. At least I saved over $100 before searching for a better job. When I learned that Mom and Dad couldn't pay the annual rent on their farm, I used the money for their rent. I decided that salaries were designed to barely cover basic living expenses and working men and women would never be able to prosper as wage earners. Perhaps, I hoped, the government paid better. I sent out civil service applications for every available position I could find and finally was accepted in a clerical position at SAC (Strategic Air Command), where Pat had taken a job while she waited to join her new husband, an army air force pilot, on his next assignment. We often took advantage of the recreational facilities provided for SAC's flying officers, meeting for lunch or after work for a dip in the pool to bring each other up to date. Mel was working in a defense factory, saving everything she made for a home when her army officer husband returned from war. Like Pat, she spent her free time writing letters and waiting.

On weekends, the three of us drove to Mississippi to check on our parents and brother, with whom Dad had talked into going into another farming venture. My brother Dick had enough of hardscrabble farming and insisted that the only way to make a living at farming was on a far larger scale with more and better land and more fertilizer. Cotton and corn were out, he insisted—the new cash crop was soybeans. He convinced Dad to borrow more money, buy a tractor, and rent the largest and richest parcel of bottomland they could find.

Dad knew it was the only way to keep Dick from leaving as his older sisters had, so they put the plan into action and planted soybeans on 100 acres of rich bottomland adjacent to Tippah River. When the fields of tall, healthy plants covered the land, we thought Dick was right, and prosperity was finally on the way. But it was not to be. The crop was nearly ripe and ready for harvest in August, and then driving rains caused the river to overflow into the fields, inundating the crop in which they had placed all their hopes and dreams. Shortly afterward, Dick was drafted into the army, leaving dad with the debts they had incurred. Dick vowed never to farm again, while Dad harassed the army to release him from service to help with the next crop. Eventually, he was released, but he vowed never to farm again. Like his sisters before him, Dick wanted no part of the poverty we had known and left home to seek his fortune after he graduated from school.

Dad lived on hope, while Mom lived on faith that the Lord will provide. Pat, Mel, and I were the providers, and we worried about our parents as much as our own needs. We continued to send them money, at the same time we questioned why we were so devoted to parents who had beaten us and shown so little affection to us. We were the victims, as they were, of the old way of rearing children: "spare the rod and spoil the child" and "children, cleave to thy parents."

Mom's devotion was written in the wrinkles in her face and the curved spine and humped back as she aged, while Dad's was in his failure to give up in the face of impossible odds. Dad simply could never believe that it was impossible to prosper when nearly half of everything he grew as a tenant farmer paid tribute to those who owned the land. We had to give him credit for finding a way to pull a rabbit out of a hat to pay for our worn-out shoes in a time when no one had money during the long depression, and where the South clung to a political system that awarded the "haves" as it raped the poor.

My siblings and I were determined to make their lives better as well as our own. It never occurred to us that the workers of the world would never again be able to attain prosperity as company employees, or that in the future it would require both husbands and wives to work in order to meet normal living expenses.

While I waited for my civil service application to be approved, there were rumors from neighbors and friends that FBI agents were asking questions about me, scaring the daylights out of everyone. "What's that girl up to now?" they asked, thinking of crimes I must have committed. Then, suddenly, I received a letter offering an appointment with the Atomic Energy Commission in Oak Ridge, Tennessee. I was elated and accepted before they could change their mind. I was so excited that I couldn't sleep on the overnight sleeper car to go hundreds of miles from home to a place I'd never heard of before. I watched the emerald fields framed in the train's windows as we rumbled through the night, and then the fog-shrouded Blue Ridge Mountains bathed in the pale moonlight. It was the most beautiful sight I'd ever seen.

Oak Ridge was a tiny hamlet in rolling hills some 20 or so miles from Knoxville that became a town of 50,000 almost overnight when the Atomic Energy Commission chose the site for its headquarters.

The internet describes the city as follows: Oak Ridge, Tenn., a city born of war, living for peace and growing through science, offers a unique blend of the past, present and future for visitors to East Tennessee.

Oak Ridge, Tennessee had geared up, as had the rest of the nation, to do its part in the war effort. By 1941, the world was at war. No one knew then that a small valley in East Tennessee would play such a big role in ending World War II. This 60,000-acre tract of land was chosen as one of the sites for the now historic Manhattan Project.

By 1947, when I went there, prefabricated houses and dormitories sprawled across thousands of acres, dominated by the huge AEC Headquarters building, laboratories, defense factories, instant shopping, and recreational centers. The little city had grown overnight to more than 50,000 mostly young civil servants, offering inexpensive housing and great recreational facilities from skating rinks to soccer fields. Most of us were to serve the top scientists in the world in one capacity or another.

The local newspaper cited statistics of the city's population as "more young people than in any city in the world" and "the best recreational facilities anywhere" and "more babies born per capita than anywhere in the world."

I was assigned to AEC Headquarters in the Research Department, where I typed thousands of pages of scientific research on a Varitypes machine (similar to a typewriter with the addition to thousands of mathematical and scientific symbols). Most of the text I wrote was unintelligible to me, but I understood why I was required to have a "top secret" clearance. At first, it was interesting to see all the studies and pictures of the Bikini tests and to chat with the eccentric nuclear scientists.

I was in my element, loving every minute—except the monotony of typing material day after day that made little sense to me. After a few months, I haunted the Personnel office to ask for a transfer to a more interesting job. Finally, I was promoted to GS-4 as a payroll clerk in the Payroll department.

# Chapter 24

Mom, Mel, and Pat wrote often. Pat had followed her husband from one military assignment to another, but when he refused to send for her when he was assigned to Germany; she understood that he was more interested in drinking and playing than he was in his young wife, so she filed for divorce. Mel had joined her husband in California and wrote glowing letters about the beauty of the area and the big trout she caught in clear mountain streams and the huge mule deer they killed around snow-capped Mt. Shasta Mountains, which towered above their home. It sounded like heaven. Mel wrote to Dick to tell him the railroad where her husband worked would be hiring soon, Dick didn't hesitate and left for California shortly after the army released him. A few weeks later, he wrote that he had the best job he ever had and loved the area and his new life. The family was scattered from the East Coast now to the West Coast, but all seemed to be well with them. I missed them, especially the frequent visits with "the folks" we once had when we were close enough to visit them often.

After I had lived in Oak Ridge several months, unaccountably, I had a vague uneasiness that wouldn't go away. I thought I was just homesick—until the nightmares began. Every night for three weeks, I had the same vivid recurring dream that woke me trembling with fear. In the dream, I saw someone lying broken and bleeding under a car. Police officers and a group of people I did not know crowded around the over-turned car. I could hear sirens in the distance. I could not shake the images even during the day. I felt something was wrong. My supervisor suggested that I take a few days' vacation and go home. After I arrived, everything seemed fine. We caught up with the news over one of mom's good dinners (called suppers) and planned a fishing trip to a favorite lake the next day.

Their house was close to a two-lane highway with a 5-6 foot incline on each side. When we returned, we had to turn across a busy traffic lane into our driveway which crossed the incline. I saw Dad slow to make the turn, signal, and check behind us for traffic before he made the turn. I also checked and saw nothing. Barely after the truck's hood crossed the on-coming lane and entered the driveway, there was the sound of screeching brakes and horrifying crash of metal against metal. Mom flew out of the passenger side and landed in the ditch. I landed nearby. The little pickup truck lay on its side in the "V" between the highway and our driveway.

A motorcycle had hit directly into the driver's door and catapulted into the edge of our yard. The operator lay crookedly between the drive and highway. It was apparent that he was dead, but where was Dad? I finally discovered him with the side of the pickup lying on top of his chest. He screamed for help. I had to do something and ran to the truck's hood, where it still rocked from the impact. If I could lift the slightly raised front long enough someone would come and drag Dad from under the truck. By that time several neighbors had arrived. Some of them saw that I could never lift the truck by myself and they held some of the weight of the truck off Dad while I ran and dragged him from beneath the truck. His injuries were restricted to a broken collar bone, a severely black eye, and numerous scrapes and bruises. Mom had a broken arm and scrapes, soreness and bruises.

I believe my dreams may have been an occult experience that led me to be present and perhaps help save Dad's life. The accident—like most—was no accident. It was caused by a fine young man acting recklessly. He had bragged to friends, "I can do that curve before Layton's place going 100." He did not live to collect the bet.

Other than this experience, my two years in Oak Ridge were one of the happiest periods in my life. I had a challenging job and earned enough to save a few dollars. My social life was filled with sports such as softball, skating, walks, swimming, and dating. I met hundreds of handsome young men who thought I was intelligent and pretty who clamored to take me to parties, movies, and dinners. I was flattered when one of the AEC Physics' asked for a date, then forgot all about it and did not show up. "I'm so sorry," he said. "I just forgot," he apologized. It didn't matter because I had more dates than I could accept.

Most of my dates were casual except for the young man (Bob) who phoned to talk to his girlfriend, Doris, then started bantering with me. Doris was not available, so he began flirting outrageously with me, calling me 'luscious baby" before he asked me out on a blind date. He was lighthearted and charming, and before long, I began to date him regularly. He kept the group we double dated with in stream-of-conscious bantering and nonsense. We had dinner together almost every night or went swimming or on long walks together. I also dated Jim (fictitious name) at the same time, who took me on a visit to Great Smoky National Park. I was torn between Jim and Bob who were attentive, attractive and personable. I never completely forgot Jim—we had an immediate, almost spiritual, connection and after the trip, we made an appointment to meet again the following day.

Bob intervened, somehow convincing me that he was my only romantic interest. In contrast to my somber nature, his optimism was contagious and he made me believe in silver linings.

Additionally, coming from an unaffectionate family, his constant demonstrations of love left me whirling. While Bob was medium height and almost scrawny, Jim's athlete's body with heavy muscles, broad back, and trim buttocks was more attractive to me than Bob. Jim's quiet gravity, contemplative nature, and quick sense of humor was enormously appealing—I sensed responsibility, sharp intellect, and strength, but I succumbed to Bob's electronic blue eyes showered by thick lashes and to his charm and wit and canceled my date with Jim.

Bob could make a glacier melt and had me in the palm of his hands. When he asked me to marry him almost a year later, I was helpless to say anything but "yes." Afterward, doubts crept in and I called it off; he just wasn't the serious, responsible man I envisioned living with for the rest of my life. I stopped answering his phone calls and visits, but he refused to give up. Finally, he came to my dormitory, saying he would wait on the porch until I met with him, no matter how long it took. After hours of buzzing my room, I could take no more and came out to tell him it was over once and for all time. But within minutes, he had me laughing and back in the palm of his hands. The next thing I knew, I was committed.

Bob wanted to be a writer, as I did. We made a plan that I would work to send him to college so that he earned enough to send me through school. We went through dozens of ideas for professions or trades where he could earn the kind of money we would need, finally deciding on photography school, which he thought would be lucrative. At the time, he was earning too little to save anything and was always broke before payday. When he financed my engagement ring, it meant that I had to pay for our meals and other expenses, even before we were married. The handwriting was on the wall. The photography school we chose in Philadelphia promised a good career as a commercial or portrait artist. Unfortunately, artist photographers were a dime a dozen and made little money, and Bob was not an artist.

I put aside my doubts and we were married in his little Baptist church in Knoxville in November 1947, attended by his best friend and his wife and Bob's parents. We skipped the honeymoon to save money for train fare and tuition for the school where Bob had enrolled in under the G.I. Bill. We loaded our meager belongings into a steamer trunk and departed for Philadelphia in early 1947, with $600 I had saved in the prior two years.

In the two years we spent there, we received an education far more valuable than in photography school. We met Jewish landlords who would steal "the coins off a dead man's eyes," as Mom would have said. Sicilians, Italians, blacks, and others sold numbers on the street outside the little two-room apartment we rented, and our eyes were opened to homeless street people who defecated in alleys shamelessly. Street vendors grabbed our arms as we walked by, entreating us to buy their stolen watches and jewels, or cheap racks of clothing or pots and pans.

I was appalled at the numbers of gamblers, prostitutes, and drunks sleeping in the filthy streets. But in time, we met a wonderful Italian family who invited us to join their 14 children for Sunday dinners and then gathered around the piano to sing magnificent Italian songs while we waited for their mother to serve the finest Italian meals I've ever eaten, served with homemade red wine. Afterward, we were invited to help stomp grapes they had gathered in huge vats in the basement to make the wine, or go bowling or to movies with younger members of the family. They made this lonely homesick young couple welcome as a part of their family.

Money was always short, especially when the Veteran's Administration benefits Bob received were lost in the mail for weeks, as they frequently were, or when I was unable to find work. Many times, we were so broke that Bob borrowed money on my little engagement ring, and even tried to borrow on a bowling ball at pawn shops. One time, we had only eight cents for food and had to choose between spaghetti sauce and spaghetti for dinner.

The little two-room walk-up apartment had a closet-size kitchen with shelves for cabinets and an old gas stove that threatened to blow up every time we turned it on. The only food in the kitchen was a box of crackers. When I opened the box, cockroaches flooded the little apartment and streaked in every direction. I was adamant that we had to move out of that place! After we moved, the landlord claimed we damaged the treads on the stairs and demanded money. There were no landlord-tenant agreements in those days.

Jobs became scarce with thousands of returning servicemen looking for work. I haunted the employment office until I found a job across the river in New Jersey, so we moved again. There was no money for recreation and little for food, and I became clinically depressed without realizing what was wrong. The young Jewish doctor I saw realized immediately that my depression was due to loneliness, poverty, and being away from family and friends. Bob's student stipend helped, but it was not enough to live on. The doctor began taking me on his rounds and invited us to his home to give us our first appreciation of classical music. I will always be grateful to that caring man and his family.

Soon, we realized that commuting from New Jersey to school in Philadelphia was an expensive and time-consuming problem and we looked for a closer, better-paying job and moved into a two-room walk-up in one of the worst sections in town. It was so dirty that we begged the landlord for paint. He agreed to supply the paint and allow a discount on the rent but never applied the discount after we scrubbed and cleaned and painted. After seeing the fights, noise, and violence in the neighborhood, we answered an ad from a young couple in a better neighborhood offering room and board in their home. The home was nice enough, but we soon learned that our hosts spend all their money gambling on horse races instead of on meals and utilities. The electricity often was cut off and meals were so scant that we were always hungry. We were forced to move again. This time, we chose a room in a lovely old grey stone in beautiful Germantown filled with the most beautiful antiques I'd ever seen. The landlady, an elderly lady and her daughter who claimed to be an actress, were gracious—but when the alcoholic son and brother visited them, he often woke us a 3:00 am demanding that we make breakfast for him. When we did, he vomited on his plate.

We had over an hour to commute via subway to work and school, but the river and park were nearby, so we spent our free time exploring and filling our souls with the sights and smells of nature that we missed so much. Occasionally, world-famous conductors presented symphony concerts in the park. We had our first experience listening to symphony orchestras play Haydn, Beethoven, Brahms, Schumann, Sibelius, and other pieces we'd never heard before.

When we could take no more of the alcoholic son waking us in the middle of the night, we finally moved into our own, tiny apartment. Money was in short supply, but Bob found part-time work photographing tissue slides for a pathologist. He brought samples of human livers, kidneys, hearts, and other parts home to be stored in the refrigerator to be photographed. I gagged each time I made a meal, but the extra money came in handy. We still had little to share, but when Bob's Dad was admitted to the hospital and subsequently diagnosed manic-depressive and schizophrenic, we were able to send his mother a few dollars for food until his father's army pension went into effect. We had little enough, but without her breadwinner husband, his mother had no income. They had bought a small piece of property and were in the process of slowly building a small house and had spent the savings they had.

When I couldn't locate a job, I claimed to be a bookkeeper and was accepted in a Philadelphia religious publication. After all, I had "an introduction to bookkeeping" in high school, and believed I could figure it out. It almost worked—I kept the job for a year by looking at old records to see how to make an entry, but in time, I was exposed and fired. In the meantime, I learned a great deal about bookkeeping.

We spend weekends and evenings in our spare time visiting museums and The Philadelphia Art Gallery, where I gawked at the world's great paintings and sculptures, then returned to our wretched apartment to try to emulate their techniques, colors, and designs. When I discovered a basic drawing class offered there in the evenings, I enrolled in it and was delighted when the instructor told me that I had a lot of ability when I did a pencil drawing of one of the sculptures. Maybe I could be a painter!

One of our friends was an unattractive, but fascinating, tall, thin Bohemian Italian who visited us often, bringing loads of books to read. As an early "hippy," Tony ranted against all "the practices of the establishment," politics, World War II, the economy, the police, and nearly everything else. He stopped attending the college he had enrolled in, saying, "They only teach lies. He read psychology, history, politics, and novels, and questioned almost everything he read. One day he appeared, wearing a bulging leather coat that he opened to reveal several thick books inside."

"Where did you get them?" I asked.

"I filtered them from the library," he told us. I was aghast to learn that our friend was a crook who sold numbers to earn extra money and stole books, but I could not resist the books that he gave me to read. He followed my puny efforts to draw and paint with pencil colors, the only art supplies I had, with great interest. He insisted that my husband provide me with my first oil painting set for my birthday, and he did. It was a wooded box filled with dozens of tubes of oil paint that Bob bought for $20. That set today would cost more than $150.00, and I still have the box and a few of the nearly dried up tubes of paint. My first efforts to use them were dismal.

When President Harry Truman made his campaign trip to Philadelphia, most of the employees in my firm crowded at windows to watch the procession go by. The candidate sat on top of the back seat, waving and smiling. At the time, I considered him to be a country boob who was a tool of the political machine that had helped him get elected to the Senate earlier. It angered me later that he was responsible for dropping bombs and killing thousands of innocent Japanese women and children. His nasal speeches turned me off at the time, but later, as he governed the country, I became a fan of his earthiness, sincerity and independent thought.

Bombing and killing thousands of innocent Japanese women anrly to returning to the South to be near our families. He now had a certificate proclaiming his expertise as a commercial and portrait photographer. We looked forward to profiting from his two-year training and having a livable income again and left Philadelphia with high hopes and big dreams.

Bob's GI stipend had stopped. We had no money, so we asked to stay at his mother's small house until he could find a job. In the meantime, I started dreaming of babies. I had thought little about having children but the dreams were vivid and compelling, night after night. I did not understand, but the dreams left me feeling an urgency that was baffling and disturbing. What in the world would I do with a baby when we had no job and no money?

When she returned from church one Sunday, she screamed at me that I was a lazy and ungrateful guest because I hadn't started the pot roast for dinner. She refused to accept my illness and berated me over and over, while I cowed in a corner. Bob tried to defend me, but it didn't help.

# Chapter 25

Bob spent every day looking for photography work—or any other job available in the Knoxville, Tennessee area. Many returning servicemen had the same experience, so he decided to strike out across the South in search of work in his chosen field. I was never more proud of him than when he hitchhiked to Atlanta and all the smaller cities in between. For over a week, he went from Atlanta to Memphis, often washing dishes for meals, reporting later that he spent nights at YMCA's or flophouses.

Finally, an "artist commercial photographer" in Memphis agreed to give him a try after Bob agreed to work night and day if necessary, to photograph store windows at 3:00 or 4:00 am when traffic was light. They agreed that Bob, in time, would open a wedding and portrait photography branch of the business. The hours were long. The pay was $25.00 a week with no overtime, holidays, or other benefits. It was all he could afford as a young commercial artist with few clients.

Bob was impressed with the high quality of his work and had great hopes of making the young firm prosper and become recognized. The Artist, who owned the small commercial studio in his home, was a young perfectionist who accepted nothing but top-quality work. Like a bulldog, he did each job over and over until it was "right" by his nearly impossible standards. Many times, both Bob and the owner worked all day, all night and the following day without stopping to produce images. The months passed, and while they continued to discuss a portrait and wedding branch of the business, there was no time or money. In retrospect, after so many years, I believe that the little studio may have become one of the best commercial photography businesses in the area and if he had stayed, could have eventually succeeded. But after trying to make ends meet on $25.00 a week, I insisted that Bob find another job.

Pat wrote that she was now happily married to the man of her dreams, a young Air Force Captain whom she met at the SAC (Strategist Air Force) base where we had worked in Memphis. She and Mel called or wrote often in anticipation of my big day giving birth to the first grandson in the family. Pat, who was there in many big events in my life, decided to be there to make sure the birth didn't happen without her. I went into labor early on the morning of September 4th but my doctor didn't send me to the hospital until 7:30 pm that night. Pat drove us through the crowded streets of Memphis, blasting the horn all the way while the contractions became closer and closer. Nevertheless, when the doctor finally came, he filled me with so much medication that I knew nothing until after 1:30 am when my new son, Bobby, arrived. My doctor's chosen medication was Demerol which caused me to scream every obscenity in the book. I remembered nothing until after the baby was born, despite an agreement with the doctor that the birth would be natural. Apparently, I called him, Bob, and everyone else every epithet known. I was sore from top to bottom and was torn so badly that I didn't heal for weeks.

When they laid that bald, squirming little piece of flesh and blood into my arms and he grasped my finger in his tiny little fist, I was captivated. He felt and smelled like a bowl of dough that I wanted to knead. When he suckled my swollen breasts until some of the pressure released and the pain subsided, I experienced a little bit of heaven. He was beautiful and perfectly shaped except for huge hands and feet and big ears like his Dad's, but restless and unhappy. Bob insisted he must be named after him and my objection that no one should be saddled with the same name as thousands of others couldn't sway him. Bob was determined to have a junior in the family.

Bobby screamed for the first three months night and day with colic or hunger. We walked him most of the night or gave him different medications the doctor ordered. Nothing worked, but at three months it suddenly stopped, only to be replaced by such energetic squirming and wiggling that it was nearly impossible to hold him. He was fighting the world with every instinct he had, but neither his doctor nor I believed it was the result of hunger.

My slender, frail mother came to see the baby but even her motherly skills didn't work with Bobby. It was all she could do to hold him—he would arch his back and almost squirm out of her arms. Her health was failing, so I took her for a medical checkup. The diagnosis was swift and shocking: she had cancer of the uterus. The doctor called me aside to tell me, suggesting that I inform none of the family, especially my mother. Although I thought it was bad advice, I told no one for a number of years, and my mother only learned about it when she was in her 80s.

I now doubt it would have made any difference because Mom accepted her lot in life without complaining. When she was discharged after surgery, she returned to their little house in Mississippi, and to her duties, gardening, canning, housework, drawing water, and taking care of Dad. The doctor told me he thought her prognosis was good. Fortunately, he was right.

# Chapter 26

It was 1950 and America was prosperous and at peace, although inflation was considered a problem. The war years had seen the fastest period of economic growth in its history as factories supported its allies' war efforts. Those plants had retooled and were producing consumer goods which caused a boom in consumer spending. The Marshall Plan, which hoped to promote political stability and assure peace, offered American aid for recovery and aid to the hungry and poor in Europe. The idea of reconstruction was partially due to the calamity of the 1930s, convinced many that a free market could not guarantee economic well-being. The New Dealer's hopes to revive the economy now sought to apply those programs to Europe. The Great Depression had shown the dangers of tariffs and protectionism, creating a belief in the need for free trade and economic integration in Europe.

The congressional campaigns that year largely concerned the Korean War and inflation. The Republicans' theme was "Liberty against Socialism," claiming Truman's Fair Deal programs were modeled on the Socialist governments in Europe. Gen. Eisenhower, expected to be the front runner as the Republican nominee in the next election, claimed the United States suffered from creeping paralysis due to the increased size of the federal government. Although the country was experiencing good times, Bob and I had a difficult time meeting our expenses on the $100.00 a month he earned as a photographer. His two years in school had not raised our income. We did not know it, but it was likely the last year that husbands/fathers would be able to support a family and the beginning of the time when wives were forced to leave their children with babysitters and go to work to help support their families.

Despite the distance that separated us, my sisters and brother were very dear to me. Perhaps the lack of affection we received from our parents caused us to cleave together. During the war years when we lived close together in Memphis, we had shared clothes, loaned (or gave) money to each other, and even occasionally double-dated before Pat and Mel married. If one of us were sick, there was always a sister to brew broth for us or fetch an aspirin.

Men had always hovered around Pat like a hive of bees, but she had searched for the perfect mate while she worried about becoming an old maid. After she started dating the young military men she worked with as a civil servant for a military base, she had met a young officer who, although imperfect, met many of her rigid requirements in a mate, such as being a good provider and occupied the right circles. Unlike her siblings, Pat knew what she wanted—the best of everything, and she accepted it as her due. She chose Johnny out of fear of poverty and of becoming an old maid. She needed Johnny's adoration and the stability of an officer's position and married him. It was a perfect marriage for the first few years. He was attentive, generous, and personable when they were together, but regrettably, the military had little consideration for new marriages, and Johnny was frequently shipped to other bases temporarily or for long periods of time. Unfortunately, Johnny loved to drink, go to parties and play golf with his friends, leaving her alone and feeling neglected. After the first few years of marriage, during which Johnny's greatest interest seemed to be one continuous party and drinking, he was sent to Germany on permanent assignment.

When he didn't send for her to join him and neglected to write her for nearly six months, Pat became more and more upset. She was not going to accept that from anyone.

As a civilian employee at a military base, Pat, despite the rings on her fingers, received a great deal of attention from young military officers. She was not ready to stay at home at her young age to wait for Johnny while he ignored her, and when a handsome young officer at her base started asking her out, she saw no reason to cling to an absent husband who ignored her. In a very short while, Pat and her new friend, Ronnie, realized that they were madly in love. She had found her perfect mate who she felt could support her need for prestige, attention, and prosperity.

Her agonizing need to make a decision about what to do about her "soul mate," as she described him, was fortunately taken from her when her doctor discovered she had a condition that required a hysterectomy. After several days in the hospital without any word from her husband, she knew what she had to do. The handwriting was on the wall, and she filed for a divorce. Soon afterward, she married Ron, without any regrets or self-condemnation. Pat received from Ronnie the attention and affection that Johnny failed to offer her, and they were serenely happy. That year, the air force sent them to San Antonio, where they settled down in a little cottage near the base.

Pat was living in Texas with her new husband. She was the fastidious, perfectly groomed, and manicured petite little blond who told Mel and me how to dress and behave and hovered over us like a mother—never quite approving of all our actions, behavior, or our friends and companions. Her habit of being both our staunchest supporter and greatest critic was both endearing and annoying for the rest of our lives. Like our mother, no one was perfect enough to completely please Pat.

She had always rejected poverty and simply never accepted it. Although she was generous with the rest of her family, she squeezed every dime until it bled, somehow managing to meet her needs, along with a few treats.

As pretty as Pat was, Mel was even more beautiful, although not as petite as, and more buxom, than Pat. With her dark hair, which she dressed elaborately in the style of the day, her grey eyes and classic features, she could have been a movie star. The only mar to her beauty was the two broken teeth which she had suffered with ever since Pat accidentally broke them as Pat innocently pushed her head into a fountain when she took a drink. She couldn't afford to get the teeth repaired for years, and suffered continual pain from raw nerves.

Mel was more casual and less critical than Pat. Live and let live. Although she suffered from a lack of self-confidence, she was confident about her attractiveness to men. Like Pat, men hovered over her—offering her a cloak to walk on in the rain. Mel was my mentor without any of the criticism I received from Pat, and I loved her for it.

Working in a hotel during her young years, where nationally known big band artists appeared regularly, she could choose her dates between musicians, servicemen, or businessmen and often dated members of major bands that were touring the South to entertain servicemen during the war. She became very popular with Harry James band members who wooed, pursued and praised her beauty. None of it seemed to increase her sense of self-worth or give her confidence. Despite her beauty and her scholarship in high school, she was steeped in the humiliation and poverty of her childhood, and would never completely get over thinking, as many people do to the present, that Southerners were stupid. So, she dated numerous men and glowed in their admiration before she became interested in any individual.

My brother Dick was a searcher, and like me, had many interests he wanted to pursue. Both of us knew from an early age that, despite our love of the South, we wanted more than it had to offer. Our unhappiness over parental fighting, poverty, and deprivation led us to the conclusion that we could never find the life we wanted there. "When can we escape this place?" was our refrain from an early age.

Perhaps Pat's marriage to a military officer—or because so many of them were available, finally attracted Mel to a tall, handsome young officer from California. Reacting to the times, in which millions of servicemen and women married in fear of becoming old maids, or having their men get killed in battle, she decided it was time and they were married in a full military service, along with crossed swords and colorful uniforms of the attendants.

But it was only a short time later that her handsome husband was sent to Germany and like so many other wives, she waited and wrote letters until his return. When the war finally ended, Pat left Memphis with Ronnie, Mel went to California with her new husband, and Dick later left to go to California. I went to Oakridge, Tennessee, then Philadelphia and back to Memphis. We loved our childhood home with a passion, but it held no promise for our future. Our poor parents were left to fend for themselves, along with an occasional check from one of us when we could afford it.

I was three months pregnant in Memphis when the phone call came through from my sister, Pat, who was living and working at an airbase in San Antonio, Texas with her new husband, Ronnie. I knew something dreadful had happened the moment I answered. She struggled to control her emotions as she told me Ronnie's plane had exploded on a hillside just out of town, scattering wreckage for miles. No, the authorities didn't know what caused it. Suddenly, the short, happiest period of her life married to her "soul mate" was over. They had been married for less than two years. Our family usually accepted tragedy stoically without exhibiting the heartbreak and pain we felt, but Pat barely held it inside. She asked me to fly to Texas to be with her, where we spent night and day discussing their remarkable love affair and marriage. I learned more about how wonderful my sister was at that time— more than I had ever known or understood before. All I could do was to listen as she poured out her devastation, shock, and pain. Decisions had to be made, and she was barely capable of making them. Ronnie's air force officer friends suggested his body be shipped by train to his childhood home in Portland, Oregon for burial. She and an honor guard accompanied the body. Later, she was sorry he was not buried in the National Cemetery in Washington. I could do nothing to help, so I was left alone in their little house until she returned a week later. I forlornly drove to the accident site and viewed the plane strewn across a mile or more, grieving for her loss.

Almost a year later, "on the rebound," she married one of the officers she worked with at the base. She had little time to make a decision because his new assignment was to Southeast Asia as the new military attaché to the embassy and he wanted her to accompany him. He was a handsome Air Force Captain and career serviceman. It concerned me that she was rushed into marriage because he needed a wife in his new assignment. It was sudden and unexpected, but Pat was never happy living alone. I cynically wondered if Ronnie's insurance had anything to do with their sudden marriage. Pat was generous with the insurance money, as she always was with her own. She had sent Mom and Dad money to complete the little home they were building. She also invested in a night club in San Antonio with a partner who raked off the profits and then turned over the remainder of the insurance money to her new husband to help pay alimony to his former wife. He invested the balance in stocks that appreciated over a long period of time, but it was always "his"—not their money.

Pat was frequently left alone during their early marriage caring for her husband's two rowdy boys while he took survival training, French classes, and indoctrination in Washington, D.C., Foreign Service in preparation for their impending tour to Southeast Asia as the military attaché. Except for annual leave every year when they returned to the States, it would be several years before all our family was together again, although long letters flew back and forth between us. I missed her terribly and feared for her safety.

# Chapter 27

In a letter to me, Pat wrote: "I arrived in Rangoon, Burma on my 30th birthday. Ty (her husband) met me in Clark Field in the Philippines. I was overwhelmed with all the attention given to me by the Chief of the Air force, Air Commander Tomie Clift and his wife Kay. Fortunately, Ty had suggested that we change clothes on the flight from Bangkok to Rangoon. The Clifts had arranged for a reception and birthday party for me. I was handed a huge bouquet of roses and greetings from many people whose names I knew I would never be able to remember—such a long way from San Antonio, Texas, where I had waited for months for orders and word from Ty so that I could join him in the cottage on Inya Lake that he had rented for us. I was still suffering from the terrible sunburn that I had gotten on the way over in Guam. Unfortunately, the airplane had been delayed there overnight because of some problems. But the pilot of the aircraft was a friend of a friend who had arranged a sight-seeing trip by boat during the lay-over for maintenance of the aircraft. The sight-seeing trip was wonderful but had disastrous results for me. I had no thought of understanding that the sun there is much more radiant and I was about the same color as a cooked lobster. The next morning, I tried to soothe the burn, and dress as well as I could for the meeting with my new husband at Clark Field. Finally, he appeared. He was not pleased to see me with this lobster colored face, nor was he happy about my being in the company of the pilot, so he started ordering me around and rushing me as if I had any control of the situation.

As it turned out, he had a car waiting to take us to Baguio, and it was imperative that we get through the hill country where the rebels were fighting before darkness set in.

I was so crushed and miserable that I broke into tears because I could not understand why Ty was behaving in such a cold manner. We arrived at the guest quarters there and Ty invited a man that we knew to play bridge with us. Needless to say, I was flabbergasted. During the four months, I had been waiting for orders to go to Burma, I had envisioned a wonderful meeting like a honeymoon, but since I had received only two or three letters from him during that period, I really didn't know what to expect. He had sent two letters to give me explicit details of what to include in household shipping, and had not sent any money to buy these things. I wanted my new husband to be proud of his wife, and I wanted to do a good job of representing the USAS wife of the Asst. Air Attaché. We did get through the few days spent there, and I did recover from the terrible sunburn I had. I was further shocked, however, when we went to bed that first night in our bunk beds that Ty said, 'I am sure you are very tired,' and jumped into his bed, indicating that I was to do the same. According to the news, things are very bad in Kashmir, and the fighting goes on between Pakistan and India over the ownership of Kashmir. The Kashmir's want to be a separate nation. I have been thinking back to the time we spent in Kashmir during our tour in Laos in about 1965, where we had a very pleasant vacation for about two weeks with another couple on a houseboat. We had a wonderful view of the mountains from our floating villa which came with a cook, houseboy, and everything we could possibly want. The floating vegetable vendors called every day to see what we wanted to buy, as well as vendors of many varied arts and crafts. We could not have a more pleasant vacation. We played bridge with our companions and went into the town of Srinagar to golf at one of the oldest of the many golf courses built and run by the British. At this time, I think it would be unsafe for tourists to attempt this type of vacation there."

Other letters followed in the same vein. She was not happy in her new marriage to a good-looking husband who practiced coolness toward his wife. At least, on the other hand, he welcomed her desire to work if she chose to do that, or to follow her interest and talents in art and collecting art and antiques. Pat had many interests, and she began to look for unusual jewelry, paintings, frames, Asian artifacts, china, and crystal. In her spare time, she either took art classes or taught art to groups that she met in the air force or among the many friends she had made. She soon added golf to the huge-time demands of the wife of a career air force officer because she had servants to do most of the cooking, housekeeping, and gardening.

With thousands of servicemen home from the war, the housing market rapidly expanded in Memphis. I longed for a home of our own. The little apartment, an interfering landlady and a growing baby were almost more than I could stand, so I asked Pat to lend us $500 for a down payment on our own little two-bedroom cottage in a new development just past Memphis city limits.

Moving to the outskirts presented us with even more problems. We had no car; it was a much longer commute for Bob to get to work. Shopping meant walking a mile to the end of the bus line to lug groceries home with a baby who tried to squirm out of my arms. We had little furniture, no window coverings, and an unplanted lawn. Within a year, we found ourselves up to our neck in debt, with an income that couldn't possibly cover payments, utilities, groceries, and costs of the new baby.

Bob's $100 a month salary simply did not cover our expenses, and expansion of the photography business into a wedding and portrait studio had not materialized. He was at work more than he was at home, leaving me, a lonely young wife, at home with all the duties of mother and homemaker. We believed in the business but did not have the luxury to wait—perhaps years—for it to pay off. The owner was achieving some success in commercial photography but it was not ready to expand or pay an adequate income. I started nagging him to find a better paying job. The baby needed new diapers!

We agonized about what to do and finally decided we would have to sell the little house we had only occupied for about a year. When the Realtor examined it for listing, he offered $500 for our equity, and we accepted it.

Moving day was heartbreaking and traumatic. The last of our personal belongings were loaded except the little gas stove. Bob disconnected it from the gas line behind the stove but forgot to turn off the gas at the meter first. A moment later, flames were climbing from the gas line to the ceiling and threatening to burn the entire house down. I yelled for him to shut off the gas meter, as I ran for a water hose to put out the flames. By the time the meter was closed, several inches of water covered the vinyl in the kitchen and crept toward the oak floors in the living room. Needless to say, the Realtor buyer was angry and threatened to sue us. Thankfully he didn't, and we moved into a duplex closer to town and work.

Bob's only experience, other than photography, was his army experience as a gunner's mate, and as a tools inventory clerk at Oak Ridge. He searched for a job where he could capitalize on his "gift of gab," which finally resulted in a job selling insurance, and he was given territory in one of the most impoverished sections of town, where his customers were mostly Negroes living in shacks. Many of them could hardly afford food, so insurance was an unaffordable luxury. Nevertheless, he started selling (mostly) burial policies and then returned the following weeks to collect premiums. Week after week, the company's newsletter wrote about their new salesman's unequaled sales record. He did indeed have a gift of gab. He won the title of "best salesman" week after week for months.

Unfortunately, his paychecks did not reflect his success, and policy cancellations (deducted against sales) often exceeded his sales. He frequently paid the premiums for his policyholders for a few weeks until they could pay him back— but they seldom did. Week after week he received an adequate check that reflected his sales, but subsequent checks were reduced to only a few dollars from cancellations. Often, his expenses exceeded his income. Despite high praise and encouragement from management, our finances continued to deteriorate.

When Bobby was nine months old, a bundle of uncontained energy and beauty, I decided to find a babysitter and get a job. My job experience included being a waitress during the summer, two weeks as a bartender at the age of 15 during the Christmas season, operating a switchboard at the summer I turned 17, clerical jobs at Chicago Airlines, Army Depot, SAC, Memphis Press, and two years computing payrolls at Atomic Energy Commission. None of the jobs paid well except AEC, and I wanted to earn enough real money to make ends meet.

# Chapter 28

It always enraged me that newspaper ads were separated into categories for men and women. When an ad appeared under "Men Wanted" in the jobs section in the local paper, *"Salesmen wanted to sell appliances,"* at a Western Auto Company Store, I decided to apply for it because it promised good wages. The manager immediately told me that they do not accept women. I looked at a number of women in the office who were pounding typewriters, adding machines, or were occupied on the phone, I told him respectfully, "I'm sorry, but your office staff is full of women." He looked exasperated and replied, "Our salesmen are all men. I don't have the authority to hire a woman."

I replied, "Then please get whoever has that authority on the phone. I want this job!" He glared at me and returned to his desk, ignoring me. When I didn't leave, he approached me again and told me to leave.

"I'm not leaving until someone interviews me for the job," I insisted. He angrily dialed the phone, and a voice asked, "What makes you think you can sell appliances?"

"I can do anything I set my mind to do. If you have never tried a woman salesperson, what do you have to lose?" I answered. After a short conversation, the District Manager agreed to fly to Memphis from Kansas City to talk with me the next day.

There were 18 salesmen in the big store with six of them specializing in selling company-made appliances. I reasoned that women who used stoves, refrigerators, T.V.s, and radios more than men would be better able to discuss the use of appliances than men who were more interested in automobile parts and tires. The pay was $35.00 a week, based on a draw against commissions. When I left after the interview with the District Manager, he agreed to give me a try, I wondered if I had stuck my neck out far enough to be decapitated. The gauntlet had been cast, so I had to show them!

Several new salesmen were hired and sent to a week of training to learn about the operation, manufacture, and uses of the appliances. We were taught how to tune and do minor repairs on the new craze—television—which was rapidly becoming in demand. We were told that each of us would be assigned to floor duty alternatively and encouraged to follow up by phone or visits after talking to customers. If they indicated a need for a certain appliance or television, we were to keep a card file with the name, date, and item they were considering buying.

I approached customers with a friendly smile and began to try to find out little things about them: where they lived, if they had children, married, single, likes and dislikes, etc. This approach surprised me at the knowledge that could be gained in a few moments. If they expressed a specific need, I acted as an authority regarding the manufacturer of the item, how it compared with others, and why our store provided savings, service, and better terms than our competitors. Soon, I had a large card file of potential customers that I phoned or visited in their homes. My sales began to mount.

The 18 male competitors in the department grumbled, "It's because she is young and pretty." The leading salesmen, Mr. Turner, (who I thought was an old man; he was probably 55) had been employed at the store for over 30 years and seemed to have a card file on half of the Memphis population. We all thought he compiled a record of every customer's name, address, and phone number, whether they mentioned buying an appliance or not. He frequently contested sales by the rest of us and produced a card to prove that he had talked to the customer on previous occasions. Our lost sales were deducted from our income and granted to him.

I worked long, hard hours, often into the late night. I had to earn more money than the men because of the $25.00 a week child care expenses and high gasoline bills driving the baby-sitter home every night after work. Mattie, a soft-spoken, caring black woman, was a god-send after my poor son came home with black eyes and bruises from a previous daycare provider who told us he'd fallen down. Nothing is more heartbreaking than seeing a child abused and we were totally unprepared and devastated about it.

Mattie managed to tame our wild son, kept the house picked up and sometimes even cooked for our little family. Bobby was a curious, intense and demanding baby who constantly got into things, climbed out of the five-foot fenced yard, or fell off the swing set. Several times he escaped from the yard and couldn't be found as we agonized that he'd fallen into the adjacent ditch, or been kidnapped. Once, we found him two blocks away at the corner store where we bought groceries. Fortunately, a neighbor who knew us finally phoned us to pick him up.

Our store frequently had weekly, monthly, and even district-wide contests, where the best producer won dress shirts, hats, sports equipment or other items—all for men. I won often, only to receive some masculine award that I did not want. After several months, the store announced a district-wide contest. Salesmen were given two points for each radio and five points for each television sold to win a grand prize of $5,000 at the end of the contest. I was determined to win that money. We had bought a new bedroom set (wholesale, thanks to store connections) and while my earnings were good, Bob's kept creeping downward until we were behind on payments. Now, we started thinking about his giving up insurance sales and working at a separate Western Auto Store.

The popular contest with a huge prize had everyone excited. As the end grew closer, the Manager started announcing each salesman's name and number points acquired over the loudspeaker. "50 points of Burke; 60 points for Anderson; add five more to Smith," etc. On the final day of the sale, Mr. Turner and I were neck and neck and every time a new score was announced, my fellow employees went wild. Everyone stopped to applaud when my name or Turner's was announced repeatedly. My sales that day—selling seven television sets, several radios, and a water heater—were a record in the entire division. Mr. Turner was slightly ahead until then but many of the customers I had called or visited the prior week miraculously came in to buy that day. Everyone started pounding on my back in congratulations. When the final tally was counted, my score was five points ahead of Turner. He refused to accept it. He brought his card file to the manager and demanded that each of my sales is checked against his file. Eventually, Turner produced a customer card showing that he had talked to one of my buyers a year earlier, and demanded credit for the sale. As the lone woman in a field of wolves, I didn't have a chance. Turner received the prize but it was a long time before I learned that women would never be able to compete against men in the business world.

# Chapter 29

I became disillusioned and unhappy in my marriage. Bob spent our money faster than we could earn it, buying name-brand clothes, charging for things we couldn't afford, and sparing no expense for restaurant meals when he was working. A consumptive spendthrift and born optimist, everything was going to be alright. Never worry. We were still making payments on my engagement ring and a watch he'd bought me for a Christmas gift years earlier, on top of the payment for our new bedroom set. The qualities that had attracted me to him now irritated me. He did not hear anything I said unless I screamed at him. It was beyond his ability to discuss our problems seriously. Everything was going to be all right. I resorted to yelling to get his attention until I considered myself the consummate "fish wife" and I hated it.

After seeing my success at selling appliances, he finally decided to get a job at another but smaller Western Auto Company Store. If he could earn as much as I did, maybe we could make ends meet. I was sick of never having enough money to meet our expenses. The Capitalist system is based on exploiting your competitor in search of profit and position, and I was determined to take advantage of it. I believed that wage earners and small farmers in American society had little chance to achieve prosperity and that entrepreneurship was the key to flourish.

But it was not to be. The store was in a poor neighborhood where new appliances and televisions were unaffordable for most customers and he was not as aggressive as I was in following up on leads. Within six months, the handwriting was on the wall. The job wasn't working.

Several months later after seeing relatively easy television sales, two other salesmen at my store and I decided we could start our own television and appliance business so we would earn profits in lieu of commissions. Television was in great demand. We would buy a set and then peddle it door to door from the trunk of the car.

The three of us each sold close to one set a day each. Within six months, the business was worth over $100,000, but soon one of the partners decided to open a separate business. The other one disclosed that he was in love with me, which broke up the three-way partnership.

I was almost ready to abandon the marriage and try to make it on my own when letters from Dick and Mel arrived from the west, urging us to come west. Dick was working for the railroad in Dunsmuir, California (where Mel lived) and he loved his job as a railroad fireman, as well the location with the beautiful mountains and clear mountain streams. Mel and Dick assured us that railroad jobs would be available, and that compensation was above average.

Tall trees sheltered all kinds of game, the rivers were full of fat trout, and the scenery was magnificent with Mt. Shasta towering over the little town. To my earth—mother nature, it sounded like heaven, especially if Bob could get a good-paying job.

When Bob and I discussed our problems, we ended up arguing bitterly about his overspending, lack of progress for eight years, and his frivolity in managing problems. I couldn't take it anymore and told him that the only way this marriage could work was for him to find a way to earn a decent living. I could no longer tolerate the creeping poverty and failure to meet our growing needs.

"You have to make a living for us someway or I will!" I demanded that he at least consider joining my sister and brother in California, where they assured us he would be able to earn a good income that a railroad job would provide.

"I love you," he said, "and it won't be easy to get rid of me." Life was a big bowl of cherries to him.

Bob's characteristics—constant demonstrations of affection, light-hearted attitude and false optimism that initially attracted me—now seemed careless, free-spending and irresponsible, and I could no longer cope with it. My early childhood with an unaffectionate, financially insecure family, had led me to marry a man like my father.

Dick wrote to us advising us to come before they started hiring to make sure he got the job because so many others wanted it too.

He wrote glowingly about the beautiful area where he worked at an amazing income from his new job. We were hopeful that we would be able to make our lives more prosperous by doing the same thing. This convinced Bob to go early and get any kind of job until the railroad started hiring again. For the first few months, he worked at a Ford automobile plant in Los Angeles before his railroad application was finally approved. I received long, loving letters every day or so that promised to be more responsible and careful with spending. Six months later, he sent me a railroad ticket for us to join him in Dunsmuir.

When I got off the train with three-year-old Bobby in my arms, his father gathered us in his arms. Bobby queried, "Mom, who is this man?" as Bob carried him from the railroad platform.

We moved into a cold, dark apartment where the sun did not penetrate until noon. I felt cold and damp as we gradually tried to adjust to living in a canyon shadowed by huge trees and Mt. Shasta. Later, we moved into the third floor of an apartment building that overlooked the Sacramento River that was lighter and much warmer.

Bob "marked up" to go to work on the Southern Pacific "extra board," which allowed firemen to take available jobs by seniority as they became available. As one of the latest hired, he was able to work long hours at first when the railroad was busy, but "lay-offs" occurred more and more often as time went on. Some weeks, he left on long trips without returning for 16 hours or more, spending the night at the destination point and returning 16 hours later.

At other times, his seniority didn't allow him to work at all. The pay was good and we were able to live on the income most of the time. When he was laid off, he accepted jobs in Alturas or Klamath Falls and we packed up and moved into temporary housing for a few months or weeks at a time until his seniority allowed him to work in Dunsmuir again. The roughest move was the next summer when we moved to a two-room motel in Alturas, where we cooked and heated water for baths and dishwashing on a wood stove. The temperature in our little residence was often 118 degrees—higher when I cooked meals. There was no escape in a town where the only relief from the heat came after midnight. We had no friends and no place for our son to play except the street. We sweltered for a month before going back to Dunsmuir.

I joined "Lady Firemen," the support group for the firemen's union, where we had pot lucks, card games, fashion shows, and rummage sales until again we were forced to move to Klamath Falls where Bob had enough seniority to work. My second child, Debbie, was born there in August 1954, and my sister, Pat was home on leave prior to returning to Vietnam and arrived in time to be with me for the big occasion—the birth of my second child.

It would be another year before my sister and her husband would return to the States again if they were granted leave from the escalating war, and they had no idea if leave would be granted.

Debbie was the most beautiful baby in the world, with long, dark lashes, piercing dark eyes, and wisps of wavy hair framing her perfectly shaped head. Her little body was perfectly shaped without her father's big hands and feet.

The next year, we moved back to Dunsmuir where I learned I was pregnant again with Jan, who was due in January 1956.

# Chapter 30

That fall as my belly swelled with the baby, we received bad news from home. Dad had fallen off the end of a wagon hauling their corn crop from fields. They didn't know if he'd had a heart attack or the tractor driver bounced him off going over ruts. He was in the Memphis hospital, paralyzed from the neck down. None of us could leave our young families to go back to Mississippi. Pat was the only one available to devote to our parents' needs but was scheduled to meet her husband overseas and would be unable to visit our parents at that time.

Dick, Mel, and I spent hours on the phone with our parents' friends and neighbors for weeks, worrying and praying for his recovery. Dad was 62 years old, now totally disabled with no income. Who would care for him? Over many years, Mom had developed a "widow's hump" and a severely crooked spine from arthritis that we believed was caused by the hard farm work she had endured her entire life.

She wrote to us bravely, "We'll manage. Don't worry about us. You have your own families to take care of." We worried, but somehow, they did manage. County Social Services sent them a little money and food boxes. Neighbors and relatives dropped in to help—but Mom bore most of the burden of caring for Dad after he was released from the hospital. We sent them a few dollars whenever we could afford it. Later, Pat bore most of the responsibility when she returned from her duties overseas. Mel, Dick, and I went on with our lives until we were able to visit when the children were old enough to manage the 2500-mile drive. We arrived to find that someone had built an exercise bar for dad to use and he had regained enough strength in his shoulders to support himself as he tried to regain some use of his legs. His hands and arms were almost useless but in time, he developed a method to lean over his plate to feed himself.

The "Lady Firemen" organized a baby shower for me a few days before I was expected to deliver the baby in January 1956. We were playing pinochle when my contractions began, so we placed a clock on the table to time them.

When they were ten minutes apart, we notified the doctor, who agreed to meet us at his office at midnight.

The snow had begun to blanket the streets and he had promised to deliver the baby in his office if we had a big snow, since the hospital was nine miles nearly straight up the mountain. After his examination, he decided the baby "wasn't ready yet," so everyone went home. At home, an hour later, I knew he was wrong and called again. He grumbled, half asleep, and agreed to meet us at the hospital. We plowed through a foot to 18 inches of snow for what seemed like hours, slipping and sliding up the steep unplowed slope, timing my contractions and worrying if we would get there in time. The doctor was in an adjacent room drinking coffee when my nurse roused him to wash his hands in time to catch the baby.

Bob celebrated the birth by stopping by Mel's house at 6:00 am, demanding that she drink to the new baby, and she gagged the drink down.

The next day, snow was piled over five feet outside the hospital. Someone had dug a tunnel to the hospital entrance and when the doctor released us, my little baby, who was wrapped warmly, gasped for breath when we left the hospital through the tunnel of snow.

While Bobby, who was exploding dynamite who went from one activity to another most of the time, and at other times sought his own quiet time alone to read or listen to records, Debbie demanded constant attention. Endlessly curious, she explored everything—cabinets and closets; the medicine cabinet especially fascinated her and it was impossible to hide anything from her. We found her eating aspirin or other drugs we kept in the medicine chest that resulted in more than one doctor's appointment. Pills fascinated her.

Once when she was about 18 months old, she climbed to a cabinet over six feet high where we kept paints and turpentine. We found her trying to drink the turpentine stored there. She was constantly exploding in dramatic laughter or anger and she never knew the difference between the truth and a lie for years—anything to get attention. There was another incident where she was playing outside near a small stream when Bobby rushed in to tell us, "Debbie is going to pick up a rattlesnake." True enough, we found her walking toward a small rattlesnake when we grabbed her away to safety.

Besides her older brother and sister, Jan appeared tranquil and happy, though slightly pale, with soft, almost colorless blond hair and blue eyes like her father. I adored her immediately for the serenity and the undemanding way she assimilated into our little family. Unlike her brother and sister who were so active, she loved being cuddled, petted, and fussed over.

It was a busy, happy, often chaotic time with Mel and Dick popping in and out, babies crying or laughing or screaming, and Dick and our husbands leaving or returning from work at all hours of the day and night. Dick and his new bride came to visit or to play pinochle with us—or Bob and me with Mel and her husband. When we could get together, we had picnics together by the roaring Sacramento River, gathered at the park to watch baseball games, or lined our brood to the street side to applaud the colorful "Railroad Days" floats as they paraded down Dunsmuir Avenue. It was a happy time for all of us.

There had been frequent rumors that SP planned to replace the big steam engines that pulled the snake-like trains through the mountains with their hissing black smoke that turned the snow into black grit along the tracks.

Most diehard engineers who operated the trains loved their belching steam engines while the firemen worried that they would not be needed on diesel engines. Another persistent rumor was disturbing that Southern Pacific planned to move to Klamath Falls from their main distribution point in Dunsmuir.

Bob was working often enough that we earned a living income as long as we were willing to move temporarily, but it would be harder with three children now. Had we moved all the way across the country for a good job only to lose it three years later? We believed that firemen would never be replaced because they were trainees as future engineers and other eyes and ears for safety. Who would operate the trains when the engineers retired?

Gradually, the rumors became reality as layoffs for three weeks or three months or more became more and more frequent and we were forced to move back to Klamath Falls so he could work more often than in Dunsmuir. Between layoffs, we lived on unemployment insurance or part-time jobs for sometimes months. Sometimes, I took a part-time or temporary job when Bob could take care of the kids. Moving became a way of life. We lived in a rundown apartment in a converted barracks for a while with noisy children, fighting families and barking dogs until I could stand it no longer, and we found a house that was being remodeled to rent.

Debbie had battled allergies that resulted in terrible skin rashes that turned her little bottom into red, raw blisters or food allergies that caused her to vomit nearly everything she ate for weeks. Doctors tried everything from salves or lotions to thick, oily ointments, changing her formula, and changing detergents I used to wash her clothes.

We finally learned that she was allergic to milk. By the time this condition disappeared, she started refusing to eat. She would spit out any meat that I fed her and some of the vegetables and fruits. My daughter had a mind of her own and never ate meat from that tender age afterward. Then suddenly, when she was nine months old, she became feverish. She was flushed, listless, and pale so I rushed her to the doctor's office, where she was diagnosed with pneumonia. I was never so frightened in my life and spent the next four or five nights sleeping next to her crib so I could sponge her hot little body, walk, or rock her when she cried and administer antibiotic drops the doctor prescribed. We came close to losing our little girl but she finally regained her health and energy to terrify the family with curiosity that led her to sample everything that life had to offer.

# Chapter 31

Railroad work became so scarce that Bob became a grocery clerk and became involved in the clerk's union negotiations when their contract came up for renewal. Most of the members were dissatisfied with the Teamsters Union due to negative publicity about Jimmy Hoffa's possible criminal activities. As a result, Bob ordered a correspondence course from ICS to study labor relations. Occasionally when he was called to work at SP, he would "mark up" to work to show he was available, then sign off (or lay off) the job in order to keep his seniority and then return to his job at Safeway. The wages he received barely kept the "wolf from the door"

Bobby was in the first grade in Klamath Falls, a holy terror who teased his younger siblings unmercifully for the attention it received. Eventually, he settled down to school, a few friends and the record player he enjoyed so much.

Debbie was still a handful with her curiosity and penchant for exploring, tasting and trying everything she could. For instance, once I had emptied the refrigerator to defrost it. Five minutes later, she disappeared. We could hear faint screams that sounded like she was under the house, but she wasn't there. A thorough search in and around the house failed to find her and I panicked until I finally thought about the refrigerator. She had climbed in and shut the door. When I opened, it a frightened little girl tumbled out.

Klamath Falls was a beautiful little town set on a mile-high desert plain, set between high ochre hills and even higher hills covered with 100-year-old Douglas fir, or Ponderosa Pine trees. Not far away was a rocky mountain dotted with caves known as Captain Jack's Stronghold, the source of the Modoc tribe's last efforts to remain free before being forced into reservations. On the morning that troops advanced on the Stronghold, the soldiers never saw a single Modoc. The Modoc, occupying excellent positions, repulsed troops advancing from the west and east. A general retreat of troops was ordered at the end of the day. In the attack, the U.S. Army lost 35 men, including five officers and 20 wounded enlisted men under Captain Jack's command. There were in all approximately 150 Modoc including women and children. Of that number, there were only 53 warriors. The Modoc suffered no casualties in the fighting. After numerous battles considered the most expensive of all Indian wars, Captain Jack, John Schonchin, Black Jim, and Boston Charley were hanged at Fort Klamath on October 3, 1873. The remainder of the band of Modoc Indians, consisting of 39 men, 64 women, and 60 children were sent to the reservation as prisoners of war.

Later, the Modoc of Oklahoma were allowed to return to the Klamath Reservation if they desired. My sympathy was with the Indians. The whites had killed, maimed, and destroyed most Native Americans, raped and stolen their lands and their culture, then forced them into shanty houses on reservations, where many of them became alcoholics. Who could blame them?

The county was a crossroads that brought settlers from the north and south to trails leading into California's central valley. Several thousand acres served as the temporary exile for thousands of Japanese-American citizens who had occupied a camp during the war at nearby Tule Lake, which was the largest of the segregation camps. It is now a national landmark.

The county was home to three major tribes: the Modoc, (or Pit River), the Piute, and the Klamath, many of whom still live in the area on the reservation. Others chose to accept a large monetary settlement in return for the right to live off the reservation. Mostly, they were a handsome peace-loving group, although a few became belligerent trouble-makers and alcoholics. After the settlement, part of the reservation was opened to the public for hunting for big mule deer and fishing for giant rainbow in the beautiful mountain creeks and lakes.

Hunting was a way of life for most of the Klamath Falls citizens, and soon became our favorite recreation during the fall deer season. I was enthralled with the idea of killing a 200-pound animal for a plentiful supply of meat for winter during Bob's long lay-offs from the railroad and decided I wanted to be a part of this thrilling sport and new (to me) sport.

When a male chauvinistic neighbor challenged me, "Women's place is in the home, cooking and making meals instead of running around in the mountains hunting for deer," I was hooked. After all, I was a good marksman as a child and had listened to my brother, sister, and her husband talk about hunting for a long time. Bob and I, sometimes with friends from Kingsley Field, spent many happy days hunting deer every season the entire ten years we lived in Klamath Falls. We brought them home and butchered, cut, and wrapped them for freezing on the dining room table. Our family ate steaks, chops, stews, and chili made from venison until we never wanted to see any more venison again.

During Bob's lay-offs, it was often the only meat we had. My poor daughter, Debbie, told us later that she believes her aversion to meat was partially due to butchering deer and cutting slabs of meat on the table.

I had one frightening adventure when I was four months pregnant that cured me from ever going hunting again. The first trip of the season was to Hargesty Mountain, which rose above a plain where we camped overnight with a young soldier and his wife from Kingsley field. I had barely had my coffee when I saw three or four deer making their way across the hill above me. Determined to get my deer, I quietly found my rifle, which had no scope, and aimed at what appeared to be the largest one of the group. Despite the fact that it was so far away that I was not entirely sure it was a buck, I aimed carefully and shot. I heard a ping as the bullet bounced off a rock and saw a dust cloud rise from the ground slightly below the deer's hooves and knew I had not accounted for the distance and rise of the steep hill. I refocused and shot again.

I saw the deer kick his hind leg as if he were swatting at a fly, and knew he had been hit, so I fired twice again as he limped out of sight. He was wounded, and good hunters never let a wounded animal escape. The hunt began to find my wounded deer. Puffing my way up the steep hill as quickly as possible, I found spots of blood and followed them for what seemed like a mile, stumbling over rocks, through heavy brush and ravines. Suddenly I heard two quick shots ahead of me. Two men stood over my deer, which had several other bullet wounds in it. I knew it was my deer, but they argued that they had shot it and told me they intended to keep it. Since they had finished it off, I felt I had no argument, and left the area.

I didn't want to climb down the steep hill, so I stayed on the slope above the old roadbed that I thought would take me back to the camp with less wear and tear on already aching muscles and bulging stomach, and started walking. Instead of taking me back to the road, it angled away from it, and hours later I finally realized that I was getting further away from camp instead of closer. It was noon before I retraced my steps, found the road back, and returned to camp with an aching back, sore legs, and near total exhaustion. What the hell was a pregnant woman doing in the wilderness anyway?

However, I was not ready to give up yet. Deer season was almost over when a friend called to ask if I wanted to go again. In spite of my bludgeoning size and ungainly body, I agreed. We decided to go to Green Springs, a thickly forested area in the Coast Mountain range. When we arrived, fir trees towered over us so thick it was nearly impossible to see the sky, and huckleberry and other bushes were so thick you couldn't see in any direction. Old logging roads permeated the area, running in every direction. I chose one to follow only to find it cut by so many others running parallel or cross to it that I recognized immediately how quickly someone could become hopelessly lost in a wilderness where no one would find them for days. I was terrified while I was still nearly in sight of our car, visualizing falling, getting lost or even giving birth in such a place. This was no place for a woman who would be giving birth in six weeks! I returned to the car, honked for my friend to return, and went home. That was enough of hunting for me.

I was dissatisfied with our frequent moves and wanted a home of our own when Kingsley Field, an air force base, was reactivated, so I applied for a civil service job there. I hated leaving the children but felt it necessary. Due to Bob's schedule, he could take care of them part of the time and neighbors agreed to fill in as care-takers when he was at work.

At first, I computed and paid the military personnel and calculated their leave and travel benefits. Then the Personnel office decided to establish a Civilian Payroll Department. I had been hired in a clerical position but a few weeks later, the Personnel Office asked if I would accept the "Payroll Certifying Officer" position after reviewing my past experience at The Atomic Energy Commission. Of course, I would! It meant better pay, more responsibility and an opportunity for advancement. But first, they decided to send me to Hamilton Air Force Base to learn the new computer system using IBM and NCR machines.

At the time, large computers filled whole rooms, and spit out hundreds or thousands of cards initiated by big machines that computed the payroll based on the data typed into them. I had never seen or used these machines and welcomed the chance to learn their use, but the training consisted of only a half-day in San Francisco and returning home the next. I was expected to set up the new system—a daunting task that I was only to master because company technicians who set up the machines tutored me the first few days. It would have been impossible without their help. Before long, the department was running smoothly. I enjoyed the challenge, the new people I met, and the prestige of being head of the department.

The job enabled us to save enough for a down payment on a house, a comfortable older cottage with enough room for Debbie and Jan to share a room, Bobby to have his own and a larger one for Bob and me. There was a screened-in porch in front, and a second one in the back of the kitchen. The house was built over a drive-in basement for a garage. We had some wonderful Thanksgiving and Christmas gatherings when Mel and her children or Dick and his wife, Eyvonne, came to Klamath Falls for the holidays. An especially memorable one was when the turkey gravy failed to brown, so I added coffee for color and it turned it almost green. They still tease me about my green gravy.

# Chapter 32

By the time Bob completed the IRS course in labor relations, Safeway employees with Teamster contracts were suspicious that "sweetheart" contracts were being negotiated and many of them were anxious to "throw the bums out." Some Teamster officials were being investigated for larceny, income tax evasions and other crimes such as misuse of pension funds. Later, suspicions were confirmed when the revelations of a Senate investigating committee led the AFL-CIO to expel the Teamsters. Dave Beck was later sent to prison for larceny and income tax violations and clerks smelled a rat about Jimmy Hoffa's influence in the union. Employees wanted a "clean" union. Bob decided to contact the Retail Clerks Union (later known as United Food and Commercial Workers International Union), whose membership had soared as the result of aggressive organizing programs and strong leadership. He wired a short telegram to them: "I can deliver the Klamath Falls grocery clerks! Call _____ (our phone number)."

The telegram received immediate attention. After some phone calls with the Seattle Retail Clerks District, some organizers arrived and meetings were scheduled to convince members to change affiliation from Teamsters to the Retail Clerks Union. Unfortunately, it was too late in the negotiation process for a new contract underway at the time, but Bob had succeeded in attracting attention to himself as a future union official. The District Manager told him, "We can use someone like you if you'd like to join our team." They promised to contact us as soon as a job became available. We were ecstatic at the prospect of Bob having a secure, well-paying labor relations career with had good prospects for advancement. Would it be possible for us to have an uninterrupted income without constant lay-offs?

The merger of the Retail Clerks and the Amalgamated Meat Cutters Union a few years later united two union powerhouses to fight for justice and economic security for working people. We believed wholeheartedly that union affiliation was the only way wage earners could ever receive an adequate income. We had already learned from our Southern Pacific railroad employer that job security was uncertain even with a powerful union. In an era when unions were rapidly losing their influence, Bob and I believed that promoting union membership among wage earners was essential to the welfare of all working Americans. He thought he had found his calling with the prospect of working as a union official.

The merger of the Retail Clerks and the Amalgamated Meat Cutters Union a few years later united two union powerhouses to fight for justice and economic security for working people. We believed wholeheartedly that union affiliation was the only way wage earners could ever receive an adequate income. We had already learned from our Southern Pacific railroad employer that job security was uncertain even with a powerful union. In an era when unions were rapidly losing their influence, Bob and I believed that promoting union membership among wage earners was essential to the welfare of all working Americans. He thought he had found his calling with the prospect of working as a union official.

In the meantime, my position at Kingsley Field continued to be exciting and fulfilling, despite missing being at home with the children. My duties had expanded into budgeting, lecturing to other department heads regarding efficient methods of records keeping, and ever more decision-making responsibilities in the Accounting and Budget departments. I was respected, well-liked, and had developed many friends among both the military and civilian population at the base.

Then one day 18 months afterward, the head of the department called my office to tell me that we were having a team of inspections from our headquarters, SAC (Strategic Air Corp) from Colorado Springs, Colorado to examine the Civilian and Military Payroll Departments. They informed us that the base Commander and the Personnel Department had established those departments without Headquarters' knowledge or approval. Everyone was astonished that this had happened and the team spent days pouring over our records, controls, budgets, and methods.

The only thing they found wrong was that they had never given Kingsley Field the authority to operate those departments locally. No one had known the need to seek authority. I had acted as the Payroll Certifying Officer for 18 months, which normally would have been at a much higher civil service rating than I had without the knowledge and approval of SAC Headquarters. Our Accounting and Budget supervisors had a number of meetings to decide what to do. Finally, a full audit was ordered, completed, and proved accurate and up to date, but Headquarters did not have copies of our records. Surprisingly, no one was fired because of this flap.

Instead, after much discussion, they demanded that I attend a three weeks class in September at Colorado Springs to learn the same methods I had used since being the head of the department. I went home to discuss the greatest shock I'd ever had with my family. How could I spend three weeks away from my three children? Who would look after them night and day? Nothing was wrong with my work. Why did I need to take classes to learn something I already understood? We agonized for days about what to do. It would mean a significant raise in my civil service rating, higher pay and a professional level career.

On the one hand, naturally, I preferred to stay at home to raise my children.

I had taken the job because we needed the money—not because I wanted a career. I still dreamed of being a writer and/or painter instead of a career civil servant. What to do?

But alas, the decision was taken away from us a few days later when my period stopped and my doctor told me I was pregnant. He had treated me for endometrioses for months, saying that the best cure was to get pregnant, although it was difficult since my painful periods were a result of the loss of the lining of the uterus.

When we told the children we were going to have another baby, Bobby was ecstatic. He wanted a baby brother to play with instead of two little sisters! He danced around the living room in frenzy. The girls were more subdued, as we were. It was a sobering development to try to live on a grocery clerks wages with another child, but we decided I should give notice and sacrifice my career at the airbase.

My doctor allowed Bob to attend the birth of our new baby, Steven on January 8th, 1961, and he had to be sent out of the room when he became dizzy and nearly fainted from the experience. Bobby was awed and half afraid of the baby, while the girls considered him their new doll. His happy nature captivated all of us and when he learned to talk, he charmed everyone around him. Like Jan, he enjoyed being held and hugged, but unlike his older sister and brother who often resisted being constrained.

The hospital bill was $100.00, a sum difficult to pay in those hard times, but somehow, we managed and life went on as before, with our dreams of achieving the American dream as we continually tried to live on a budget short of basic family needs.

I decided the Capitalist system was designed to reward the rich by depriving the hard-working poor and near-poor working class in America. Although unions had lost much of their power, we believed they were the only way to advance the cause of working people and we dreamed of the time when the

Retail Clerks would hire Bob as promised. John F. Kennedy, the youngest and first Catholic in American history, was elected as President and we had hopes that his social service programs and pro-union position would provide some help to millions who faced the same problems we did. Angry because I thought big money had bought his election, I rebelled and voted against him despite my approval of his platform. In a letter from Mom, she called it "cutting off your nose to spite your face." Of course, she was right.

So, we waited for the Clerks Union to find a job for Bob and waited and waited, worried that it would not happen. I urged Bob to call to remind them.

"We're so sorry," his contact said, "We had forgotten all about it." It was nearly Christmas before they finally hired him as the Acting Secretary-Treasurer for a small Local Union in Hood River, Oregon, where there were few retail employees in a territory that covered a sparse population in most of Central Oregon, Hood River, and The Dalles, where later he would be elected by union members. His duties were to manage the office, account for dues, hold meetings, negotiate contracts, and act as a liaison between the district office in Seattle and Washington, D. C., headquarters.

We were elated and immediately put our house on the market. Our for-sale ad was answered by a Native American family who had recently received a large sum of money from the Bureau of Indian Affairs for giving up their reservation rights. Hoping for a large sum of cash, we toured them through our little cottage, around the yard and our beloved peach tree, and into the basement. They seemed delighted with the house until we got to the basement; Bobby pointed out, "We float boats down here in the winter."

He was referring to a few hard rains we had at times ran down our sloping driveway into the basement, resulting in a little pool of water where he played with a toy boat.

There was never over a gallon or two but apparently, it frightened them from buying. A new buyer soon showed up.

The New Year felt like a fresh new beginning for us. Although Bob's income was not expected to be very high, we did not expect there to be lay-offs and interrupted income. Nor would he have to be away from home 16 hours a day as he had on the railroad or different shifts at a grocery store. There would be some evening work for union meetings, and occasionally short trips to adjacent towns, but he could expect to be at home with the family in the evenings most of the time. More important, he was dedicated to helping union members attain a better living wage, better working conditions, and job security. American employers no longer considered loyalty to their employees essential to their welfare, which we considered short-sighted and self-serving.

# Chapter 33

So, we packed our meager household goods, the children's toys, books and clothing, and arrived at the new tiny four-bedroom home on a hill we had selected that overlooked the new Columbia River dam in The Dalles on a cold, windy evening of December 31, 1960. The bedrooms were little bigger than closets, but at least the girls would have one to share, and Bobby, the oldest, chose the almost unfinished basement bedroom for privacy, and Steve would occupy "the nursery"—an even smaller room next to our bedroom. There was a small dinette that was once was an enclosed porch with an awesome view of the Columbia River, and a living room and kitchen. It would do.

After the holidays ended, I enrolled Debbie in a small, ancient school only a short distance from our house and Bobby into Jr. High School. Steve was nearly a year old and Jan would not start school until the following year.

Bob seemed to take his new duties in stride and won the election several months later as the official Secretary-Treasury of the local union. Since he did not have a secretary, I filled in as needed a few times each week to answer phones, type letters, file, or whatever needed doing while the older children were in school, and became interested in union activities. The work was like a drug to Bob and he talked of little else. It was a passion, a calling, a cause that occupied his mind 24 hours a day, seven days a week. I welcomed the time I spent in the office to type or file for him as an escape from household duties, children, PTAs, cooking, laundry, and sewing clothes for the children.

Bob was at home most evenings, which allowed all the family to eat together for the first time in months. The subject of conversation nearly always concerned events going on at the local union. Bob was the focus of family conversations. He demanded to be the center of attention. Fortunately, between the time Debbie and Bob got home from school until dinner time, I listened to their discussions about friends, school activities. Sometimes, I played or practiced baseball with Bobby or helped Debbie practice her lines in a school play. After dinner, I helped with the kids' school assignments and ironed or sewed dresses for the girls after reading a story and tucking them into bed.

The weeks and months flew by until a year passed. We began to catch up on old bills ran up during previous lay-offs or unemployment. I began to believe that our needs—dental care, better furniture, clothes, and a night at the movies occasionally could soon be expected. We soon managed to buy a slightly larger house, close enough to school that Debbie could walk and look out for her little sister when she started the first grade.

When the letter came from Southern Pacific Company, we had given up hope of ever having enough seniority for Bob to work regularly or to have the lifestyle we wanted when we migrated to the northwest. Good pay, good benefits, living near my sister and brother and promise of a great future retirement were more important than the irregular hours that often started in the middle of the night. The letter explained that many of the railroad firemen hired after a certain date had the choice of going back to work to become future engineers, or to accept a buy-out agreement based on seniority. Only those who "marked up" for work by a certain date would be eligible for the compensation of over $10,000 if they chose to leave the company. I studied the letter carefully, but Bob only glanced at it, saying, "That was another chapter."

I urged him to comply with their rules in order to get the compensation, but he simply was not interested. All he needed to do was drive back to Klamath Falls, mark up for work as required, then chose to give up the seniority he had acquired. He refused. In subsequent years, we learned that either option would have given us security and a better life. The compensation would have paid everything we owed and much more if he accepted a buy-out. If he had chosen to keep his seniority, he would have been able to work regularly. Bob was deaf to my pleas and chose to not even respond. Thus, ten years of railroad lay-offs and relocating time after time went for naught. I was furious, and although I still cared deeply for him, I thought it was the most stubborn decision he could have made.

Gradually, our lives began to have order and predictability, and I was grateful, but the constancy of busy, full days with children, cooking, laundry, shopping, school activities, cleaning, and immersion with everyone's life but my own began to take its toll. Like many mothers of small children, I began to feel like a non-person who was programmed by my loved ones. My previous need to paint and write re-surfaced. My old habit of "writing" words, sentences, and paragraphs in my mind returned after I fell into bed at night and refused to switch off. I yearned for the paints I'd received as a gift years before and visualized finished paintings spreading over canvases in bright splashes of color.

Loss of sleep while "writing" all those words at night left me tired and listless in the following days until I became impatient with Bob and the children's constant demands. My family owned me. They commanded: "Froggie jump" and I answered, "How far?" I did not exist. Bob showered affection, but he saw me as his reflection instead of a person. We argued but my views had no validity. The only time anyone heard me was when I shouted and screamed as my mother had often done. We lived in a world where women were accessories with no power of their own.

I thought of my childhood where my parents viewed me as their subject and serf required growing and harvesting crops. I found myself punishing my children for infractions the same way my parents had with switches on their little backsides that left them rebellious and angry instead of contrite. Before long, I developed severe psychopathic back pain and my doctor ordered me to bed for a week, where I regretfully ruled my little castle as my duties mounted. I attempted to follow the doctor's orders, but family needs and demands prohibited it. Subconsciously, I knew my problem was caused by severe depression and a need to express those old yearnings that had always been with me. I wanted to stop being a machine and to experience, learn, create and grow toward self-realization. There had to be a way to manage the family and my own needs, so I started to search for creative outlets.

Our neighbor was a sweet older lady who had a ceramics business in her garage, so I found a second neighbor to trade child care with me and started painting ceramic molds under her tutorage for a while and although it wasn't entirely satisfactory, it later led to some watercolor classes that were.

I was just a beginner, but at the urge of the instructor, I exhibited a couple of paintings for the first time that year. It was a state-wide competition, and I was elated to over-hear one of Oregon's most renowned watercolorist say, "This is the best painting here," about my painting. The few hours I spent in that class encouraged me to seek further channels to meet my emotional, intellectual, and creative needs, and I found a group called the "Writer's Workshop." An investigation found that about ten to 15 men and women met to critique their writings that varied from short stories, novels, journalism, feature stories, and essays and it soon became my creative home.

Bob was at home most evenings, and I announced that he had to care for the family on the nights the group met. It forced me to write something on a weekly basis to be read and criticized at the following meeting, in addition to an introduction to some of the tricks of the trade. Even better, I met a teacher, a retired postmaster, a feature story writer of a small rural paper, and a published author who became the best friends I ever had. Judy was one of them and the author of two children's books and became my best friend until her death 50 years later. Disney had bought the rights to one of her children's books and made a movie of it, and a second was released shortly after she became a member of our little group. That was big news in our little town of about 7,000 populations, and The Writer's Workshop decided to hold an autograph party to introduce Judy and her new book. The occasion was well attended and brought new members into our group. I was elected President of the group later, and that honor no doubt lent some credence to the editors of our local paper because they accepted some articles and feature stories I wrote, but insisted that my by-line be my married name, which infuriated me. It appeared that the masculine gender dominated the writing field, and my protest did not change their mind.

I started sending out queries, articles, or short stories, without much luck. Undoubtedly, I needed to practice writing and to learn more about the craft. After our meeting, a few of us gathered at the local coffee shop to discuss the books we read on politics, religion, or any other subject that might come up. Kip, a school teacher, discussed her writing about a unique and powerful way to teach math that no one had tried before.

From being a poor math student in school, I learned more math from her methods than I ever learned in school. Florence wrote interesting and informative feature stories for a rural publication about things like Indian pictographs found along the bluffs, little known stories of Sam Hill's castle (now an art museum) across the river from The Dalles, or about the past practice of growing asparagus in the rich soil beneath the cliffs bordering the Columbia River. Our retired postmaster introduced us to his literature of a little-known metaphysic sect that seemed to encompass some Biblical text, a little astrology, and outrageous claims of predicting America's future and that of the planet we live on.

My friend, Judy, was interested in and questioned everything. She was an astrology graduate and handwriting expert. Others had a deep need to understand our purpose, why are we here, what happens after death, etc. Someone mentioned *Life and Teachings of the Masters of the Far East*, and someone else brought up *The Tibetan Book of the Dead*, while someone else mentioned the wonders of the Russian author's *Devine Wisdom* and Yogananda Paramahansaar book *Autobiography of a Yogi*. There was nothing we were afraid to delve into. We shared The Oasbe Bible, Jung, and books about reincarnation. One of our out-of-world experiences was when we decided to play with the Ouija board.

Kip and Florence placed their hands on the guide and it immediately began to move furiously across the board, spelling out words as fast as we could write them down. The words spelled out, "Future trip, long-distance, promotion, move to another destination, and beware of water." I didn't connect it to anything until several months later some of it applied to my family. Another time, the board spelled out the most atrocious epithets I had ever heard. It scared us so badly that we never used it again.

We were all fascinated, so we decided to meet on a regular basis to share knowledge of little-known books and to investigate anything or everything that made us curious to know more, especially a popular subject in books and periodicals at the time. We decided to investigate ourselves to determine if we had any extrasensory perception. One of our members would write a series of letters or numbers on a piece of paper and another would try to read them from a distance. Sometimes, we would telephone each other late at night for the result. Almost all our group was slightly above average in perceiving what was written on the paper, though none of us could be considered gifted.

We explored table tipping, automatic writing, handwriting analysis, psychology, parapsychology, astrology, and the Oasbe Bible, supposedly written by a dentist with automatic writing on one of the first typewriters made. We read one book that led to another to another and exchanged the books with each other after we discussed them.

Bob did not get too upset when Judy and I came home after our meetings for more talk and to eat my "cheese dream" sandwiches at two or three in the morning, but he became very upset when we discussed some of the books that interested us. He would angrily retort, "You can't believe all that crap!"

It became a contentious subject for a long time afterward and a threat to his Southern Baptist upbringing. My answer was, "I didn't say I believed it, I'm just trying to learn what to believe." That did not pacify him in the least. I continued to enjoy the Writer's Workshop and what we began to call our "goofball club."

Our finances improved, and in three years had our first "mortgage burning" by placing all old bills (except the mortgage) in a metal container and setting them on fire. Some of those bills dated back to 1947 and had been refinanced time after time.

After the "mortgage burning," Bob agreed not to ever go in debt again, but a few days later, he bought a $50 tape recorder on credit. Apparently, there were some scratches on it, so he bought some black spray paint to obliterate them. The paint destroyed the mechanism, so the next day he charged a new similar one that cost over $250.00.

I was enraged! I told him that I would not continue to stay up at night to sew the children's clothes to save money if he couldn't even compare prices, or wait until he had cash to buy things he needed. Finally, I decided that if I can't beat him, I would join him. The next day, I renewed our Penny's card and charged over $100.00 worth of children's clothes. It was a mistake that I later regretted.

# Chapter 34

Bobby, who was now in high school, was fascinated with the songs of Bob Dylan and spent most of his time in his room listening to his records. He saved enough money from his paper route to buy his first car—a classic black Chevy 1956. I was so proud of him that I made him a tailored corduroy blazer which he wore until it was tattered and torn. He loved it and refused to throw it away for years.

Debbie surrounded herself with friends and spent much of her time directing them in plays, using our shed in the backyard for a dressing room. She made up inventive stories for them to play. Her practice of inventing stories applied to daily life; I never knew when she actually saw men exposing themselves behind a tree or if it actually happened. Moreover, she tortured Jan unmercifully or excluded her from activities. Once, she walked to a nearby store and stole some candy bars and I had to march her back to apologize to the owner. Jan was good-humored and happy and Steven was a delightful toddler.

The small local union started experiencing troubles in 1963 when the grocery clerks' contract ran out. Bob was determined to at least negotiate raises that were closer to that paid to clerks in more populated Oregon cities. While negotiating, he spent long hours at the table in the rural areas of Central Oregon and was often away from home for days at a time. When he was at home, he had a distant look in his eyes and was totally unaware of family events. It was obvious that things were going badly before he told us he planned to take the clerks on strike.

I worried that a strike would be impossible to win with the small number of members in Central Oregon. They didn't have the strength or power of the local stores and the larger chain stores. The Retail Clerks District Office advised him to accept the small settlement offered, but Bob was adamant. He believed the local would prevail only if the members voted for a strike, and convinced them it was the only way to get a good settlement.

The strike was nasty. A few members harassed the strikebreakers that the stores hired and others vandalized stores, despite pleas from officials to remain peaceful. The District sent organizers or other local union officials to the area to help walk the picket line. As Bob's local gradually exhausted its treasury, the District sent small amounts of money for food for the strikers, but the strike continued.

Bob seldom came home, but when he did, he was haggard with exhaustion. When the strike finally ended in November 1963, he couldn't eat or sleep and restlessly paced the floor at night. On November 23rd, Bob called me from the union office, crying uncontrollably. "Turn on the TV," he said. "Kennedy has been assassinated." He was grief-stricken and inconsolable.

I turned on the television shortly after noon to watch re-winds of President Kennedy's limousine as it entered Dealey Plaza and approach the Texas School Book Depository. Mrs. Connelly, wife of the governor of Texas, turned to the President and commented, "Mr. President, you can't say Dallas doesn't love you."

There was little reaction in the crowd to the first shot. Later witnesses thought they had heard a firecracker or the exhaust backfire of a vehicle. President Kennedy and Governor John Connelly, sitting beside his wife in front of the Kennedys, both turned abruptly from looking to their left to looking to their right.

Connelly, upon recognizing the sound of a high-powered rifle, said, "Oh, no, no, no," as he turned further right and then to the left in an effort to see President Kennedy behind him. As President Kennedy waved to the crowds to his right, a shot entered his upper back, penetrated his neck and exited his throat. He raised his fist to his neck and leaned forward and to his left as Jackie Kennedy put her arms around him. Governor Connelly reacted as the same bullet penetrated his back, chest, right wrist, and left thigh. He yelled, "My God, they are going to kill us all!"

As the final shot was heard, a fist-size hole exploded out from the right side of President Kennedy's head, covering the interior of the car and a nearby motorcycle officer with blood and brain tissue. Shortly after the shot that hit the president in the back, Secret Service agent Clint Hill, who was riding on the left front running board of the car behind the Presidential limousine, jumped off and ran to overtake the limousine. Mrs. Kennedy climbed onto the rear of the car, perhaps reaching for something, and Clint Hill jumped onto the back of the car and pushed her back into her seat as it exited Dealey Plaza and sped away to Parkland Memorial Hospital.

Bob was grief-stricken. A union member called a few minutes later to tell me he had taken Bob to the hospital where he was diagnosed with a nervous breakdown. He lay grief-stricken and heartbroken for the next four days. The long, difficult strike and the loss of President Kennedy left him shaken and tormented.

Several days later, he was released to attend a district-wide Retail Clerks' convention in Portland, where in his speech he made an impassioned plea for more effective union leadership and participation. As a result of the speech, the District manager offered him a chance to become a Retail Clerks Coordinator, working directly under headquarters. He was offered a new car, a generous expense allowance, and a much larger salary than he was earning as the Secretary-Treasurer of a local union office.

The job would entail moving to Eugene in the central Willamette Valley and require him to travel more. They explained that he would be away from home only two or three days a week. We were all jubilant and excited except Bobby, who told us that he didn't want to move and leave all the friends and the paper route where he had earned enough to buy his first car. There was no way that we could turn down this wonderful chance to improve our lives, even if it meant our son was unhappy about it.

My friend, Judy, had lived in Eugene prior to coming to The Dalles, where her husband led a construction crew. Occasionally, we shared dinners at their trailer or in my house for further discussions. Their little trailer was so cramped that two people could not pass in the hallway, but some way, she had reared five children and written several books in that trailer while they traveled to and from construction sites. The bedroom was overstuffed. In the corner, there was a small desk piled with papers and an old typewriter. I felt ashamed that she had accomplished so much in those circumstances, and I so little in mine. She seemed serene in her unsettled environment while I was angry and unhappy with my husband's ever-increasing demands for attention and addiction to debt. After our meal, her husband immediately fell asleep on the table, snoring loudly. When I told her about Bob's promotion and our projected move to Eugene, she was thrilled for us.

Her two older sons had gone to school in an area close to Eugene, and her three younger children had spent most of their lives there, so she explained what the area was like and gave me a long list of her old friends and metaphysical groups to look up once we settled there. I would miss all the friends I had made in The Dalles but there were new ones to be made in Eugene, and I eagerly anticipated the move.

Judy was not as serene as she seemed and shortly after we moved to Eugene, she took her two remaining children still at home, left her husband and moved to Chicago to advance her writing career. It surprised and outraged me when she unexpectedly divorced her stable, hardworking husband to pursue her own dreams. I did not consider personal ambition a good reason to break up a marriage, although I could sympathize with her primitive life in their tiny, crowded trailer, traveling from area to area on his construction jobs.

# Chapter 35

Moving had become a way of life—a temporary, barely noticed inconvenience. By the time we moved to Eugene in 1966, I couldn't even count the number of times we had moved in the past 20 years, nor even in the last ten years during my husband's railroad employment (or unemployment) and grocery clerk years. America was a mobile country and everyone seemed to constantly be moving to advance a career, start one, or exchange one for another. Leaving friends and family was an American way that we had come to accept.

Bob had had an honest-to-god career, and he was moving up in his position as the Regional Coordinator for a flourishing union to do the work he loved. He was issued a new "company" car and a credit card for all his on-job expenses, with an admonition to use them wisely. His only restriction was to pay for fuel for family use when he was at home. His dream of being a writer or photographer fell into oblivion. My personal goals and ambitions were put aside in favor of a better life for the family, and I was content and optimistic about our future. Bob was jubilant and proud, although he grieved over the loss of President Kennedy for months afterward, as most of America did.

We rented an old home, but after learning it was in a poor neighborhood, we moved again to a split-level rental in a better area. What was another move? It was so close to a good grade school that the children could walk to in minutes. I enrolled Steve into the first grade with mixed feelings—sadness at losing my "baby," and joy for the free time his absence would mean for me to be creative.

As promised, Bob was at home three or more days a week. His travels were mostly to cities or towns in the Willamette Valley, from Portland South to Medford. None were over three hours driving time away. A far longer trip each month was a three or more day's trip to Eastern Oregon or Idaho to meet with local union officials and members. There were other conferences with District union officials, as well as periodic conventions attended by hundreds of union members, where wives were encouraged to attend.

Bob began the new job with great determination and commitment, while I returned to my household duties, bill paying, chauffeuring the children to school events, doctors, dentists, violin and drum practice, shopping and gardening. In summer, preteen Debbie and teenager Bobby picked beans or berries at a local farm, while I entered Jan and Steve in church camps, Red Cross swimming classes and children's park activities. Picking beans apparently was a great new experience. Deb and Bobby earned some of their own spending money, met new peers, and had a wonderful time. Unknown to me, it was also a place to pick up the cultural mores so popular in the '60s—smoking pot, drinking, and partying. At day's end, they told me about swimming after work in the clear fast-moving waters of the near-by river and jumping off railroad trestles into nearby swift, rock-filled rivers. I would have had a heart attack if I had known.

In school, Steve soon signed up for drum classes, Jan into violin lessons, and Debbie into school plays, sports, glee club, and almost everything that was offered, while Bobby joined the high school print shop and the school newspaper. It was a defining point for him academically, turning him from a comfortable student into a dedicated one with a four-point average. He was offered summer courses at the university when he graduated from high school, where he earned perfect grades. I was immensely proud of him and encouraged him to continue, but he chose to go to Community college instead.

Between chauffeuring the kids to all their activities, I contacted Judy's old friends who lived in the area and got to know and love them as friends. Many of them frequented the Theosophy Library, where all of us explored metaphysics and various philosophies. The group consisted of several writers and artists, nurses, teachers, and inquiring housewives who were exploring views that might give more meaning to their lives. The Library was well stocked with little known or out of print books varying from studies of the world's great religions to reincarnation, ESP, and exploration of the unexplained occult phenomenon.

This group opened my intellectual eyes to possibilities and demanded answers to age-old questions: where did we come from, why are we here, and what is our purpose? It opened my mind to new friends, new organizations, and new knowledge. It led me to an art gallery where I took my first class in drawing and painting, and where I exhibited and sold my first painting.

Bob viewed my intellectual and spiritual quest as "way-out," ridiculous, and a total waste of time, although he approved of my painting efforts. If I mentioned books about reincarnation, for example, it was a threat to his Southern Baptist upbringing that distressed him. He refused to discuss ideas or themes I read about, and it became a sore subject to him. Hungry to discover, I turned to new friends that Judy had suggested I meet. I urged Bob to attend meetings with me so he could view ideas in a non-threatening way, but he shut me out when the subject was mentioned. Marge, an astrologist and writer, visited me only when Bob was away, and I visited others in their homes.

Although I disapproved of our locally famous writer, Ken Kasey (author of *Sometimes a Great Notion* and *One Flew over the Cuckoo's Nest*)'s use of drugs and alternative life-style, I considered him a compelling and charismatic character that I visited on a few times on special occasions. After I met Mary M, she became a special friend who both captivated and bewildered me with her insight and incredible intellectual capacity. Her mind was like a sponge gathering data and processing it like a computer. She was able to memorize entire pages of complex books and recite them verbatim and had the reputation of being psychic, in which I put little credence. She would frighten me even more after I got to know her better, but she inspired me in our early relationship. She showed me reams of poetry and other writings— much of which was too diverse for my poor brain to absorb.

Our first year in Eugene went by quickly, with my new friends and busy times with children's activities. When Bob returned from his travels, everything changed as he dominated all our discussions and habits. We had established routines, such as when I gave (or refused) the children permission to visit their friends or stay after school. They would ask me first or if I denied them the privilege they wanted; they would then ask their father.

Bob usually countered with an absent-minded, "Fine, what's the problem?" He was intent on re-establishing his authority and standing in the family that I had unintentionally usurped in his frequent absences. I pleaded with him to present a united front in our parenting, but gradually it became a "good guy" vs. "bad guy" with the children, with me being the disciplinarian and Bob the good guy. When we fought over issues, he usually won. The kids adored him because when he was at home, he allowed them to do anything they wanted.

# Chapter 36

My sisters visited us, or vice-versa, several times each year. Pat and her husband received extended vacations at least once a year, and usually made trips back to Mississippi as well as visiting Mel in California and my family in Oregon. At times, they returned to the States for further training and/or Pentagon conferences and she took that opportunity to visit us without him. Her visits were always a treat, although I was baffled that she usually came without her husband.

During her travels, she generously picked up souvenirs or jewelry or other gifts for each of us but her loving presence was her greatest gift to us. She considered us her family since she never had children of her own. She delighted in "mothering" me as her "little sister." To us, her travels, especially in Southeast Asia as the wife of the military attaché were exotic and exciting. Sometimes, she referred to her job as "a glorified spy" who entertained foreign diplomats, military and governmental officials. She described the elaborate parties they held to entertain officials, their staff of servants, and the varied menus and flower arranging she had to plan and prepare for with the aid of their servants. In my little world of children and simple household duties, it sounded exhilarating. Sometimes I felt envious, compared to my ho-hum existence washing clothes and dishes and trying to make ends meet.

Other facets of her life made me more grateful for my own little world. She had married too soon without getting to know her husband well after the death of her "soul mate," and soon learned that he was domineering, demanding, and unaffectionate.

No one needed love more than Pat did. She had entered into a loveless marriage to a handsome, charming Air Force officer who intimidated and degraded her. She fought back the same way we had been taught by our parents by nagging, screaming, and fighting. She was bitterly unhappy in her gold-plated world despite the prestige and luxurious life-style. When I coached her that there were alternatives to living in an unhappy situation, she was too insecure emotionally and financially to change her life, so she endured—kicking and screaming.

"Stand up to him!" I advised her. "No one can treat you that way unless you accept it." But she had allowed him to invest her insurance benefits from her former husband and was afraid to rock her security boat. If Pat failed to fulfill his directives, he fumed, pouted, or threatened to divorce her. He had her firmly under his emotional and physical control. Their money was his—and if she spent for things he did not approve of, there was hell to pay. In time, she almost succumbed to this thinking: money was to be used to earn more money. By the time they were in their 80s in age, they owned a condo in Hawaii, another one in Washington State, and a house in Arizona, with cars and golf carts in each location. She broke out of this kind of thinking occasionally to buy a computer or painting supplies, but she bought clothes, furniture, and household items from garage sales and thrift stores to save money even after they had piled up a fortune in stocks and bonds. I couldn't fault their spending habits but could not understand his hoarding money. He made the decisions, and his decisions were not to be questioned. I asked him once when I visited them, "Do you plan to take it with you?" I thought my sister paid a very high price for financial security!

For instance, he hated gardening, while she loved it. He frequently went into the yard and removed some of her plantings without consulting her, resulting in huge arguments. She planted fruit trees and he removed them. Although he loved the vegetables she loved to grow, he complained about the water bill or her occasional expense for landscaping help. By that time, her money management was almost as stingy as his, although spending for expensive golf club memberships, dwellings, and cars was not questioned. It seemed that the only thing her husband didn't complain about was her interest in art. She took classes and workshops and later taught The Old Master's Technique as she traveled around in Texas, Vietnam, Laos, Thailand, and other countries. Her paintings were exhibited in galleries around the world.

Furthermore, Pat complained, during earlier years—the times when they were in the States for extended periods of time—he moved his 50-year-old mother in with them, who immediately assumed the role of the female head of the house. He insisted that the mother he adored needed to be taken care of at the age of 50. Pat felt she had no definitive role. Pat's mother-in-law took over and Pat was delegated to the junior position in the family until her vehemence objections won and "Mom" was sent away, over her husband's objections. At times, the only way Pat was able to force her mother-in-law to move out was to threaten divorce. On other occasions, she simply moved out herself to return only after her husband ejected his mother. She was healthy, active and perfectly capable of looking after herself. It was a co-dependent relationship that lasted for many years and caused extreme pain for my sister.

# Chapter 37

Pat also took most of the responsible for Mom and Dad. She helped them buy a small parcel of land and build a basic little cottage in Mississippi and sent them money from time to time trying to make them as comfortable as possible under the circumstances. After Dad's accident that left him paralyzed, she made many trips to arrange for part-time helpers, transportation, or see to other needs they had while Mel and I were busy with our growing families.

I don't know how they could have survived their difficulties without her. Mom had to learn to drive for the first time at over 60 years of age after Dad's accident, which caused even more problems. She had two accidents, in which she lost an eye in one and broken limbs in another. Their problems seemed insurmountable, with Mom's arthritis growing worse and worse, on top of her duties as my dad's caregiver and her own frequent hospitalizations.

Mel had settled into a family routine in the tiny canyon in Dunsmuir, California with Mt. Shasta and adjacent mountains towering above them. She and her tall, handsome 1st Lt. Husband, Bob, who she had met in Memphis when she was working at a Hotel, had returned to his home town after the war ended to resume his career as a railroad engineer. For the first eight years of their marriage, they were frustrated when Mel failed to get pregnant. They had tests after test to ascertain why they were unable to start the family they wanted. The only cause they found was that Mel had a thyroid condition. After therapy to correct that problem, she apparently was so thrilled about my pregnancy with my oldest child that they "forgot to try." After her first child was born (nine months after Bobby), four more beautiful children followed.

Bob and Mel's lives were dominated by family activities as new babies were born one after another. They doted over the children, depriving them of nothing. She changed from a near-glamorous object of attraction to worshipful men into a devoted mother, cook, gardener, and housewife who hovered over her little brood with total devotion. Her children could do no wrong. She herded her beautiful oldest child into various activities and spent her evenings sewing costumes for her dancing pageants and beautiful new dresses to show her off. A whirlwind of activities kept her moving from one chore to the next, and she was never still. Somewhere along the way, she lost some of her old intellectual curiosity and devotion to literature that she had as a teenager in high school. She had found her calling as a wife, mother and "friend who lived by the side of the road and be a friend to man." She never met a friend she didn't like, and everyone adored her. People would drop in with their families for a cup of coffee or to share a recipe and end up having dinner and card parties with no apologies. The house was always filled with children, noise, and constant interruptions, and she loved it.

Their life in a town consisting of about 2500 people was routine, dominated by children's activities, Southern Pacific railroad events, picnics, fishing and hunting, and an occasional outing at the local bar, where her husband, Bob, loved to stop in for a drink after his long hours at work. He was a loving father, a good provider for the family; stable and conventional except for his occasionally bar-hopping episodes with his friends. His occasional drinking caused their unsatisfactory life to fall through the cracks and she became frustrated and unhappy.

Mel was still young, glamorous and beautiful. She missed the accolades she had once received from world-famous musicians and actors who had showered her with candy, flowers, dining, and dancing at the hotel where she worked before their marriage. Her husband was devoted to the family, but he was never demonstratively affectionate—the one thing my siblings needed above all else since our parents had shown little love for us.

I realized I had married Bob because he provided a semblance of the love I needed, but neither of my sisters was receiving enough affection from their spouses to fulfill them and make them happy. My visits with my sisters were dominated by complaints about the failure of their husbands' to exhibit attention and love for them. They were both starved for love. In Mel's case, in time, the result was to look for it somewhere else.

After the children because old enough to look after themselves, Mel decided that if her husband could stop by bars for drinks with his friends, two could play that game. Her beauty attracted the local men to shower her with attention. One of them was a married-with-children railroad employee who gave her what she needed—romantic attention. In time, it resulted in what she considered to be the biggest mistake of her life—the breakup of her family and marriage to a man who gave her little besides the attention she needed. For the remainder of her life, she was married to a man who adored her, but whose intellectual capacity and stability were far less than her former husband. She grieved over breaking up her marriage mistake for years afterward.

Over a period of time, her new husband became a periodic alcoholic, couch potato, and poor decision-maker. Further, the breakup of their family threw the children into a tail-spin where the younger two started using drugs and spun out of control emotionally. The youngest son was diagnosed with a mental illness, and the youngest daughter became an alcoholic. Both died at an early age, with one who committed suicide, and the daughter died of chronic liver disease. She grieves over this tragedy daily.

Mel took her big family home to Mississippi as often as possible, as Bob and I did on several occasions. All of us felt responsible for taking care of them but our pleas that they move to the northwest were rejected for many years. Dad was a diehard Mississippian and said he would never be happy living anywhere else—nor was he, when years later, they were forced by circumstances to move closer to us. By that time, all of the children lived on the West Coast, and they had no better options.

My brother, Dick, found a sweet, loving Nebraska native and fell in love and started a family. After several years as a fireman on the railroad, like Bob and I, he found that he didn't have enough seniority to depend on the job for a livelihood, and started looking for a different way to earn a living. Dick started by placing a pair of coin laundry machines into apartment buildings around Dunsmuir until he gradually built up a supplementary income to his railroad earnings. As lay-offs became more and more frequent, he increased his secondary income, and eventually purchased a Laundromat. Like our father and me, he did not believe that working for wages was the way to make progress financially.

The laundry-mat became his primary income for the coming years. He repaired machines, collected the money, cleaned the premises for an hour or two each day, and spent the remainder of his time with his family. An intense and inventive person, he built the children little scooters made from old lawnmower engines and watched them as they happily rode across the lawn on them. In his free time, Dick got a pilot's license, a big float boat and finally took a course in hypnotism. My children loved to visit them because Dick entertained them with ingenious contraptions he built or took them swimming or floating the adjacent swift-flowing creek on old tire tubes. They had a blast, as we did play pinochle or other games with each other and the children, picnicking and talking the night away. The closeness of my siblings and their families was central to my happiness, but I only wished that our families were closer in distance.

# Chapter 38

The 1960s were possibly one of the most important decades in American history. Dominated by the conflict between the East and West, Communism vs. Capitalism, peace vs. violence and the disenfranchised against the establishment, the country was in constant disruption. Fire hoses and dogs confronted the young charismatic civic rights leader, Martin Luther King and the hordes of protestors he led in Alabama and elsewhere. The Civil Rights Act of 1964 and The Voting Rights Act of 1965 gradually changed the lives of minorities. It also contributed to, if not actually caused, the assassination of Martin Luther King, John F. Kennedy and later Robert Kennedy, which perhaps issued in an effective progressive movement that attempted to change America for the better. The effects of the Vietnam War were felt throughout the world as students and minorities learned that protests were getting attention.

Perhaps the anguish Americans felt over the war led to the drug culture that started in the late '50s and early '60s. My friends and I hated the war machine that caused the massive explosion of spending on war materials and weapons, as well as American's interference in other countries. How could Communism spread to America? What had happened to our country?

We worried that my son, Bob would be drafted and become another statistic. *"No way! I won't go,"* he told us when he finished high school and was subject to the draft. His risky but creative, non-conformist plan to avoid the draft worked and he avoided the draft. I was proud of him. During his high school and college years, he became involved in school newspaper printing and it soon led to a good career in the printing industry.

The longest and most costly conflict in American history at that point, the Vietnam War claimed the lives of over 58,000 Americans and wounded another 304,000 as well as three to four million Vietnamese between 1959 and 1975. Afterward, Laotians and Cambodians were drawn into the war and 1.5 to two million of them was slaughtered.

When Debbie was 12 years old, I decided to give my charming, charismatic daughter a birthday party and invited her numerous friends to help her celebrate. We decorated the family room on the lower floor of the split level, and I made mounds of treats for the party, monitoring their games and activities from the deck above or quick surveys into the room. When their music or laughter and play became too loud, I went downstairs to control the noise to avoid neighbors' complaints. When, later, I noticed a number of children chasing each other around the back yard, screeching with laughter, I returned to oversee their activities and was shocked to find a keg of beer hidden under the deck. Debbie was furious when I ordered her friends off the premises. An argument ensued with my husband taking her side. He thought it was fine for 12-year-olds to have a beer. I was the "bad guy" and he was the "good guy." That was the end of any effective control of my ubiquitous teenage daughter. The incident was disquieting to me as the young mother, but it would have been more distressing if I had known it was prophetic of her future behavior.

When Bob returned home one day in October, he informed me that he wanted me to attend an upcoming two-day convention with him. "All the wives will be there," he said, "It is expected."

"But who will take care of the kids?" I asked.

"You will find someone," he answered. I started calling all my unencumbered friends to stay with the kids that weekend. My new friend, Mary, finally agreed to the task. It was my first time away from my children, but I felt they would be safe with her as she had a child of her own. Off to the convention we went for two days of speeches, food, and relaxation.

We returned on Sunday evening too late for Mary to go home, so she spent another night at our house. Bob left again early Monday morning, and I prepared breakfast for Mary and the children before they left for school. When I started our usual free and open conversation with Mary, she was strangely reticent; refusing to reply when I asked her if something was wrong. Repeatedly, I asked her, "What's wrong?" and she refused to reply. At last, finally, she grunted, "What the hell is the matter with you?"

"What does that mean?" I asked.

"You are a fool," she said. "Why can't you see what is going on?" Her voice was angry and scornful.

"I don't know what you are talking about. What have I done?" I asked incredulously.

I begged her to tell me what she was thinking, but she refused to say any more. Finally, I pleaded again, "If you know something I don't know then you have an obligation to tell me!" By this time, both of us were angry, and I was upset. Back and forth the conversation went until once more she finally blurted out, "You're a fool! You only see what you want to see."

"Then tell me why," I demanded.

After repeated urging, she told me that Bob was hiding things from me that any sensible wife could see and that I should be more aware. "I can't tell you what you don't want to know," she said, "But I will tell you this much. Something is going on that will disrupt this family and agonize all of you."

I begged her to tell me more, "When will I know whatever it is that I need to know?"

"It'll come to a head by the end of the year. It will involve pain and illness, negotiation and hospitalization. There will be confession on Christmas Eve." I stared at her vacantly, not having the least idea what she meant, but nothing could force her to say anymore. When she left the house, the only thing she added was, "Just open your eyes."

In October of 1962, I noticed that when Bob was at home, he often paced the floor and slept poorly or not at all. Sometimes, he stared at the television without seeing it, and his eyes appeared vacant when I spoke to him. He ignored the kids and no longer joined into conversations at meals. Instead of grabbing me for hugs as I made meals, he told me, "I love you," repeatedly—almost desperately. I watched his actions in horror with no comprehension of what was happening. It got worse. In the weeks before Christmas, he was awake all night, pacing the floor or sitting in his chair staring at the wall. He couldn't eat or sleep during the week he was at home for the holidays but refused to see a doctor. From being an enthusiastic shopper for Christmas gifts, he now had no interest in buying gifts for the children or in the festive dinner I planned. When I wrapped the gifts to put under the tree for the children, he was oblivious. After I settled the children into bed that night, I approached him, "What in the hell is wrong with you?"

And it all poured out… he was so ashamed of himself—he had betrayed me, the one he loved most in the world. He proceeded to confess that he had slept with 32 women during the past year and could I ever forgive him, he didn't know why he did it, he couldn't help himself, and why did he do it and on and on and on. He sobbed uncontrollably until I took him to the emergency ward of the hospital, where he was admitted, diagnosed with his second nervous breakdown. The doctor told me he couldn't sleep for the following four days, despite heavy doses of narcotics. "I've never seen anyone so resistant to sleeping," he told me.

I spent the week he was in the hospital in a fog, crying copious tears and trying to understand. I called a neighbor friend, weeping uncontrollably, in an effort to talk it out and make sense of it all. His confession did not compute. I always had complete blind trust in him, without a clue that he was capable of doing what he had done. His actions were no match for the affection and love he always showered on me. It was the last thing I would have accused him of.

Yes, he was a poor money manager, and yes, he talked and called attention to himself too much, but he had always been extraordinarily affectionate. I had not considered Bob extremely neurotic—although very narcissistic. I was completely baffled that Mary had somehow predicted exactly what and when the events occurred.

When I visited Bob after he finally was able to sleep on his fourth day at the hospital, all he could say was, "I'm so very, very sorry. I hope you can forgive me."

I asked, "Why?"

He replied, "I don't know. I wish I did."

I returned home in agony, trying to figure out what to do. Should I get a divorce? How could I take care of and support four children? With my limited skills, how could I pay for child care and earn enough to pay rent, a car, transport the kids to their activities, and manage a one-parent family? I was a good typist and had experience in payroll and other clerical work, but could I trade an adequate income from a philandering husband for a job that paid little? The questions went on in my mind over and over without an answer. What affect would a divorce from their beloved father do to the children? What to do—what to do? How would the children react? It could destroy their love for their father if I explained why I had to divorce him. On the other hand, wasn't it harmful to all of us when our disputes, arguments, and disagreements exploded when he was at home? They considered me the "old nag" when I begged Bob to back me up when I corrected the kids or took away their freedom when they ignored my wishes or orders. He was the "good guy" and I was the "bad guy." Was divorce better than the bickering the children had to endure?

# Chapter 39

The past 20 years flooded back to me: the good years when he was railroading and our tight budgeting trying to live on disrupted income; the wonder and delight of the births of our children; games, swimming and barbeques with my sister and brother's families; the struggles of trying to balance our household budget with Bob's reckless spending habits; his insistence that he buys whatever he wanted whether the family had money for food, clothing, and groceries.

My heart was shattered into a million pieces. I had been deceived, betrayed—yet I was certain he was in love with me and cared deeply for the children. My love for Bob had been tested for 20 years and despite each of our idiosyncrasies and failures, I thought he had been a good but emotionally fragile husband. I had promised to love, honor, and cherish him in our marriage vows, and he told me that he was still committed to those vows, despite having broken them. I wasn't perfect either. He was aware of his inadequacies and begged me to stay with him so that therapy would help him overcome them.

When he left Monday morning to go to Washington, D. C., for a conference, he asked, "What are you going to do?"

I answered, "I don't know. I'll have to think more about it. Call me in later and I'll let you know what I decide."

He called the next day after both of us went through a sleepless night. "I've decided to stay on one condition that you enter a counseling program— not only to work on your betrayal but to learn better parental and money-management skills. I'll go with you if you want. Both of us need marital counseling."

Bob seemed overjoyed, promising to start therapy immediately after his return home.

For the first few months, he met with therapists twice a week, and then gradually reduced his visits to alternate weeks, then to once a month, with the excuse that it interfered with his work schedule and cost too much. After five or six months, he announced that he was cured and didn't need that "bullshit" anymore.

Often when he came home from a trip, he said he needed some recreation to "unwind." Both of us loved to fish and spent many happy hours on weekends or holidays casting for rainbow trout from the banks of a river, creek or lake, sometimes taking the children and picnic food. This changed suddenly—the minute he entered the house, he announced, "Come on, let's go fishing."

It became a routine that summer that caused me to worry about leaving the kids without enough supervision. Steve was only eight, and I was concerned that babysitting him was too much responsibility for his 11 and 13-year-old sisters.

"Ok, but let's take the kids," I answered. Sometimes, the girls had their own plans, but more often, Bob would insist on leaving them at home to care for Steve. I felt guilty most of the time we went fishing without the kids. If I suggested taking Steve, Bob would object that it would cause us to spend all our time retrieving lost lures and kinks in his line. Invariably it caused arguments and disagreements between us and little joy in it for me.

"I work hard all the time and I deserve some playtime," he would say adamantly. So off I went to placate him, guilt-ridden for leaving the kids behind.

I did not understand for years why I was losing the ability to control and discipline my teenage children when Bob was at home from his travels. It had started after he became The Regional Coordinator and started traveling. We were having dinner one night after he returned from a trip and the kids started misbehaving at the table. Bobby initiated it when he dropped a roll on the floor, picked it up and tossed it across the table. Everyone thought it was extremely funny.

Determined to make it even more hilarious, Bobby picked some dough from one, rolled into a small ball and threw it across the table at his sisters. I was incensed to see the meal I had worked so hard to prepare so abused, but everyone was shaking with laughter. "Stop it, stop it. You don't behave this way at the table," I demanded. They persisted. They ignored me as another child tossed a roll across the table.

"Bob, speak to the children!" I demanded.

"Hello, children," he said. They thought this was the funniest thing they had ever heard, and rolled on the floor in merriment. It turned out to be a repeated performance over the years—a way for Bob to assert his control.

It escaped my attention for a long time that Jan's jealousy of Debbie's personality and popularity overwhelmed everyone around her or that Jan was acquiring an inferiority complex. She was a delight to me, but it did not occur to me that she was developing "the third child syndrome." Her older sister and brother demanded and received most of the attention, while Jan seemed to enjoy reading, quiet times, and companionship with two or three of her best friends. We had open and candid discussions, her grades were good, and I respected her quiet scholarship and interests, and I saw no reason to be concerned for her.

On the other hand, it seemed impossible to contain Debbie's curiosity and constant activities. One minute she would tell me she was going to a friend's house, and the next they were off with a group of friends at another house. I could not keep up with her, but efforts to restrain her became nearly impossible. She'd tell me her plans—without following them.

Bobby became more and more self-reliant and independent, spending hours in his room reading or joining his two best friends for swimming or high school activities. However, he loved making jokes at the table.

After he tossed dough across the table, and I couldn't make him stop, I resorted to the way my parents disciplined us by slapping him. He grabbed my hand, threw me over his shoulder and turned me around and around. Bob and the children were laughing hysterically. He was larger than me. Nothing is more humiliating than having a 16-year-old son pick up his mother and refuse to be disciplined. Once, he produced a gun which turned out to be a toy when I entered his room to find out what he was doing that was so important that he couldn't join us for dinner. He was often volatile and secretive, while at other times he was positive and upbeat, treating everything as a huge joke. By the age of 17, he had declared his independence. Disciplined control of my two oldest children was impossible.

Another incident occurred when he was working on his car in the garage one day when his father interrupted him. He turned on Bob with a string of harsh, disrespectful epithets, yelling, "Leave me alone." Bob was furious after his tirade became more and more abusive and uncontrolled. I was standing by the door begging both of them to control themselves, with my pleas totally ignored. The argument became worse until Bob picked up a pop bottle and threatened to hit Bobby with it, leaving me close to hysteria over the fear of killing or badly wounding our son. Fortunately, Bobby walked away but the incident left us with the knowledge that our son refused to be controlled. Both of them were headstrong and wrong. Like most arguments, I could only hope they had learned something about losing control. So much for my ability to handle my volatile family!

Steve was my sweet, compliant child. He joined his friends to ride bicycles at the school grounds, played quietly with his Lego's or cars and trucks

or helped me without complaint when I asked him to take the garbage out—
or other little chores.

# Chapter 40

Debbie was in Junior High School, a leader in all the music programs and theatrical productions, girl's athletic programs, and a charismatic student. She earned good grades and was a teacher favorite. Everyone predicted future great things for her—especially her mother. Yet, despite her enthusiasm, intellectual curiosity, and optimism, she periodically had bouts of debilitating depression and discouragement that was hard to comprehend. To those around her, she had the world on a string and was capable of doing and being whatever she chose to be. We spent hours discussing her endless questions, ranging from friend and family relationships to sex, her future, her aptitudes and interests, and even world affairs. She was open and honest about her relationships with friends, and of her activities. I thought I knew my daughter better than any mother could know a child, and I both adored her and had high expectations for her. She was talented, beautiful, bright, and a born leader.

When we weren't exploring relationships or aptitudes and interests, we explored endless ideas, including my fervent interest in metaphysics. From the age of around 13, Debbie began calling me "the ghost worshiper," and couldn't get enough of my insights into the esoteric subjects I was exploring. Her constant questions revealed her innermost need to know that had consumed me. I felt that she was "an old soul" with a quest for deep spirituality, wisdom, and a need to know the mind of God. This search led her not only to questions but to dangerous experiments in ways that I would never have dared. Unknown to me during this period, she was smoking marijuana, drinking, and experimenting with a variety of other drugs. It wasn't long before she went to San Francisco to join the "flower children" and protest the Vietnam war.

Like many of her friends, my distrust of President Nixon and the war machine Eisenhower had warned us about angered and frustrated me to the point of wanting to join peace marches and war protests, although I never did.

Nixon's administration turned America from a democratically ruled country into an arrogant, authoritative system dominated by weapons manufacturers and corporations intent on dominating all other world countries and governments. From this administration to the present one, lobbyists for "big money" effectively controlled most government political decisions. The military-industrial power structure turned the United States into a war machine that spread over 700 military bases, arms caches, and CIA and FBI snoops all over the globe to monitor the actions of every world country. Presidential executive power expanded, secrecy reigned, and America's previously good media coverage was reigned in, to the point that citizens would never hear the complete truth again.

Nixon's election and power were bought by oilmen, industrialists, and the wealthy, which soon controlled most government decisions and actions. Nixon's images on television left me with feelings of apprehension. I saw the lies, deceptions, and arrogance of his administration and wondered what had happened to my beloved country. Fortunately, in time, our constitutional principles allowed us to depose those whose wrong thinking and acts had brought the country so close to ruin. The investigation into Nixon's lies led to his resignation.

Debbie's insight into the political and sociological realities of the times was astonishing for a young girl. Her intelligence was amazing, while she seemed to have little control over her emotions. Her moods varied from being appallingly depressed to excessive euphoria. Admiring friends flocked to her side to aid and comfort her in whatever mood she was in. Remembering my own teenage moods, I thought her behavior was reasonably normal for her age.

I felt it was a critical time to consider getting a job during my children's teenage years, but we needed the money. Although Bob's earnings were good, inflation and the costs of raising four children had increased. Further, Bob's away-from-home expenses seemed to be higher than his allowance. For the first time in our marriage, we had a regular paycheck but somehow, it never seemed to fill all our needs. A part-time job would fill the gap, I thought. My years of extreme need for financial security began to overwhelm my life.

I found a part-time, temporary job at the University of Oregon as a relief clerical worker, where I filled in for clerks, typists, bookkeepers, or other staff, to replace those who were sick or on vacation. It was a fascinating, intellectual, and rewarding job where I traveled from one department to another as a short-time replacement for the full-time job occupant. It also filled my need for sociability and relief from "the housewife's dilemma."

# Chapter 41

I came home from work one day to made dinner and took care of endless household chores. Debbie was resting in her bedroom when I called her to dinner. She staggered out, leaning against a door post crazily with shaking knees and wild, distorted expressions on her face. What in the world? When I questioned her, she first giggled and then exploded into uncontrolled crying and hysteria. After continual questions, she gave no indication of what, if anything, she had ingested, or why she was behaving as she was. I managed to get her into the car and to the hospital, where they pumped her stomach. This was the first of many similar incidents that were to follow.

Once it was alcohol, later it was LSD, and there were many incidents to come that ranged from depression to drug use. I was devastated and grief-stricken.

When the episodes were over, Debbie returned to her usual stable, normal self, while I blithely assumed that it is just raging teenage hormones. She always found ways to dramatize every event in her young life, even to invent little lies about them for effect.

I reached the point where I asked, "Is this true, or are you making it up?" Sometimes, she would sheepishly agree that she was exaggerating, or at other times stick with her story. I remembered the story she told when she was about 11 when she claimed that a man jumped from behind a tree and exposed himself as she walked by. I thought she was making it up, but she was traumatized by the event for days or weeks and was afraid to go to sleep at night. It seemed that she saw a boogie man behind every tree.

Bob came home one weekend and suggested that just he and I go out for dinner—a rare and infrequent treat. I agreed if 15-year-old Debbie would stay at home with the younger children. Debbie agreed but wanted to visit a friend after we returned. I asked her to clean up the kitchen while we were gone, and told her we would return by 9:30 pm. Bob told her she didn't need to clean the kitchen.

Foiled again! When we returned home, Debbie was gone and a black cloud gathered around my head in a persistent feeling of dread, with no clue why I had such a powerful sense of doom and approaching catastrophe. Was my ESP working overtime, and should I heed such overpowering feelings? I was frantic, certain that something was terribly wrong.

I visualized my daughter in every kind of horrible consequence imaginable. I knew. I knew. I started calling all her known friends and acquaintances to find out where she had gone and what she was doing. After dozens of phone calls, I learned that some of her closest friends were also missing, with their parents almost as frantic as I was. From about ten o'clock that night until four in the morning, I called all of her friends I knew and their parents. Gradually, I picked up clues after learning that four of her other friends were not to be found either.

"They were all here, but left about midnight," one parent told me. Another friend admitted that he had seen the four 15 and 16-year-old kids smoking "grass," and then he had gone home.

I called the parent who had seen them last again, asking, "Do you have any clue where they could have gone? Do you have relatives somewhere they could be visiting?" It was four o'clock in the morning by then. Like me, they had been awake all night, questioning and worrying.

"Greg's father is in Washington State," she said.

"Who is he, and what is his phone number?" I asked.

"He is a psychologist," she answered, and then I knew. Debbie had mentioned him on occasions, and I knew Greg well enough to know that he might want to visit a man that he obviously appreciated.

Since Greg was the only child who owned a car, the next call I made was to the Washington phone number. I dialed the number anxiously, only to get a sleepy, disgruntled voice demanding to know why I was calling him in the middle of the night. He calmed down when I told him about the missing children, but told me that they weren't there. I told him I had a feeling the kids could be on the way there and left him with my phone number to call in case they showed up. He promised he would call me if they arrived.

A few hours later, Greg's father called to tell me the five children had arrived safely. I asked him to put my daughter on a bus home with a police escort if necessary, as soon as they slept a few hours, and he agreed that he would. "Don't worry," he said, "I'll take good care of them." The following day we picked up an irate, exhausted Debbie at the bus station. Bob and I agreed that she needed a lesson that she would remember, so we drove straight to the juvenile detention center with our defiant 15-year-old, where authorities put her into a bare cell with no window to recover from the experience.

She was open about what happened, explaining that the five children met at a friend's place, smoked some pot, or had a couple of beers. After midnight, one of them suggested that they try some LSD. All of them took it except her, she said. Debbie said she ingested LSD out of anger and spite after their Washington host informed her of my phone call.

The psychologist gave the children some food, and then put them in bed for a few hours' sleep before he drove Debbie to the bus station for the return trip home. Debbie also explained that none of the four other children were in any condition to drive, so she had to. She was the only one who had not taken LSD before leaving on the trip—it just seemed like a great trip to make, she explained. She had no driver's license and little knowledge or experience in driving. I could only thank god that they made the five-hour trip with no incidents or accidents. My precious daughter, the delight of everyone who knew her, seemed to defy her own talents, intelligence, and all her future potential to choose her own path through life.

We spent hours on a daily basis discussing her prolific aptitudes and abilities. Her writing ability was uncanny for a child so young—so insightful, full of life and abstract thought that I encouraged this facet of her near-genius as a career goal to consider. She had musical abilities and talents as well, but she seemed less serious about them than the possibility of a theatrical career. Gradually in her high school years, her interests turned into acting and show business after she got the lead in her junior year play at high school, where she brought the house down with her portrayal of an English maid with a cockney accent.

She settled down to school and study for a while after the running-away incident, but periodic episodes of highs and lows continued at intervals. If her boyfriend disappointed her, or if she felt left out of her peer group, depression or elation followed. She was an emotional child, as our entire family was—*what else can you expect*, I thought.

I was going through my own emotional upheavals from being a single parent when Bob was traveling, too much responsibility and too little recognition. The weight of working part-time, coming home to cook, clean, sew, and care for the children was taking its toll on my psyche. I felt overworked and underappreciated. The hardest part was trying to keep the bills paid when Bob's expenses exceeded his allowance. It was driving me crazy because his fellow "Regional Coordinators" reported that their allowance was more than adequate, and the wives received their salaries for the family to live on.

When Bob came home, I questioned him about his expenses, but he just shrugged, saying, "Well, it cost a lot of money to live on the road."

I replied, "But you are on the road only two or three days a week. Why are your expenses higher than others?" I never received a definitive answer, so I started offering to type his weekly expense and activity reports each weekend as a way to understand where the money went. I found bar bills and restaurant receipts for five to ten people for drinks and meals. When I questioned him, he stated that "he was expected to entertain" fellow union officials and members. I also found weekends fuel receipts—a violation of the rules that we were expected to pay for our own personal gasoline bills. "Don't you understand that filling your car with gas on weekends is a violation of the rules?"

Bob answered, "Well, I don't do it often."

"You can be fired for doing it at all," I nagged. "Do you value your job so little that you would take that chance?" My typing his expense reports became a routine that I hated. It ended in huge arguments about his unnecessary use of union funds.

His overspending habits now included both his expense allowance as well as our household budget. He bought what he wanted whether or not the family had money left for living expenses. My nagging and complaining only seemed to make it worse, and I felt more and more angry, distressed and controlled by events over which I had no power. I demanded that he take over the household budget so he would become more aware that it was becoming uncontrollable. He agreed, with dire results. He would forget to stub checks, or make mistakes in deducting them until I was forced to regain custody of the family finances and attempt to balance a checkbook that consisted of more debits than credits. My experiment resulted in a greater disaster than ever.

Bob usually gave me his salary check to pay household bills and kept the check for his travel allowance. One Friday evening, he returned from his travels and stopped at the bank to cash both checks. When he gave me the cash, which was $200.00 less than usual.

"What happened to the rest of the money?" I asked.

"A puff of wind blew the cash out of the drive-in drawer," he told me. "I got out of the car and tried to catch it, but couldn't find it, but I got the bills that stuck to the windshield."

The credibility of his story did not compute, but I was naïve enough to almost believe it. He still wrapped me around his finger, as he did the children. It was hopeless—many of our household bills did not get paid. It seemed we were getting further behind on our bills every month.

My frustration was taking a toll on my ability to maintain all the household duties, spend enough time with Steve and Jan, and pay the mounting bills that Bob ran up. My job gave me almost the only satisfaction I had, filling my intellectual curiosity as well as my social life with students and professors I met at the college. At the same time, it renewed my passionate need to know and desire to learn topics that my work allowed only a slight glimpse. When I had time to think about it, I dreamed of being a part of the student body in order to fill those empty spaces in my mind. My household duties consumed my time and energy while I agonized over my inability to find time to write, paint and read.

Undoubtedly, these frustrations contributed to guilt feelings over my failure to give Steve and Jan the attention they needed. They demanded little. Steven had his little friends and his drum set, while Jan had some close friends, the books she loved to read quietly in her room, and her violin. Her only need seemed to be her twice-weekly ride to practice at the University with the Junior Symphony, where she was the second chair. In hindsight, in view of later problems, I now know they needed more of my personal attention. My self-involvement, hectic schedule, and worry all contributed to the neglect of their needs that I failed to see.

Jan was jealous of her big sister's popularity and her demands for attention received more of my involvement. Debbie's habit of tormenting her little sister escaped my attention. I just was not there for Jan and Steve just as I was not there when Bob tormented Debbie in earlier years. My cup was too full, my attention span too short, and my ability to cope was causing more stress than I could manage. Something had to give.

# Chapter 42

During this period, my employment at the University took me from one department to another: History, Economics, Personnel, Geology, Education, etc. At this time, I was working for the Business Department in Real Estate, when I was asked to type an exam for the Real Estate Professor. When I read the exam, I asked him, "Gee, this test is easy. I could pass it and I've never had a class in real estate." He laughed, and said, "Want to make a bet?"

"Sure," I answered. He bet that I couldn't pass the test, and was astonished when I did.

The examination and my growing friendship with the Professor led me into considering real estate as a future career. It seemed easy enough. I questioned him relentlessly about the duties and responsibilities, earnings possibilities, etc., and his answers satisfied me. I needed a way to earn a large sum of money to pay old bills, send children to college, and start saving for future retirement.

At the age of 45, there were few years left for security and a decent retirement and I was resolute that my children's future would never reflect the financial insecurity our family had endured in the past. The handwriting was on the wall. I needed a chance to end my nearly 25-year-old marriage, although it was a sub-conscious decision rather than a conscious one.

There were lots of hoops to jump through. I needed the credentials, a car, money for a license, and some time. I found a school where I could get the credentials quickly—money and a car were the only problems. I went home, told Bob what I intended to do, over his heated objections, and enrolled in the school. Bills would have to wait because I intended to use whatever money I needed to go forward.

I received my real estate license in December 1971 and bought an inexpensive car that would have to do until I earned enough commissions for a better one.

I spent my small salary from the part-time job at the University for grocery bills, or to buy material for the children's clothes and sat up until midnight to make them, while my husband threw money to the four winds to buy things he wanted without considering the family's needs. All the past years of deprivation and sacrifice were being repeated while he became more demanding and selfish. He wanted to take weekend trips, go fishing without the children, and spend the weekend at the coast without considering the family's needs for clothes, utility, and grocery bills or other needs.

When I asked him to return to psychological counseling, he repeatedly denied that he needed that "bullshit." I became more and more frustrated, angry, and upset. For the first time in years, Bob earned an adequate salary and a generous expense allowance. It made no sense at all that we were drowning in debt and uncovered household, medical and dental needs. We could never afford to buy adequate furniture, pay for a canvas to paint on, or a book to read. The money seemed to evaporate uncontrollably. Nearly 25 years of financial insecurity was making me crazy.

When I started working with my new license, my husband would become infuriated when someone called to ask about a property I had listed, yelling into my ear, "No wife of mine is going to work," as I tried to converse with my customer. Sometimes, he screamed out, "Don't you understand that we are having dinner?" I was embarrassed and humiliated, but quietly asked if I could call them back. Bob degraded me continually, that I was working to make some broker rich and, "You'll never make a hill of beans!"

I confronted him calmly, saying, "This is what I'm going to do and you and no one else can stop me." Clearly, he was threatened by the prospect that I might become self-sufficient.

In January, my first full month, I made 11 sales. Some of them fell through for one reason or another. I would not receive commissions for any of the sales until they closed, which could be from one to three or more months.

I left for work early in the morning and did not return until late at night, discussing real estate with everyone from my gasoline attendant to sales clerks, and even total strangers I met. They all seemed interested. Bob could make dinner for the children, or they could all starve. I was determined to succeed. I had to succeed. Failure was not an option. There was going to be security for my family or I would die trying.

The house we had rented for two years would soon be mine. I made an agreement to purchase it by "work-credit" for the down payment and was well on the way through the requirements. After work each evening, I spent two or more hours sanding the kitchen cabinets and performing the other work for-credit conditions before falling into bed, exhausted. With no credit in my own name, my broker interceded with the mortgage banker, predicting that I would have a successful future in real estate. Closing the transaction was expected a month later in June. Despite almost desperate apprehension, I can think of nothing that gave me more pride and satisfaction that signing the closing check, depleting my checking account to the price of a loaf of bread. Fortunately, some of my earlier sales began to close, and it worked out.

Debbie settled down to school and study for a while after the running-away incident, but periodic episodes of highs and lows continued at intervals. If her boyfriend disappointed her, or if she felt left out of her peer group, depression or elation followed. She finished her Junior High School year as a dedicated drug-using "hippy" and dropped out of school to attend Community College classes. I was devastated.

While my life was more interesting and satisfactory, my children's lives were not. Debbie was moving from one squalid living arrangement into another one with almost no income except loans or haphazard fundraising ideas. She had garage sales or sold her books and clothes. She returned home to ask for money but rejected my pleas to return home to live. I was heartsick and frantic with worry.

It wasn't long before Jan got into the act. At 15 years of age, her normal self-containment and happy, carefree attitudes changed—possibly as a cause of my commitment to real estate and emersion into this new venture.

So undoubtedly, I neglected both my younger children during that time. I was split into too many directions between work, household duties, and my determination to succeed in my new field. My insecurity over our financial failures for so many years made me determined and dedicated to a more secure future, whatever it took. Real estate is demanding. There were phone calls late at night in addition to showing property, paperwork, and meetings to attend. In my hectic life, I did not see Jan's resentment at being left alone, or that Steve was spending more time with his friends than at home. What child would want to live at home alone without a mother present, or with an older sister more interested in her friends than she was with him?

I threw myself into work and neglected my two youngest children for my first year in the business before I was able to organize my time and life better. It resulted in my ability to earn expenses and our household bills, but little else. Next year, I promised, it would be better. Selling inexpensive houses for a $300 to $600 commission was not getting me where I wanted to go. I analyzed the market carefully. Many of my home sales failed when the buyer didn't have the required down payment, his credit was unsatisfactory, or the house failed to meet the lender's requirements.

There had to be another way. I would try to sell only very expensive properties, I reasoned, because wealthy buyers could afford to pay cash or at least qualify for loans. I loved the rural life I had experienced in my early years and I thought that selling farms, ranches and timberland would be more interesting than urban house sales, so I decided to specialize. My dad's insistence that land ownership was equivalent to wealth convinced me of this truth. He dreamed of land all of his life and passed the dream onto his youngest daughter. In the following year, I decided to specialize in the sale of rural properties, farms, and timberland to satisfy the passion my father and his ancestors had aroused in me for land.

I decided that poverty was a state of mind, determined by thought processes and expectations. In a world of plenty, we only need to choose what we want, visualize its manifestation to receive it. I wanted love, a stable, reliable mate, and freedom from financial needs. My children would never have to suffer the pain of poverty! I lay in bed night after night, feeling frightened and insecure about needing to break up the marriage.

Would I be able to provide for my family? I tried to crowd out doubts, grief, and insecurities with a vision of health, happiness, and prosperity in my mind. One of my friends, a graphologist, once wrote that I was a member of the "talk-to-myself" club. She was right. I knew I had to accept those things I could not change and concentrate on those that I could.

My sister Pat and Mel were perfect examples. They had seldom had financial worries and had experienced the kind of lifestyle they wanted. They believed, as I did, that you only have to decide what you want and the universe will help you produce it. I wanted economic security for my children, a good home, some land, and an opportunity to retire to paint and write someday.

My children loved me and their disappointment in me would change in time. In the meantime, all I could do was to try to support them emotionally until they became more mature, try to bring better balance in my personal needs, love myself, and continue to seek fulfillment. It was a daunting task.

# Chapter 43

February 14th was Bob's birthday. Out of respect for our 25-year marriage, I made a cake for him. We were sitting down to eat it when a customer called, and Bob screamed at me in a tyrannical rage that his dinner was being disrupted. I had to ask the customer if I could return his call and calmly told Bob: "Leave. Leave NOW. Don't come back." At last, I felt that I could not—would not—tolerate any more. It was over, I thought. Unfortunately, it wasn't.

Jan made a remark to him that angered Bob further. He brutally slapped her across the face and I had to intervene to protect her. Clearly, he was totally out of control. I quietly packed his suitcase and threw it out the front door, "Get out. NOW!"

I wanted the marriage to be over, but Bob would not accept it, nor did our financial problems allow it. A few days later, he was back, arguing that he did not earn enough to pay the bills in the family household, in addition to separate expenses if he moved out permanently. There would have to be a compromise. After a great deal of discussion, we reached an agreement that the marriage was over, but we would have to live in the same house until we could get the bills under control. I had forgiven him once for multiple affairs with many different women, but I could not cope with continued financial instability. I'd had enough, yet it was obvious that he was not ready to give up the marriage.

My friends in the Theosophy Society were helpful. One of Judy's old friends was an astrologist, and when I consulted her, she told me that my chart was in a decidedly precarious position, with all kinds of distractions and disruptions. She saw me alone with the children but encouraged me that my mental, emotional, and intellectual assets would see me through the coming hard times.

She said, "God doesn't make any junk," and, "You will not only survive but progress in your life's pursuits." She told me that I was a loving mother devoted to my children, who would be able to guide them if I decided to take a giant step. She was especially concerned for Debbie's difficulties that I told her about, but without a chart to read, she was unable to guide me—or her. She encouraged me to continue to read and study—especially Gnostic literature, and listed some books that might help in my struggle. At this time, I was reading some Unity literature that I found to be helpful. Love will conquer; God answers our needs and is a part of our divine mind, available as necessary. God and I are one, it repeated again and again. It rang true, and I left my friends feeling more hopeful and optimistic despite only half believing in astrology.

My old friend, Judy, was living and working in Chicago, and we continued to correspond regularly. Her brilliance had landed her a writing job as an editor for a local newspaper, where she continued to write books, do feature stories, and engage with local community affairs. Her insight into my problems, similar to some she had experienced in her marriage, was open, honest and incredibly accurate. I will be eternally grateful for my friends who helped guide me through those hard times.

My frustration was taking a toll on my ability to maintain all the household duties, spend enough time with Steve and Jan and pay the mounting bills that Bob ran up. My job gave me almost the only satisfaction I had, filling my intellectual curiosity as well as my social life with students and professors I met at the college. At the same time, it renewed my passionate need to know and desire to learn topics that my work allowed only a slight glimpse. When I had time to think about it, I dreamed of being a part of the student body in order to fill those empty spaces in my mind. My household duties consumed my time and energy while I agonized over my inability to find time to write, paint, and read.

The bills spiraled more and more out of control. I told Bob that I would no longer cope with his money mismanagement, and demanded that he agree to use his three weeks' vacation pay to catch up on bills. He finally agreed, while at the same time, he persistently bombarded the children with the idea of a Canadian vacation in July.

# Chapter 44

"We'll just drive up and back and spend the night at Pat and Ty's. It won't cost much. I've worked so hard and I need it."

"There's no way in hell we're going to Canada or anywhere else," I stated emphatically. "That money must be used to catch up on bills. You agreed," but the children became more and more enthusiastic about the Canadian trip, while I consistently told them, "No way." As July grew closer, I was adamant. I refused to go even after the children begged and pleaded with me.

"Mom, it won't be a vacation without you," they begged. Bob told them, "Get packed. We're going."

The departure day arrived and everyone packed their suitcases into the car, only to return to the house and gang up on me to beg me to go with them. How could I disappoint my children? At the last moment, I reluctantly threw a few things into a suitcase and joined them.

The trip was a disaster from start to finish. We stopped at a children's recreation center en route to Seattle to allow the children to exercise and play, then proceeded to spend the night with Pat and her husband in Seattle. The next day, we left early to drive two days without stopping except for fuel and food until we arrived at the cabin Bob had engaged for the night. It was nine o'clock at night by then and we were all famished and exhausted, but Bob insisted that we go for a boat ride before eating. He could still wrap the children around his finger and they were enthusiastic to do it. The lake was beautiful, surrounded by towering trees, the sound of loons in the distance, and ducks and geese grazing on plankton near the banks. The sun had set with the dying rays painting the water in pinks until it disappeared behind trees into near-total darkness where we could see only the outline of the shore. An hour later, we could see almost no light or features anywhere except water, and then a frigid wind came up that left us all trembling with cold.

Bob ignored our plea to take us back to the cabin until we were all close to hypothermic. We searched for a landmark marking our cabin's location only to learn that all the landmarks looked exactly alike. We were lost in a wild, remote area where we had no idea where we were. With many suggestions from all of us, we eventually found our way back to our cabin almost out of control with cold, hunger, and fatigue. We unloaded our suitcases and coolers and I quickly stirred together some food and then fell into bed in exhaustion.

Early the next day, Bob let the children take a quick ride trip on rented horses before we proceeded to a lake he wanted to see. It was 25 miles on a one-lane, bumpy road surrounded by forests. We traveled only a few miles before Steve and Jan had to stop to vomit. They were burning with fever, unable to keep anything on their stomach at all. I pleaded with Bob to turn around and go back to the main highway, but he refused. The 25-mile trip consumed another four hours of 10 to 15 miles an hour of travel, with frequent stops for vomiting.

When we finally arrived, Debbie and her boyfriend immediately found a boat to tour the lake while I took Jan inside to bathe her with cold mountain water to reduce her fever. She was so hot that the soaked towel I used dried out in minutes. I was sick with worry over her high fever. Steve seemed to be getting slightly better.

After trying to reduce Jan's fever with cold water for another two hours, I demanded that Bob call Debbie and Bill back to the car, so we could find a doctor for what I considered a seriously ill child. Finally, he agreed, and we re-packed and returned to drive the rutted road back to a more civilized area. Unfortunately, none of the Canadian outback could be considered very civilized.

We drove until ten that night before we found a small town with a hospital to take the children. The emergency room doctor treated the children and we left again with all of us begging for a place to sleep and eat. It was another day with little food or water, exhaustion, and trauma because Bob refused to stop for anything except fuel and toilet stops. We finally found a motel several hours later and piled into an exhausted sleep.

Bob had agreed that the vacation would be short and cost little but failed to fulfill that promise. We left for the two-day return trip the next morning, having spent most of the money I wanted to use for bills. I was frustrated with so much anger and despair that I was ready to commit murder or suicide. The trip cured all my caring for my husband and our marriage completely, although I still was uncertain what action to take. I told him that as far as I was concerned the marriage was over, but we could survive financially if he continued to live at home temporarily to save on housing, utility and child care expenses until I could afford to file for divorce. There was no way

I could afford to hire someone to take care of Steve while I worked. He was nearly 11 and would be with Jan when she was at home, but it seemed preferable to have his father with him when I was gone instead of a 15-year-old sister. I felt we had no other choice.

In August 1971, the annual Clerks' Convention was in a nearby city, and both Bob and I were expected to attend. As an interested observer, I attended many of the lectures on the first day but decided to spend the second day doing my own thing. I read in the hotel room for a few hours and then decided to go swimming that afternoon for some exercise and sun and fun at the pool. I took my book with me, alternatively reading, tanning, and then swimming to cool off. There were few people there, but I struck up a conversation with a large, dark young man who was tanning in an adjacent chair. He told me he was a scout for a California baseball team and was there to recruit ballplayers for his team. We casually discussed topics from baseball to politics to religion without exploring any personal information other than our names and why we were there. It was a delightful, but innocent exchange of thoughts and ideas that I believe both of us enjoyed.

After the evening banquet and a few drinks, the delegates decided to go for a midnight swim to cool off after the hard workday. I joined the crowd at the pool to discuss the day's events to find Bob chasing a dark-skinned woman around the deck, or lifting her onto his shoulders in the pool, ducking her, or laughing at full volume. What the hell was going on? Was he drunk? I had met her casually, and knew that she was the local union president in Idaho, but why was he acting like a teenager with her?

The delegates started looking at me as if I had two heads. Some of them avoided my eyes in embarrassment. It immediately reached my consciousness that he was flirting outrageously with her, and I was so embarrassed that I felt like melting through the pool's concrete deck. My loving husband seemed to ignore my presence entirely, with his whole concentration on a relatively unattractive female. My first instinct was to call him from the pool and slap some sense into him, but I couldn't do that with an audience of his peers. I tried to think of some method of easing his method of humiliating me for several moments before I thought of something that might work. I left the pool and found the name of the baseball scout (we'll call him John) I'd met at the pool earlier in the day and found his name in the registry to call him. "Come on down," I requested, "There's a party going on at the pool."

A few minutes later he appeared, wearing his swimsuit. Bob's antics continued except for a brief moment when he got out of the pool long enough to introduce him to my new friend, and then he continued his flirtation with the dark-skinned Indian woman. John was no fool. He became immediately aware that calling him was my effort to create a reaction in my husband, and decided he wanted no part in it. He departed, and because I had enough of being humiliated, I went back to the hotel and to bed.

Strangely, I never confronted Bob about the incident. Life as we knew it resumed until one weekend, he came home saying that his nerves were shot and he couldn't stand the children's activities going on at our house. It was too noisy, he was too tired and too distracted, and he needed the quiet of a typical hotel room he was more used to. He took his unpacked bags to a local motel and left. I tried to call him on several occasions, but his line was busy. On Sunday afternoon, he called to request that I come to help him type his weekly report, and I complied.

I found a telephone bill for over $400 to Idaho when I typed his report for him. He sheepishly admitted that the phone call was to the Indian woman to break up an apparently on-going relationship that I was too blind to see. I never knew how long it had been going on. Although I seldom considered breaking up my marriage until after his first indiscretion and after the Canadian trip, I was aware that his promises could not be taken seriously after this betrayal.

I made an appointment with a psychologist with Catholic Charities, since I couldn't afford any others. When I explained the past history of our marriage, he said, simply, "You've got to get out now!"

Bob would not accept that the marriage was over even after I filed for a divorce. I was granted custody of the children, and $50.00 a month child support for all four children. Our cache of bills was not even mentioned in the divorce papers, but I was forced to pay them because Bob couldn't—or wouldn't.

Debbie adored her father, and when Bob got an apartment, she visited and even occasionally lived with him while she treated me with disrespect bordering on hatred. I was at fault and she could not forgive me for breaking up the family.

Later that year, there was an even greater challenge after I filed for a divorce. Bob called from the airport asking if I would pick him up. He had been fired and they kept his car. His salary ceased and he had no income for the following two years to pay child support. He appeared to still depend on me as his mother figure.

"Get a cab," I told him.

# Chapter 45

One of my needs was for companionship, love, and sex in my life. Now 50 years old, I had no intention of spending the remainder of my life alone. I needed more time for creativity in gardening, painting, and self-expression. Foremost of all, I needed a father for my youngest child, Steve, who seemed totally bewildered at the change in our family.

A local singles dance club began to provide me with the sociability I lacked. Every Saturday night, a group of several hundred singles gathered at the club to mingle and dance the night away and I began to accept dates occasionally with a few of the men I met there. I met more acceptable and interesting men in my work. During the following years, I must have dated dozens of two and three-time divorced "losers" who were looking for future mates that I rejected almost immediately. The dance club provided wonderful exercise and companionship but no acceptable mates. I only wanted a "winner" and a good father for Steve.

When I met a handsome Italian–American real estate broker from the Southern part of the state, I knew he was a winner. He was intelligent and stimulating with a great sense of humor. We had an immediate rapport and started seeing each other regularly. For most of the following year, I drove south to visit him or he came to see me as often as our business allowed. Unfortunately, he finally told me he was burnt out with real estate and had decided to retire early and move back to Texas. Although we corresponded for months later, that was the end of that romance.

During my work-week, I searched for large parcels of land and farms, pouring over multiple listings, advertisements, and signs. Timber was in great demand and some of the farms and large parcels in outlying areas had stands of timber. I spent many days driving through the countryside to inspect listings. My love for exploring the scenic beautify of Oregon filled me with joy. I loved my work.

One day as I glanced through new listings, I noticed an ad for a 309-acre farm for $309,000 about 20 miles from town and immediately called one of my customers to see if he wanted to look at it. He did, and we had hiked only through the edge of a grove of large Douglas fir trees before he turned to me, saying, "Let's go. I'll drive, and you write!" He was shaking with excitement at our find. He dictated his offer as he drove back to town.

When I presented the offer to the sellers the next day, I noticed that they offered to pay a 12% fee. The owner was dying and wanted his estate settled before his death. I couldn't even imagine a $36,000 commission, although my broker would get half and the listings broker another half. It still left me with a $12,000 commission if they accepted the offer. I sweated blood while the family considered the offer, but they finally did. I was ecstatic. Even in my dreams, I never imagined that kind of money for one sale.

When I received the commission check, I cashed it, depositing all but $1,000 in $100 bills in my bank account. At home, I called Jan and Steve together and threw the $100 bills into the air to celebrate. Their eyes were as big as saucers, and I could not believe our good luck.

I used some of the money to buy an inexpensive car for Debbie, who was attending classes at the local college, a motorbike for Steve, and filled Jan's wants and needs. Bobby had a good job and needed nothing, although I offered help if he needed it.

The multiple listing services sent out a special bulletin to inform agents of the largest real estate commissions anyone had ever received at the time. My broker wrote a cynical poem about my big dreams and unexpected triumph.

The purchaser and I had a good relationship for years to come, resulting in dozens of sales and purchases. He bought and sold hundreds of acres of land in the following years, with me as his agent. When he decided to sell 160 acres of logged-over timberland he owned, I bought it in partnership with another customer, Wanda, whom I met when I ran an ad to sell it.

Wanda was a big, rawboned Chicagoan who appeared in my office one day after I returned from viewing another large parcel of land, soaked to the bone from touring the property through mud and rain. "Where the hell have you been?" she demanded. "I've have been trying to contact you for days to see this land." I apologized over my busy schedule and invited her to stay at my home while she looked for a property. It was to be the beginning of the closest friendship I had except my old friendship with Judy and it continued until their deaths.

I found Wanda to be a kindred soul. Like me, she had been reared on a rural farm and experienced the agony of picking cotton and the same poverty and deprivation I had during the depression. Although she was married, now very wealthy, and had a degree in microbiology, she wanted the security that land ownership offered in the event of a major economic catastrophe in the US. When we inspected the 160-acre logged over timberland, she wanted to buy it, asking if I wanted to be a partner to manage it when she returned to Chicago. I used part of my commission to pay one-fourth of the purchase price, with Wanda contributing the balance in cash.

We planned to re-plant the land with new Douglas fir seedlings which would generate another crop of merchantable timber in 35-50 years. I estimated the timber value by the time we were 75 years old to be at least half a million dollars, which would secure our retirement income no matter what happened to the economy. Both of us felt that the Capitalist system would fall sooner or later due to the overspending of the military-industrial complex and to the greed of the top 1-2% richest citizens who controlled America. We wanted a place to ensure survival for our children in that eventuality.

I showed land during the week and spent weekends with the children except for the usual Saturday night dances I continued to attend. One Friday after work, I received a call from a realtor in another office who, like me, specialized in farm and timberland sales. They wanted me to sell some of their listings. Their staff was gathered in the office with a bottle of scotch to celebrate after a long week at work. "Come join us," the broker commanded, "You work too hard."

The real estate broker was attractive to me because he was a dedicated fisherman, although somewhat laid-back and casual, and I loved to go fishing. One of the sales associates with him was a younger man who was grieving because his wife had left him, and the second was a tall, balding new real estate licensee, Curt, who had recently joined the firm after a long career as an army Colonel. He poured a drink for me and the group started telling jokes for a while. Curt told me about a new listing he wanted me to sell. They poured another drink before I had finished the first one. Suddenly, I realized that Curt was hovering and flirting outrageously with me.

I wondered, *what the hell does this old guy want?* He towered over me by at least a foot and was not especially attractive, although he had a commanding presence that demanded attention. I was curious about him. In the next hour, he talked about his career as the head of the ROTC program at the University of Oregon which had been forced out by hordes of student protesters who took over the President's office to rid the campus of a military presence. They insisted I have another drink. Curt asked me to help him find a new country residence for one of his clients since they had no access to the Multiple Listing Service as I did. I agreed to look for a suitable property and left for home.

# Chapter 46

Perhaps my need for male companionship led me to show Curt potential properties that might satisfy his customer, or perhaps it was more to do with enhancing my ego by showing my knowledge of rural properties that could propel a new agent toward success. In any event, we drove through the countryside to view numerous for-sale properties for several days, talking about our lives as we drove. He told me about his army career, his terminally ill wife who had severe kidney disease, and as her caregiver his duty to operate her kidney dialysis machine every other day. I shared my thoughts and ideas about my specialty in timberland sales, some of my past marital problems, and some of my current difficulties with my children. I found him to be stimulating, interesting, and highly intelligent.

We continued to tour properties together, and later with his home-seeking client, who rejected all of them. I thought they were unreasonable, but we had spent so much time with them that both of us were determined to make the sale. When his customer finally bought a very expensive place, it was entirely different than their description of the kind of property they had asked for. Some buyers just didn't know what they wanted.

A day later, Curt called me at home. "How about some bread and wine and thou? We deserve some R & R," he joked. "I've prepared a picnic lunch and we're going to enjoy it on the bank of the prettiest creek I know. Will you go with me to celebrate my first big sale?"

Although we were still virtual strangers, the idea appealed to me. Although I considered him too old for me and married, what harm could it do? He was interesting but I had no romantic notions what so ever. He drove to a sun-dappled spot on a lovely creek, produced a bottle of wine, a loaf of bread, and some grapes. How intriguing! After sipping the wine and bread, I challenged him to a swim in the cold creek, and he removed his pants and jumped into the shallow water in his underwear. I thought it was hilarious to see his long, wet legs beneath his dripping boxers as he climbed out of the pool to dry himself on the blanket spread in the sun.

For years afterward, I never understood my motive when I joined him on the blanket. The next thing, strangely, I found myself sheltered in his arms with our lips locked together, followed by the natural consequence. Was I that love-starved? *What the hell was the matter with me*, I wondered. A romantic liaison with a married man was simply foreign to my beliefs or values that I would never compromise. Yet, something more powerful propelled me that I only understood after the romance blossomed and both of us fell hopelessly, incurably in love.

"We are just lonely," I told myself. Perhaps his grief over his wife's condition led him to seek comfort. Whatever it was, I had no intention of pursuing the relationship further. He refused to accept it.

When he continued to call, I told him I wouldn't see him anymore. I was guilt-ridden for our cheating on his ill wife. My refusal to see him continued for weeks before I finally relented when we reached an agreement that our relationship would not interfere with caring for his wife, and that she would always come first. He told me that love doesn't divide—it multiplies, and our love allowed him greater compassion for his sick wife. He said, "I'm not giving you anything I have to give to her. She is my patient now. My wife is gone." The statement did not reduce my guilt feelings, but I felt hopeless to change our compelling love.

After that, we began seeing each other on a regular basis. The only time we were separated was when he took his wife to a club party where she fell asleep in her plate, or when he gave her dialysis. His effect on me was beyond fascination due to his almost psychic, perceptive acceptance of me as a person, his brilliant mind, his empathy, and his egalitarian attitude. No man I ever knew treated women as equals—they always had a superior air and demanded subservience. He continually assured me of his love, respect, and appreciation. It was novel to me that Curt had no concept of male-female roles. He made meals if I was busy bringing in wood or repairing something around the house. Whatever needed to be done was done by the one who was not occupied in some other way.

I returned from work one day to find that my nearly 16-year-old daughter, Jan, was gone. Steve told me she had left with some friends, saying that she would not be back. I panicked and started making calls to search for her. No one knew, but my detective instincts were alive and well and soon learned about a "hippy" commune in a nearby town that someone had mentioned. Within a few hours, I deducted that maybe they had all gone there. A phone call to the local police in the town confirmed that a group of children was living in an old house on the outskirts of town, smoking pot and drinking beer. They had problems at the location for some time. When I asked him to check it out, he agreed to go look for my daughter and hold her until I could pick her up. The next day, Curt went with me to pick up my angry, insolent, unrepentant daughter at the police station, cursing at me in a blue streak of profanity. She hovered in the back seat with arms folded across her chest in defiance and refused to discuss her absence except to say that she was looking for a better home.

I felt that the world had carved in on top of me when I thought of losing another beloved child to the drug culture. Of all my children, the closeness and open dialogue I thought Jan and I had could never have prepared me for this possibility of losing her devotion. It never reached my consciousness that I had followed in my parents' footsteps by failing to demonstrate enough love and affection for her during her emotional teenage years. I considered her my most well-balanced, bright, and capable child. Like her sister, she blamed me for the breakup of our family. While Jan admired and respected Curt, she was not ready to accept him as a father. She was unable to articulate my failure to provide the support and affection she needed then, but it cropped up repeatedly in the future. It was not long before she bailed and moved out. I grieved, but my work demands and my absorption with Curt prevented me from fully understanding her distress.

A few months later, Curt began occasionally spending the night with me when possible and entering into family discussions and activities. Steve adored him, and when Debbie or Bob dropped by after school or work, they accepted the situation fully, although none of us discussed the future.

Curt's wife had lived over two years past her doctor's expectancy and gradually deteriorated to a shell of the vibrant wife she had been. She had frequent hospitalizations, and occasionally the shunt that fed her blood supply fell out and she almost bled to death before Curt awoke to discover the accident. After that, he stayed at her side all night to ensure that would not happen again. Sometimes, he had to drive to a military base in Seattle to buy supplies for her and asked me to accompany him to pick them up.

Christmas came. It was hard with Curt being with his own family while my family was forlorn without him, but he showed up in the afternoon with a load of gifts for everyone. I grieved over my illicit, though powerful love affair that separated not just one family, but two on the major celebration of the year.

Curt was getting a feel for the real estate business. He and his broker were the only other agents in town who specialized in the sale of farms, ranches, and timberland, so we had common goals. When his broker listed a 680 track of land they were considering buying, they asked for my opinion. They were working with a logger, who would log the trees and sell them, and later replant and sell the land. "Go for it!" I advised. Curt, the broker, and the logger purchased the property and began the logging.

# Chapter 47

A few months later, they made a similar arrangement on a parcel of land and timber between town and the coast and Curt often traveled from the one they recently bought to the coastal property to oversee the logging. Other than brief trips away that I had to make, Curt and I met in the early morning, set a time to meet for lunch, or traveled together in our work.

Curt spent the night with me and my family one night almost two years into our relationship. We were constantly together except when he had to be at home to operate the dialysis machine. He was restless throughout the entire night, waking time after time to tell me that no one could love anyone as much as he loved me. Repeatedly, he reached for me during the night to almost desperately hold and cling to me. Previously, he had explained a new insurance policy the army had for dependents and wanted to buy the policy with me as the beneficiary, but I had refused. "Not as long as you have a wife and children," I told him. I wondered if my refusal had something to do with his restless sleep, but the clinging continued throughout the night. Later, it occurred to me that he somehow knew what was to come.

The next morning, he made breakfast for me before I left for a 60-mile trip to see a client and kissed me goodbye. Usually, we met for lunch, but nothing was said that day. It was after one o'clock when I returned to find no calls from him, and I wondered where he was. Tired from my trip, I decided to rest before my next appointment at 4:00 pm at my office, but soon awakened and left early to go to my office. Fortunately, my buyer came early also. I had just completed the paperwork on his offer to purchase some property when the phone rang.

It was Curt's attorney. He told me that Curt had been killed in an automobile crash when two drunken, drug-crazed men who were playing leapfrog on the two-lane, winding coastal road had hit his car after he had pulled to the side of the road to avoid them. He had been killed instantly. My grief overwhelmed me. I was blind with rage, anger, and incomprehension. After uncontrollable sobbing, the secretary drove me home and spent hours with me while I poured out my grief and pain.

The pain of "the other woman" and being unable to attend his funeral services humiliated and distressed me. I went in to view the body after everyone had left, struggling for enough control to keep from screaming. That wonderful, kind, gentle face that I loved so deeply, appeared peacefully content, and I felt some comfort in that. They shipped his body to his home state, which prevented me from even visiting his grave. I would have to grieve alone except for the consolation of my two sisters and my children. It would take time, but I lived through my divorce, children's problems and starting anew at nearly 50 years of age. I had to endure. "It was better to have loved and lost than never to have loved," I told myself.

# Chapter 48

Mom and Dad's situation kept my sisters and me sick with worry. Mom was getting too feeble to care for a quadriplegic while insisting that she could still do it. Her most difficult chore was assisting him to the bathroom, where he insisted on repeated enemas. Sometimes, they spent almost all morning there. Nothing could convince Dad that he had completely emptied his bowels. We developed a theory that he was getting sexual satisfaction from this exercise. When nothing else worked, he insisted on getting over-the-counter medications like Ex-Lax to relieve his "obstruction." It was a fetish that continued as long as he lived.

Finally, we received word from friends that Mom had fallen and broke her hip while trying to change his pants to help him into bed. For a while, friends came in to help until we found a wonderful lady who would come in on a daily basis. While Mom insisted they could afford to hire her regularly, the children chipped in to pay her, over her objections.

But in 1980, when I went back to the South with a friend to see the World Fair in Knoxville, I stopped in their little town of Potts Camp to check on them. Although I planned on only a few days there, Mom started having severe pain in her abdomen and I took her to visit her doctor. The doctor shrugged, saying that the pain was caused by her repeated use of aspirin products to relieve her pain from arthritis. But the next day, the pain was unbearable, so I took her to the hospital. She almost immediately began to vomit blood in copious quantities. Doctors told me that she "wouldn't make it" and advised me to let her go, at the same time trying to staunch the blood to save her life. The following day, they called an ambulance to take her to the larger hospital in Memphis.

We moved Dad into the small local hospital in Holly Springs, kicking and screaming all the way. He wanted someone to stay at home to take care of him. I finally was angry enough to give him a piece of my mind about his selfishness, knowing full well that he was so used to getting everything he wanted that he wouldn't listen. I went to Memphis with Mom, where Doctors operated immediately to stop the bleeding, with no hopes or indication that it would save her life. Everyone thought the surgery was contraindicated, and that she would die anyway.

Pat happened to be on leave, and flew south to relieve me after a few days of helpless waiting for the outcome of the surgery, and sat by her side for days while she was in intensive care. But gradually, she started recovering and several weeks later, she was released to go home.

What to do? Mom was 80 and Dad was 88. She was so crippled with arthritis that she could barely control her pain. For many years we had urged them to move to the northwest, where we could help take care of them, but Dad would have nothing to do with it. They had made two or three short trips here, including one six months residence that Pat arranged for them to live near her home, but Dad's constant complaints finally won and they returned to their little mobile home in Potts Camp. This was no longer possible, and Pat told them they had no more options: they would have to move to a local nursing home or move to the northwest to be near their children. Dad's prejudice against black aids and nurses in Southern nursing homes led him to choose the northwest. He didn't want "no niggers" to take care of him. Nothing we could say about his prejudice against blacks changed his mind although, in time, he was less vocal about it. With no other options, they chose to come west. I agreed to take care of them in my home. When they arrived, I found a nice nursing home where they were admitted until I could arrange to find nursing aids for 24-hour care. Dad complained bitterly, while Mom accepted whatever fate awaited them.

Now, in addition to operating a real estate business, I was in charge of three nursing care shifts to care for them. They complained about the food, which "wasn't cooked enough." I planned and cooked most of the meals in the Southern style and taste, but it was never really good enough to please them, although Dad managed to eat it with a hearty appetite. I took them for doctor's visits, including checking Dad's progressive sight loss, but nothing could be done. He had macular degeneration and his sight was only slightly less than total blindness.

When I took Mom to see a doctor about the little lump in her breast, she was diagnosed with breast cancer. They considered her free of cancer after they excised the lump.

Mom was ecstatic about the huge cabbages I grew in the garden and amazed at the beautiful flowers in the yard. She teetered around the yard, pointing at the luscious profusion of color in amazement and joy. On special occasions, she made her wonderful yeast rolls for family gatherings, rejoicing at the chance to be busy cooking again. I am grateful for these small efforts to give her joy after the difficult times she had in her life.

In time I had to nearly completely give up my business to devote most of my time to try to make them happy. But Dad was not happy. He wanted to go "home" and would never accept any place other than Mississippi as home. He repeatedly tried to convince Mom to take him home. Even black nursing aids were better than the three devoted, caring ones I hired. He nagged the aids I hired, and he erupted in anger at me for every kind of offense he could think of. They gave me their tiny bank account to manage, but before long, I was stealing Dad's money. He was never happy with his bowel problems and constantly demanded that Mom get him a powerful drug to take to relieve his constipation even after he had numerous bowel movements a day. Finally, Mom did give him Ex-Lax, which caused him to lose complete control. Bed sheets, cushions, mattresses, his clothes—everything he had touched—was flooded, until I was completely out of patience and refused to take it anymore.

I arranged for another nursing home for them, where Dad was no less dissatisfied, so I moved them again. After the third one, I refused to move them again.

Debbie had married and started a family in an adjacent town where I had enrolled my parents in a fine assisted-living facility where she visited her grandparents nearly every day, which relieved me of some of my duties.

Dad's 100th birthday arrived and Debbie arranged a huge family reunion to be held at her home. All my sisters, brothers, and their children attended. We arranged for all their old friends back home to call and wish him a happy birthday. Over 50 attended. It was a wonderful occasion that Dad appreciated, and he glowed all day from the good food and attention.

# Chapter 49

One day, I found a listing for a 107-acre parcel that was new on the market. It consisted of around 70 to 80 acres of old-growth forest on a mountain top with a year-round salmon-filled river at the base. There was a lovely little furnished residence framed in the forest, with a little spring-fed pond filled with flowering water lilies. The owner had bought it years before to escape his Southern California home, but subsequently started a business on the Oregon Coast and became too busy to use it, so he wanted to sell. The first time I saw it, I thought I had died and gone to heaven. It was the most beautiful property I had ever seen, and I dreamed of owning it. But my obligation was to my best client and I offered it to him. He made repeated offers to buy it over the next few months, but the seller rejected them all. He wanted all cash.

"That property had my name written all over it," I told one of my customers who wanted to buy it, and, "If you can't write an acceptable offer, I will—sooner or later." Obviously, I could not afford his demand for cash-on-sale so it was a wild dream for me to think I could have it.

I met other buyers who anticipated the need for large parcels of land suitable for growing timber in Oregon and were acquiring land as fast as they could find it. One was a division of a large corporation, so I contacted them to see if they were interested. Yes, they were, but they did not want houses or pastureland unsuitable for timber growth. I informed them of my interest in the house on the lower portion of the land and 11 acres of river frontage.

Their agent made a verbal offer on the timberland portion for the full asking price if I would write an offer to buy the entire parcel and transfer the timberland portion to them at closing in exchange for their cash. Their offer for the timberland was enough to pay for the entire 107 acres. Frightened out of my mind at my audacity at offering to purchase the property for cash I didn't have, I wrote the offer. The timberland that the Company wanted would go directly to them, and the houses and small acreage would go to me, free and clear after closing.

When it was accepted, my jubilation was almost uncontrollable. Sudden-ly, I was the owner of my dream property that my customer had paid for. It seemed too good to be true, but the seller received what he asked for, the timber company had what they wanted, and I received the house with six acres—11 acres of river frontage and a two and a half-acre parcel that could be sold separately under existing land use regulations. At closing, I received a commission of $500 for selling the land to myself and deeding a portion of it to the timber company. It was a formula that I followed in the years to come.

Shortly afterward, I acquired a farm in a nearby town with two houses and 17 acres, and a parcel with 11 acres and two houses in another area, plus a 50-acre farm with two dwellings on it by using the same formula. In addi-tion to my acquisitions, I received commissions on every sale. Now, I owned over 100 acres of land, plus ten houses in addition to my one-fourth interest in the 160-acre tree farm Wanda and I owned. Poverty was behind me.

In addition to my purchases, I located large rural parcels all over the state to sell. I listed 300 acres of beachfront property, 8,000 acres in Central Ore-gon that I did not sell, and a gold mine in the foothills of the Cascades that I sold with the aid of 3D aerial photos from the seat of a Piper Cub flown by the timber companies' acquisition manager.

Until I learned that aerial photos could be used to find all the corners of large parcels, I usually walked the entire parcel to locate the corners and es-timate the timber value. I was 50 years of age now and in good health, but when I walked the entire 680 acres of one parcel, climbed over downed trees, waded through creeks and struggled up steep mountains for hours at a time, I felt as if I was a 100 years old with my body wracked with pain and over-flowing monthly periods and menstrual pain. I made a doctor's appointment, who told me I needed a D&C immediately, and possibly a hysterectomy. When the D&C did not correct the problem, the hysterectomy was scheduled a few weeks later.

After the hysterectomy, I developed an infection that left me reeling for almost a year. Jan came home one day to find me lying on the couch in pain. I asked her if she would make some food for me, and she walked out, slam-ming the door behind her. Joy went out of my life.

The combination of health problems, grief over Curt's loss and distress over the loss of Debbie and Jan, threw me into a tailspin of depression and anxiety. Steve and I consoled and supported each other. We told each other that it was us against the world. He seemed to assume responsibility by en-couraging me and taking on some of the household chores. I worried when he said that he was the man of the family now—a too heavy responsibility for a 13-year-old, but one he had chosen. Instead of surrounding himself with his young friends and joining them to play, he often hovered around the house for long talks with me, sometimes about his lack of confidence, possibly caused by dyslexia he'd had at a younger age that still plagued him. He hated to read and had to work harder than his older sisters to keep up with his school homework. His grief over Curt's loss hit him like a ton of bricks. His father had never shown much attention to Steve, and he seemed to feel that Curt was the only father he ever had.

Steve's personality attracted everyone, but he was unsure of himself and chose only a few close neighborhood friends, where they rode bikes, played basketball and football at the nearby park, played his drum set or went fishing on the nearby river. Steve was a delight to me, but in my harried, hectic life, I was not aware of my failure to give him all the love and support he needed. Curt had filled a deep hunger in his life that I couldn't as a single mother.

In my relationship with Curt, I had learned for the first time the definition of a near-perfect mate: a loyal, devoted, fulfilling man who was a good companion, equal partner, and loving father with shared aspirations and goals. I had received that gift and I wanted to find that joy again more than anything in the world—especially a good father for Steve, who now seemed lost without him.

# Chapter 50

My memories of Curt and our happiness were with me for subsequent months as I continued my work. He seemed to direct me in my property searches, and assist in managing the properties I acquired. I owned ten houses and many acres of land scattered all over the county. They all needed my attention. Vacancies had to be filled; houses repaired and maintained, and taxes and insurance to be paid, loans to acquire. Tenants would move out and leave destruction or messes to be cleaned up, trees to plant—on top of showing large parcels of land all over the state. I had more buyers than I could handle. In the following year, I started looking for help. I could sell all the large parcels of rural property I could find, especially if it was suitable for forestry but the problem was finding them. I began questioning other agents in my office to see if they were interested in a partnership, where they would locate listings and I would sell them. My health had not fully recovered, and walking large parcels of land became too physically difficult for me. A couple of the agents were interested but didn't work out.

Cal, an agent in the office, told me he wanted to work with me. He was the divorced father of a mortgage broker I worked with. When I was hospitalized for the hysterectomy, he visited me and offered to assist me any way he could. Later, we agreed to a partnership where he would find properties and share the commissions when I sold them. He had watched me making one sale after another, and was enthusiastic about joining me. Instead, he found his own buyer and started to emulate my techniques. A year later, he had written dozens of offers for his buyers to purchase land, only to have the sales fall through. None of his sales were closed the entire year. His commissions were zilch that year.

He was also working on a project that he was certain would bring him fame and fortune. He and a partner were writing a computer program that would provide analyses of real estate investments. He borrowed $30,000 on the small shopping center he owned to raise money for the project, dreaming of the millions to come. Anyone could use the system, he and his partner stated, and it would turn the real estate business into a product for every novice investor. I studied it, but couldn't understand it. It was over my head as a professional. How could a novice understand it? I wished them luck and good fortune.

But soon, Cal and I started seeing each other on a social basis. He attracted me because I viewed him as a good father to his three girls—fine, well-adjusted people, I thought. Further, he loved fishing and the great outdoors, and we spent hours discussing future fishing trips we would take together. His 15-year-old son was capable, handsome, and charming. His father had taught that child a few things about carpentry and how to work. Cal was a former contractor and I admired that.

The romantic relationship began when he asked me to climb Spencer Butte, a nearby 2,000-foothill and park nearby, and I accepted the challenge. After that, we went out to dinner or a movie with Steve and his son Greg occasionally. Once, when we attended a realtor's convention, we danced together many times, discussing real estate and the computer program between dances.

One night, our broker invited us to join him and his wife for a few drinks at their house and began pouring us black Russians, which I had never had before. Before the evening ended, we found ourselves in bed together. I was not a drinker and was totally unaware of the effect of that drink. I was drunker than a skunk, as the saying goes.

After that, the romance blossomed in spite of Cal's apparent helplessness to communicate openly. He seemed secretive and guarded, afraid to expose his innermost thoughts and feelings. I thought—due to his children—that he had been a wonderful father, and I needed a father for Steve, one who would spend time to teach him, encourage him, and help give him greater confidence and self-worth. I was also searching for someone to help me care for my properties and to assist me in my real estate career. There was no possible way I could do it all alone.

As the weeks passed, each week we worked together he stopped by a flower shop to buy me a single rose to celebrate that week's anniversary.

After I received my broker's license, I opened my own office. My work had become less time consuming and more and more profitable. I was able to work a few days a month and earn a great deal of money. Once, I showed five properties in one day. One was almost 1,000 acres, with a commission of $18,000. In that one day, I earned over $50,000. I had the world on a string on a down-hill pull and thought I was invincible. Poverty and uncertainty were behind me, but my physical health declined and my emotional needs increased with the growing demands of rental management, children's problems and the developing recession of the early '80s.

Several months later at dinner one evening, we discussed a partnership again. In spite of my uncertainties over his failure to perform as a partner the prior year, I was desperate, full of unmet needs and loneliness. He eagerly agreed that a partnership would benefit both of us.

Later, when he asked me and Steve to move into a big house he owned behind the shopping center so his son could stay in his same school, no consideration was given to my son's changing schools, but I decided to move anyway. He and his son came first. Anticipating a loving, mutually beneficial relationship and love that I had found with Curt, I found a renter for my house and moved into his larger, older home, and in September, Steve enrolled in the new school as a junior.

My former broker told me I had gone crazy, but I ignored his warning. Others warned me that Cal could not be depended on to follow through as I had seen. One fellow broker told me he was a crook. I disregarded all the advice anyone gave me.

Cal's business partnership unraveled after they found that no one was interested in a computer program to guide investors. Most of us already knew how to do that. They never made a sale, and the partnership was dissolved with the loss of all $30,000 they had invested in it.

Cal seemed obsessed about the $30,000 debt on the little shopping center he owned—well over a third of its value. Although he never discussed it with me, I overheard quiet phone calls to others when he tried to raise money to pay off debt on the only asset he owned.

He wanted to go to Hawaii, so we spent a week there with our sons. Later, he wanted to go to Disneyland, so we went there, stopping along the way at wine tasting rooms, motels, and tourist attractions, all on my money. He didn't have any.

Cal suggested that I buy his little shopping center on a contract-of-sale with a $10,000 down payment because it would save me thousands of dollars in income taxes with all the write-offs. My $10,000 down payment would serve as an income tax credits for me as well as reduce his loan. We're in this together, aren't we?

"It will save you thousands of dollars in taxes," he said. The agreement stipulated that I would pay a monthly payment to satisfy the IRS's requirement for legitimate sale. I was well aware that I was sticking my neck out a mile, but his lawyers drew up some papers and I signed them. We were living together, which meant the commitment to share, didn't it?

We changed the address of my business to the new address and bought new desks and equipment, and went back to work with Cal as the Sales Associate and me as the agency broker. Apparently, the fact that I was the executive in the firm threatened his male ego, and he started studying to get his license. No problem, I thought.

# Chapter 51

After I made a statement that I believed in sharing everything with a mate and partner, Cal asked me to marry him. I hated living alone; so, we flew to Reno and were married in December, to the astonishment of all my friends, children and sisters. I was filled with my own doubts. But the commitment was made, and I was determined to make it work. I knew people are unlikely to change after marriage, but I believed he would lose his guarded, secret nature after he learned to trust me. My love and sharing and would cause him to change. My sisters were aghast that I so unexpectedly married without talking to anyone. I set myself up for events that were to come.

While he studied for his license, I poured over real estate ads, called potential sellers, and other brokers to locate property to sell. One day, I noticed an ad for a large farm in an adjacent town. Knowing the area, I felt sure there was timber on the property. I made the appointment and then asked Cal if he wanted to inspect it with me. There was a big, old farmhouse dating from the 1930s, a tenant's house, and about 17 acres of flat pasture land covered with ten-foot-high scotch broom so thick that it was nearly impossible to get through it. Behind that was a hillside covered with 30 to 50-year-old Douglas fir timber. It perfectly matched the kind of land my timberland clients wanted. I called my client, showed the property, and he made an agreement to purchase it. They would pay cash for the timbered portion, and we would receive the pasture land and houses. When the transaction closed, I told the escrow officer to write the deed to both of us. I had to honor my agreement to share, didn't I?

A few weeks later, Cal was re-building an old boat we found in the back yard on the place we'd bought, while I searched for other property to buy or sell. He seemed to be more interested in studying for his license, cleaning out the garage, or re-building a rotten old boat than selling real estate.

The next property I found was even more attractive than the previous one, so I made an appointment to see it and asked Cal to accompany me. It was perfect. There were around 250 acres for my timberland client, leaving

50 acres of pasture, a lovely little stream, and a huge, old—but very sturdy—farmhouse covered with blackberries. An old commune, the land around the house was littered with old cars, truck beds, motorcycles, blackberries, old bottles, and dilapidated tools and equipment sheds of little value. But my obsession to own land—any kind of land—was not resolved. I had to have the place. We bought it, while simultaneously deeding the timberland to the buyer in return for the cash they provided, leaving a mortgage of $80,000 for the balance that we would pay. Again, the deed was written to us as husband and wife.

Another property came up, which I asked Cal to inspect and show. It was the only property that he showed and sold during our marriage.

When it came time to file my income taxes in February two months after we were married, Cal approached me: "I saved you over $20,000 in income taxes by selling the shopping center to you. I think you should give me half of the money you saved."

I stared at him in incomprehension. Every month, I paid a monthly payment on the shopping center which he deposited in his individual account, while all our rental receipts and commissions were deposited into a joint account. What kind of logic was this? I was too baffled to even reply.

His thinking was, "What is mine is mine and what's yours is mine too." I knew then, that there was no way to reconcile that kind of thinking. I was sharing my business, my creative approach to making sales, my buyers and every dollar I owned, but he wanted more. Still, I could not accept that my marriage would end after two months. I did not know how to extradite myself from the disaster I had created. If I loved him enough, I reasoned, he would soon see another point of view. I was living in an illusory world. I had the companionship I needed, a father for Steve and a new son in Greg, and decided to ignore my husband's lack of logic. My attempts to reason with him were met with silence, rejection, and failure to communicate for weeks. He pouted and left the house to clean the garage, rake the leaves, or find little projects to do while I worked at making the old house a cozy, attractive home.

When his second and third $10,000 payment came due on his loan, he wrote a check from our joint account to pay it. While the shopping center was in my possession, the lien needed to be paid, I reasoned. But he continued to keep the monthly payments I made to him.

I tried to reason with him for months. We were two people who had thrown our lives together for mutual benefit and shared obligations. We would file income taxes as husband and wife next year. It made no sense for me to pay monthly payments to him for the shopping center now that all our income came from joint resources. "Why don't we change the deed on the shopping center to 'tenants by the entirety' (as husband and wife), since we're sharing everything else?

"Why should I make monthly payments to you while you are receiving an equal share of the income from my rentals and from the shopping center?" I argued. Eventually, he agreed, and I signed a document that relinquished my ownership in the shopping center and wrote a new deed showing ownership of the property in our married name. He took the documents and left for the courthouse to record them. I was satisfied that the conflict was over.

Cal was cold and distant for weeks afterward. Nothing seemed to engage his interest or attention except maintenance projects at the shopping center. He seemed to lose interest in finding or selling real estate.

During the same period, when we went to inspect our new acquisition—the old farmhouse we bought—Cal said, "You know, this old place can be remodeled." I looked at the ancient old cabinets, the big hole burned in the living room floor, un-level floors, and rotting window sills with broken panes of glass, and I wondered how it could be salvaged. It had a charming old claw foot tub, an attractive built-in china cabinet, and wonderful light from its many windows, plus a three-car garage to its credit. There was a dormitory-style second floor that could be divided into separate bedrooms. Suddenly, I saw the possibilities he saw and became enthusiastic about the big project.

"Yes, it would be lovely with new carpets, windows, a cozy wood stove, and separate bedrooms upstairs, remodeled with wallpaper in the '30's motif."

So, we began the project. As a former contractor, Cal had seen the possibilities I hadn't. Maybe a shared project could bring us back together in a common cause. For the next three months, we devoted our energy to remodeling the old house. He did the construction and installed new kitchen cabinets while I hung wallpaper, painted, disposed of old materials, and bought supplies. We hired plumbers and electricians to modernize the old '30s house. We chose a new, but antique looking, pull chain toilet with a hanging water closet to go with the old claw foot tub. When flushed, it had a loud sucking sound and was charming. I laughingly called it my goodbye Charley toilet.

We finished the project about three months later except for curtains and drapes. I hired a drapery expect to help me choose beautiful off-white cotton satin drapes over sheer white curtains that would let light in, and it was beautiful.

Cal's ego problem surfaced again and again. He seemed threatened and insecure when I insisted on retaining my own name for business reasons. The familiarity of my name and history in the real estate industry attracted cooperation from other brokerage firms. He acted insulted when one of them called and asked for me instead of him. He was the macho co-broker now since he had passed the broker's test.

An incident when we attended a statewide *Trader's Group of Realtors* illustrated his inferiority complex. The organizers of the group walked up to me and asked if I would give a talk about selling farms, ranches, and timberland to the group. As I started to agree, Cal entered the conversation. "I'll be glad to do that," he said. He had only a few months of experience in what I had been doing for years. The other brokers rolled their eyes and moved on. When someone in the group called him Mr. Smith, I thought he was going to have a heart attack; he was thoroughly deflated. When we drove home from the meeting he was seething in dejection.

Cal suggested that we move from the big old house behind the shopping center into the newly remodeled house in Veneta. I had always wanted to live in the country, and I hoped the move would reunite us as a couple. After Cal received his broker's license, I wrote a press release for the local paper that Timberland Realty now had husband and wife co-brokers in our new rural location. He read and approved the letter and left to take it to the newspaper office. The write-up never appeared in the paper. I didn't understand why until months later.

# Chapter 52

A few months after we moved to the Veneta farm, I felt I had time to visit Mom and Dad in Mississippi, who I had neglected too long, and booked the trip for Steve and me in hopes our absence would resolve whatever was bothering my new husband. Mom's health was failing from her constant struggle to care for my quadriplegic father and I hoped to find a way to help. Mom's thin frame was twisted and crooked from rheumatoid arthritis, and her "widow's hump" was more pronounced, but her condition did not keep dad from making constant demands. She struggled with helping him get up and down, taking him to the bathroom several times a day, cooking, cleaning and feeding him.

Dad was incontinent and believed that good health required his bowels to be emptied several times a day. His doctor prescribed stool softeners and fruit juices but dad wanted enemas several times a day. This required Mom to lift him repeatedly to help him to the bathroom. It was never enough no matter how many times she took him. He had no concept of the burden he placed on my mother. I thought he had become the most selfish man on earth. He sat in his wheelchair hour after hour, demanding an audience to listen to his endless stories. My plea for them to enter a nursing home or move to the northwest fell on deaf ears—even for Mom.

She could never have lifted him without the crutches he used to help her lift him. At 80 years of age, he was in better health than she was, despite his quadriplegia. She sometimes kidded him, "You'll live to a 100, and then have to be shot!" I could not visualize the same fate for my poor mother. She had an almost impossible job of taking care of him, so I started looking for alternatives. He had resorted to a self-centered, selfish old man, determined to have his way. The only thing I could do was find a local woman to come in to help on a regular basis, while they rejected all other proposals I made. I had to return to Steve and my new husband, sick with worry for them—especially my exhausted, sick mother, who did not know how to relinquish what she saw as her duty.

When we returned home to the farm, I was unloading my suitcases and began putting things away when Cal walked into the room.

"You'd better not have found it," he said irritably. The remark was a wake-up call to discover what I was supposed to "not find."

"I don't know what you're talking about," I answered. I was totally mystified and shocked. What was going on here? He was short and uncommunicative as if he was trying to punish me. I knew something was terribly wrong, but until then, I was naive and unsuspicious that he was capable of theft and deceit.

The following day, I visited my favorite Title Company Officer and asked him to check for the recorded deed to the shopping center. He found the quitclaim deed I had signed, but there was no record of the new deed showing title as husband and wife. So that was what Cal meant when he said, "You'd better not have found it."

I was curious and worried, wondering what else had happened in my absence, so I checked all the deposit receipts while I was gone and learned that Cal had written a huge check for a new air conditioning system for the shopping center from our joint account, but there were no deposits in that account. I found them in his personal bank account. When I started looking for the shopping center deed, I found it on a clipboard in his car, along with the press release to the newspaper. I was livid.

Everything then came into perspective. Cal had fallen in love with me, manipulated himself into my life and business, used thousands of dollars from our company earnings to bail out the debt on the shopping center, and then schemed to take it back after the debt was paid. He had planned and timed his every action carefully. I had been thoroughly screwed. What seemed even more stupid, Cal had regained his ownership in a shopping center that was less than 10% the value of my assets that I was willing to share with him. It was incomprehensible. I was devastated. After less than nine months of marriage, I lost thousands of dollars in addition to the money I paid to buy the shopping center, not to mention my dreams of dying old with the mate I'd foolishly chosen.

It took me only minutes to engage an attorney to file for divorce and to fall apart mentally, physically, and psychologically. I could not sleep, eat, or think. The world was a black, forbidding place with no tranquility or joy and I wanted no part in it. For the following several months, I suffered every agony that is possible in one lifetime. I blamed Cal for his dishonesty as well as for my own idiocy. I was an intelligent woman who acted stupidly out of my own suffocating need for love, companionship, and greater meaning in life. My anger at my own complicity was as bad, or perhaps worse than at him.

I wondered if any of the metaphysics I had embraced held any truth. Do we attract events from which we have the most to learn? Do we subconsciously (or consciously) seek pain? Life without love had been unbearable for me, but did I deserve the consequences because of my deep-seated need? I had made a pact with the devil and deserved the consequences. Without pain, there can be no joy, but how much joy had I received relative to the pain I was suffering? Early in our relationship, I told Cal, "You have to be vulnerable to love." I was vulnerable, which he used for his own advantage. Who was the culprit—me or him? How could I have been so stupid?

I believed my positive attitude had attracted my successes. Did my negativity attract my present torture? Were my stress, anxiety, and pain some kind of karma from prior lives, or karma from my feelings of guilt over my love affair with Curt, a married man? Questions plagued me night and day. I wallowed in self-pity and anger and tried to engage my children in my misery. My son, Bob, told me, "No one wants to hear your troubles." Debbie told me I needed help, suggesting I get admitted to the hospital. Jan was working in a print shop, too busy with her current live-in lover to be interested in my problems. Steve had moved to a nearby town, working in a grocery store, and had financial and drug problems to solve—he still seemed like a lost young man. But there were many things that had to be done and I could not afford the luxury of giving up.

My attorney asked me if I wanted to stay in the old farmhouse or move back to my family home in town. I replied that I wanted to go back home—the farmhouse was filled with a black cloud that overwhelmed me with evil. But my former home was in the process of a complete remodel and there was no stove, toilets, or flooring in it, but I told him that I would move back there within a week. Nothing was finished when I moved the next week. I slept on a mattress in the family room with no cooking or bathroom facilities for another week before the work was finished.

A week after I filed for divorce, I returned to the farmhouse to pick up a few things I had left and found the house occupied by another woman. You have to hand it to Cal—he moved fast! There was a note on a bedroom table in flowing female script from Tiney expressing her love and gratitude for the new love in her life.

My lawyer failed to council me to see the district attorney because Cal had committed a crime. Instead, he insisted that I turn over my books to an accountant to determine all the money, assets, and commissions that Cal and I had co-mingled since our relationship. In my distraught thinking processes, I blindly followed his suggestions. In the process, the attorney milked me for thousands of dollars in fees for a year as he prolonged the divorce, month after month. In the meantime, he had set up a trust account for all our rental receipts that came in.

Cal made one demand after another to settle. He wanted the caterpillar tractor we had bought during the marriage; he wanted the riverboat he had "given" me as a birthday gift, and he demanded the shopping center he had stolen. He even asked for a small bowl he had brought from his home that was worth less than ten cents. In return, he would relinquish the old farm in Veneta, where he had paid no rent during the entire year he and his lover lived there, and grant me the 50-acre farm in Crow. I balked at giving up the McKenzie riverboat, which was a gift from him paid for from our joint account and the attorneys argued endlessly for a year at a cost of thousands of dollars in fees.

When we finally went to court, after a short argument by my attorneys, the judge said that it was in the best interest of all to settle. He said that a property settlement the size of this one would result in thousands of dollars in income taxes to the spouse who received the assets. I thought this argument was ridiculous since the only asset Cal had brought into the marriage was the shopping center before he sold it to me. We broke for lunch, while my attorney and accountant hard-pressed me to settle. Only a fool refuses to take his attorney's advice, I thought.

Cal and his lady-love embraced lovingly after the judge announced the settlement.

I received the two properties we'd bought during the relationship and Cal received the shopping center back—free from the liens against it. I would get the $10,000 in my attorney's trust account.

I went home, raging because thousands of dollars that should have been in the trust account had vanished. What happened to all the year's rents that had accumulated during the year? But I was too sick to care—at least a year of torment and unhappiness was finally over.

The next day, Debbie called, asking if I would care for her four-year-old son, and I agreed. It was a distraction from thinking about my own trials. The little boy probably was the victim of childhood Attention Deficit Disorder, as he was never still or quiet, talked a mile a minute, and could not be trusted out of my sight. His hyperactivity suggested that I get a playmate for him, so I phoned a neighbor and asked if she wanted to send over her little 5-year-old.

She brought him over. As I thanked her and bid her goodbye at the door, her son rushed outdoors. Before I realized it, he had climbed a ladder into a huge tree house in my back yard. I ran out as quickly as I could to find bees swarming and stinging him all over his little body. There was a huge beehive that my grandson knew to leave alone, but he didn't. I climbed a couple of steps up the ladder, urging him to jump, "Jump, I'll catch you." He was large for his age, and when he jumped, he knocked me down, landing on top of me on the ground. My whole body was wracked with pain, and I barely made it into the house to collapse on the floor before I realized that I was badly injured. Somehow, I managed to get the child into a tub of tepid water I hoped would relieve the pain from multiple bee stings, and then called his mother to return. She said, "Are you OK?" I said, "Yes," but seconds later realized I was not all right. I asked her to call an ambulance.

For four days, I lay in a hospital bed, diagnosed with three or four fractured vertebras. They told me that I would need to lie upside down in a sling and that recovery could take six months or more and I might never walk again. Instead, the fourth day, they fitted me with a prosthetic back brace and sent me home to my empty house with no one to even help me to the bathroom or make a meal for me. When Debbie dropped by a few days later, I was lying on the couch in too much pain to move. The children were still upset because of divorcing their beloved father. I would have to manage.

I was lying on the couch—unable to move without excruciating pain—when I received the attorney's check from his client's trust account. The check was for about $3,000 instead of $10,000. He had confiscated the remainder of our real estate accumulated receipts for his fees. It was a violation of attorney ethics, and I was so furious, I decided to sue him. I have never seen a more panicked and distressed attorney when we finally had a hearing some months later. Unfortunately, I only won slightly more than the cost of the attorney I hired, but it was a moral victory that made me feel slightly better. The look on his face when the verdict came was enough to almost atone for the loss of money he had stolen.

The attorney's lack of honesty reminded me once more that women could never compete in a man's world.

# Chapter 53

My fractured back slowly healed. Life went on as I painfully cared for the most expedient needs and left everything else undone. I was able to drive again within a few weeks and there was work to be done. I started remodeling the farmhouse outside of the little town of Crow, hiring trucks to haul tons of old cars, tires, needles, and accumulated junk that hippies had left at the site. One of the prior owners returned to the site and broke out all the windows, knocked down doors and broken toilets. I joked that the broken toilet was for my "half-assed friends."

My life's ambition was to make my children self-sufficient, so it occurred to me to get them involved in the project. I needed help and they needed to acquire a measure of security and more responsibility. What about making them partners in the venture? My son Bob had re-built a school bus to live in to save money on rent. Jan was going from one relationship into another, moving often. Debbie relied on her lovers to support her and frequently asked for loans that she never repaid.

I approached them with the idea of making them partners in the farm. Land ownership was the most security anyone could have—a retreat, a method to earn a decent living, and a future if the economy fell. We discussed working together for my vision of a family farm that would provide security for our old age. The big house was large enough to accommodate two of them if we divided it into two dwellings. We would renovate the second house and have three dwellings on the property. I already had too many houses to live in. They were delighted with my offer to share in the profits in exchange for the work they did, so we drew up an agreement that they would receive equity in proportion to the work they performed. The only objection they had was to allow Debbie to be a partner because she was "too flaky" and unwilling to work. Debbie never forgave Bob and Jan for their position, but unfortunately, they were right. Debbie just was not dependable.

My son, Bob, moved his remodeled bus to the farm to live in while we renovated the big house. The first need was a potable supply of water after we discovered the prior owners had filled the well with rocks and other debris. Bob yelled at me for digging a water line to the house with the brace still on my back. We then removed doors, an old wood stove, and cabinets and hauled away more junk. Bob and I took turns operating the old caterpillar tractor, scraping and piling weeds, blackberries, and brush that had grown up around the big house. The tractor glanced into a huge five-gallon gas tank under one big patch of blackberries that could have blown us up if fuel remained in it.

The Reagan recession, high-interest rates, and my rapidly depleting savings required selling some of my properties, but little was selling because of high-interest rates and unemployment. Few people could afford a mortgage to buy a home. When I advertised both my house in town and the big farmhouse in Veneta, there was little response, but a young attorney finally agreed to purchase my house in town on a lease-option purchase; I grabbed it. I accepted his offer and moved back to the Veneta farm, which was closer to Crow and the renovation project. Less than a year later, the attorney who bought my house lost his job and could no longer afford to pay the lease payments, so he signed it back to me.

The loneliness I experienced in the rural setting was depressing me. I spent my time gardening and renovating the Crow farm, too depressed to work at my real estate profession and decided to move back to town as soon as I could sell one of the farms.

At that point, I thought my life was over at the young age of 55. Depression was eating me alive. I needed more social and creative outlets which meant changing my circumstances to include more people and a greater creative outlet. I decided to join a larger real estate firm where there were people to work with and an art group in hopes it would inspire me to paint and write.

Finally, a couple I'll call "the Jones" approached me about giving them a lease with an option to purchase the Veneta farm, praising the Lord for finding "just the kind of place we want." Mr. Jones stated that he and his wife were escapees from California, where he had worked as a swimming pool maintenance worker for a large company that handled apartment buildings. The city, they said, was too evil, with too much crime and unprincipled people who did not share their religious views.

They stated that their earnings were in the $50,000 to $100,000 range, and he would continue to receive a salary for the next six months before getting a final lump sum payment at the first of the year. In the meantime, he said he was working at a local plant and needed a home to settle into. He asked, "Would you be would be willing to wait five months for the down payment?" I was glad to get a sale—any sale—to avoid another vacancy. I wrote up the offer for a lease-option agreement with them. They would make a monthly payment from August through December and pay the down payment and close the sale in January after he received the lump sum payment from his prior employer. After they signed the agreement, I allowed them to move in.

Complaints started in the following month. The water was muddy, Jones said, before they told me that had left the sprinklers on all night. I had made them aware that the well supplied only about five gallons of water per minute, and insufficient for irrigating except for short periods.

Before Christmas, Jones called, "We are not going to buy the house. We are going to sue you and get it for nothing. We had that water problem, and you did not get permits when you remodeled the house." I had carefully explained to them before making the agreement that all the remodeling was completed by licensed electricians and plumbers to code specifications, but because Cal was the owner-contractor, it was unnecessary to buy permits. We had no problems with any function in the house when we lived there. I was completely straight-forward in disclosing every facet of the property details and description. They had no legitimate complaints. The following month, I was served by papers claiming that no permits had been taken out for the work we did. None were necessary since Cal had a contractor's license and was the co-owner at the time. It was a frivolous lawsuit by a religious couple who wanted something for nothing. They had stated, "If the Lord wants us to have this property, He will arrange it." Was the Lord arranging for them to receive the property without paying for it?

I hired an attorney to reject their claims, but they continued to file new outlandish false claims month after month. My attorney cost me $1,000 or more a month, while I continued to pay the mortgage payments and the Jones made no payments at all. My bank account was dwindling by thousands of dollars every month, while I was earning little money with my license hanging in an office where commissions were divided between other brokers, the parent company, and other salespeople. After I made a large sale and only received a small percentage of the commission, I had had enough. I needed to make money to pay for all my mistakes, so I re-opened my own office again.

My troubles were monumental. My attorney informed me that the only way we could force the Jones' out of my house was to get a summary judgment to prove that they lied about their claim of inadequate plumbing and wiring and other false claims. That was easy enough to prove. I applied for all the permits and inspections, and all was well. All of them passed. The problem was getting our case before the judge, which took almost a year, while the Jones lived free of the required monthly payment. There were no laws that covered lease-with-option sales, so I went to Salem to try state congressmen to get a law to cover my situation. The new law was written about the time we finally received a summary judgment a year later that required them to move. The judgment gave me the equivalent of two months lease payments, which the Jones couldn't pay. They wanted to make payments; they had no money. They had succeeded in defrauding me in thousands of dollars of unpaid rents, mortgage costs, and attorney fees, but there was nothing I could do about it. After they finally moved out, they left bank statements showing that they lied about their income and the lump sum payment he said he expected. I also found old lawsuit papers in the debris they left that showed I was not the first landlord they had defrauded.

It was not easy to tell myself "live and learn." Leasing to the Jones was a chance I thought I needed to take at the time. Although I made the mistake, I blamed myself for being naïve and too trusting almost as much as I blamed the Jones' for taking advantage of me. I had often learned that men will take advantage of a woman in business anytime they can. The business world was cut-throat, but I was my own worst enemy. At the same time, I saw that untrusting people were often the least trustworthy—like Cal and the Jones'. I had no desire to live in a world where I had to suspect that everyone was out to get me.

But the "ox was in the ditch" and I was forced to borrow money at 16 percent to hang on until I could sell some more property.

# Chapter 54

I put the most beautiful property I had, six acres near the Siuslaw River, on the market to sell. I loved the little one-bedroom house with an efficiency apartment on the second floor, in a setting of beautiful fir forest, and the little spring-fed pond below the house filled with water lilies and huge frogs that croaked musically in the background. I felt only tranquility when I went there, but dependable renters were hard to find and were often undesirable when they could be found. Few working people wanted to live 20 five miles from town and the property was difficult to manage at that distance from town. Showing the property entailed a long, time-consuming drive. After months of showings, I found no buyers and I became anxious over the high-interest loan I had secured on the property. It must be sold.

Finally, a young couple approached me about buying it on contract with a small cash down payment and acceptable monthly payments. I was skeptical but I needed cash and a solution to management problems. What could I do but take a chance? If they didn't pay as agreed, what did I have to lose? I felt forced to take a chance.

The payments came in on time for three months, but nearby neighbors started to call me about cars roaring by their remote farms, people coming and going all hours of the day and night, and numerous cars parked in the front yard. They suggested I find out what was going on. Investigation proved they were right. Something was going on there that I could only suspect that drugs were involved. I phoned the Sheriff's office, asking them to investigate, but before they reported their findings, an article in the paper came out about a huge wreck on the winding highway leading to the location. Six people were killed, and methamphetamine was found outside one of the wrecked cars. My buyers were responsible for the accident when they crashed into a family car while playing leapfrog with a friend on the busy two-lane highway. My buyer was arrested and put in jail for drug possession.

I found his girlfriend and her child still living in my beautiful place, with piles of rubbish, litter, and the worst order I ever smelled. "My God, what's next," I asked myself as I examined the mess. The efficiency apartment upstairs was uninhabitable, and the lower unit little better. I wondered if I could handle another huge problem, but what option did I have?

I went to work on it. My sister Mel and her husband visited to help tear out walls, kitchen cabinets, woodwork, and insulation and haul it away. When completed, I contacted a chemical engineer from an environmental contracting company to test the property for safety. They found the property to be clean and safe after the remodel.

Shortly afterward, an article appeared in the newspaper about the proliferation of "meth" labs in Oregon. The state legislators enacted a new law that required owners of "meth" labs to get a "certificate of fitness to occupy" from the State Health Department before they could be rented, sold or even occupied by the owner.

The State was going to license a new drug "clean-up contractors" who would be trained specifically to clean "meth" houses. They would be given seven days of training to qualify to issue "certification of fitness to occupy" to owners of drug houses. Previously existing environmental contractors, who had been cleaning environmental hazards for generations, were exempt from the program. When I contacted the State Health Division, I was told that the tests I had done were not acceptable, and I would have to hire one of the new contractors they were training. It made no sense.

Oregon civil servants rejected my argument that the chemical engineer with a Doctorate degree I had hired was more qualified than any of the new contractors would be. I was forced to wait for several more months for the state to license the new contractors before I could hire one. I fumed in anger and frustration.

I argued, wrote letters, pleaded, cursed, and seethed in my frustration with the State Health Department for almost a year, to no avail. I was forced to engage one of the new contractors after they received their license. Only six of them were available in the entire state. The nearest one was 70 miles away, so I contacted them in hopes they could issue a "certification of fitness" based on the tests I had already had done.

"We'll have to walk the entire six acres and thoroughly inspect and test the house," they told me. I told them to go ahead.

The following day I received an invoice for $1,200 for their afternoon inspection. I was outraged to learn that the State had given licenses to these contractors and allowed them to charge such outrageous fees. I could do nothing about the state's role, but I would not be ripped off by a brand-new company that had only eight days of training. I phoned and gave them an irate dismissal, agreeing to pay them $300 for the trip but they could whistle for the rest of their bill. I had enough of being scammed by con artists and charlatans.

There had to be another way. It took another two years before it occurred to me to sue the State for applying the "meth house" law retroactively. My house was clean before the law went into effect. In less than a week, they removed the property from the "unfit to occupy" list so it could be sold again.

Jan helped clean up and renovate the farm at Crow for about a year before she bailed out and moved back into town. Bob and his new bride moved into one side of the big house after we completed the remodeling for another year before they decided to move to Seattle to get a better job in the printing trade.

# Chapter 55

I retired in 1989 to nurse my wounds and try to restore my soul. My sisters and I visited each other several times a year, in addition to their visits to see Mom and Dad after they had moved to the Northwest.

I now had time to follow my own wants and desires, and gradually life became good again. I could travel, garden, read, paint – or do nothing except spend time with my parent until their deaths.

Mom contracted pneumonia in March 1983, and in less than 36 hours she was gone. She had told us repeatedly that she wouldn't last much longer, and was ready for the other side. I couldn't grieve for her death as much as for all those years of pain and suffering she had endured.

Dad had many near-death illnesses when his doctors expected him to die, but he had a mind of his own. He was not ready to die. Several times, doctors asked him if he was ready, and he always said, "No." Finally, three days before his 102nd birthday, Debbie spent hours with him in an effort to relieve his mind that he wasn't going to hell for drinking an occasional glass of blackberry liquor at Christmas. The "Old Southern Religion" had indoctrinated him well. Other than his fear of dying, his mind was clear and unclouded until the day he finally gave up, with useless arms and legs hardened into rigid positions.

Pat and I took a wonderful five-day trip to Canada with a group of artists on an artist's watercolor workshop together. We stayed in an old Mounted Police Headquarters where bears and elk roamed outside our cabins, which nearly scared our host to death when she encountered a bear wondering around, completely ignoring people coming and going.

We spent an hour or two in the morning watching our host give a demonstration, and then moved to a gorgeous nearby mountain or stream in the magnificent Canadian wilderness to work our own magic on our own watercolor paper.

We also took a seventeen-day trip to England with twenty other artists, where we were bused to most of the tourist attractions in the country with a

British tourist host who explained everything about each attraction in great detail. It became clear where America got its land use legislation after touring the narrow roads for many miles without seeing anything except expanses of land with an occasional castle in the distance. Again, we had an artist demonstration at least once a day or more, and later practiced what we had learned. When I exhibited my work later it was obvious that my work had improved a great deal. I still have several paintings that I haven't even exhibited since the trip.

Both Mel and Pat, along with their husbands and I went on other trips – some to Canada and others to explore lakes and rivers in Oregon or Washington. One of the trips we took was to Central Oregon, where a friend of mine urged us to use his cabin while we fished for a rare striped bass that was supposed to the best fishing anywhere. We were so grateful that we had taken Mel and Dan's RV with us after we found the cabin full of rodents roaming around in the filthy interior.

Mel, Dan and I also went to Canada several times to fish for the might salmon – some weighing up to ninety or more pounds. One trip was especially memorable when we stopped for fuel and we mistakenly filled the diesel truck with gasoline instead. We had to waste a whole day or more to empty the tank and repair the engine after it was almost ruined by the mistake. After that trip, we decided that we could fish for salmon from a travel trailer park on the beautiful Oregon coast easier, less expensive and for a longer period of time. Mel and Dan drove their RV to an Oregon campsite every fall for over ten years, where we fished for about a month during August through October. My sister and I grieve that our advanced age makes this no longer possible, but we live with wonderful memories of those trips.

# Chapter 56

Jan had seldom given me cause for concern in her younger life: I had worried about her choice of the men in her life and the continued drug culture of the '60s. She had held a stable, well-paying job in the printing industry for a number of years, and seemed to manage her life adequately.

She had my devotion and expectations for continued success. Her bubbling personality attracted friends and lovers, and she was seldom negative or unhappy except when a lover disappointed her. She made her contented way in the world and seemed to be happy most of the time. I was pleased with the progress she made and would only have changed the choice of her lovers, many of whom drank excessively. It never occurred to me that her low self-esteem led her to make such relationships—but then don't mothers usually think that way? When we were together, we had a loving relationship and I did not want to risk criticizing her arrangements. That was her business.

When the printing trades began laying off local workers, Jan moved to Portland where there was a larger market.

In the late 1980s, Jan told me that she had a new mate, Matt, and asked me to visit them in their new place. I found her living in a tiny travel trailer with the genial, bearded Matt in a wooded area outside of town. Beer bottles were strewn around the premises and the little trailer was crowded and unkempt. She told me her employer had cut back on her hours so she was only working part-time. Nearing the end of her child producing years, she told me she wanted to have children before it was too late. In a short time, she became pregnant with her first child.

She bought a manufactured home and they placed it on the land Matt owned. She seemed content and happy with her life and especially her pregnancy. I visited her several times during her first pregnancy and she called and asked me to attend the biggest event her life—the birth of her first child. Mat stood next to her head, encouraging her as the birth approached, while I held her hand until the tiny figure emerged. It was my first experience at the birth of a grandchild, and I treasured the experience. It was a beautiful baby boy that everyone adored.

Two years later, she gave birth to a strikingly handsome baby girl, attended by both me and her sister. All of us were crying with joy after the delivery.

Unfortunately, the relationship with Matt became strained and unsatisfactory because of his love of drinking beer at the local pub with his brother and friends, and they broke up.

She spent thousands of dollars to move the manufactured home into a park, but then later unexpectedly decided to marry Matt for a father to her children. The marriage was doomed from the start, resulting in divorce two years later.

In the next few years, Jan's employers began to cut back until she was unemployed for the first time in 20 years. Never one to give up, she told me that if she couldn't beat the printing trade, she would join them by starting her own computer graphics business in her home so she could stay home with the children she adored. In the following months, she taught herself digital publishing of advertising brochures and other high-quality graphics. I admired her for her newly acquired skills, devotion to her children, and failure to give up. She approached local businesses, schools, and individuals for work to do for them to replace the high income she was used to. Unfortunately, in a small town over 20 miles from the city, the work entailed picking up and delivering jobs once or more a day, requiring time-consuming and costly travel. Jan was terrified when little new income resulted from her efforts. She called me almost daily to ask for advice.

Jan was alone now, a single mother dedicated to her business in an area too remote to promote, create, and deliver her product. I told her the family would back her up and I would sponsor her until the business was established if she wanted to move back to Eugene, where there was a ready market for the graphics she produced. She was amenable to the idea and asked me to find a house for them. It was the worst mistake I ever made in the relationship with the daughter I loved and admired so much.

The owner of a for-sale-by-owner home agreed to sell a nice home for a low-down payment and assume her payments. Jan and I agreed that she could rent it from me, with the payments to apply to the original purchase price when she could afford to buy it from me for the amount I invested in it. It was a chance to own a home for her family with no cash outlay except the monthly rent.

I invested a down payment to buy the house, but it needed a new carpet, a new roof, and some repairs. Even with the repairs, it was an excellent investment and Jan was pleased.

Determined to make sure her business succeeded, I purchased additional equipment she needed to make it work. Within six months she acquired enough clients to earn a living wage. I was proud of her. I often cared for my grandchildren or helped with housework while she managed the workload.

One day when I went there some months later, I watched in horror as Jan swallowed a hand full of Advil.

"I have a migraine headache," she explained.

"What are you doing?" I gasped. "That many pills could kill you!"

The headaches became more and more debilitating until she found a doctor who diagnosed the cause as damage to her iris from ultraviolet machines, she had previously used in the printing trade. She was given a prescription for opiates for relief and in a short while, she became addicted, resulting in emotional outbursts and abnormal behavior in which she berated me for "interfering" in her life. One minute she loved and expressed appreciation for my help and the next, I was her worst enemy. I was aghast at the changes to my beloved daughter and best friend, without understanding what was happening to her. In the meantime, I subsidized her income when necessary to pay expenses.

Six months later, Jan's new boyfriend moved into the house. I thought a student who was studying for a degree in early childhood development would be helpful in caring for her three and five-year-old children. Instead, he spent his time studying, reading the paper, and dropping his cigarette butts on the floor for her to clean up. He contributed nothing to the family. He had no income except loans and grants for school, so Jan cleaned and cooked for him on the money I spent to subsidize them. I felt he not only was using her, but he was using me as well. I asked Jan to get him to mow the grass or weed the unkempt yard, but he had better things to do.

When Jan's boyfriend ran an electric line across the yard to a shed behind the house and renovated it as a place to study away from the noise of the children, he went too far. I told Jan that if he wanted to live there, he would have to sign the required rental agreement. As the official owner of the house, I was liable for the care of problems.

Jan became very angry, "He is my tenant—not yours."

"If he is your tenant, why isn't he paying any rent?" I asked.

Jan had no answer except to advise him not to sign a rental agreement. He had been living there for six months, and when I insisted that state law required a written agreement, Jan sent me an angry email stating they would move out before he would sign.

They moved out, leaving the house filthy with cigarette burns in the new carpet I had installed, and a yard full of clutter. *The story of my life*, I thought, as I hired a crew to restore the property at a cost of thousands of dollars.

Jan's irrational behavior disturbed me so much that I decided to confront her doctor to inquire about possible addiction after finding a prescription bottle of morphine in her medicine chest.

The doctor was out, so I discussed the drastic changes in Jan with the nurse.

"I'm not allowed to discuss this matter with you," she told me.

"Then maybe you don't care if she dies," I replied. "Her behavior has changed so much that I don't even know her anymore. The only change that I know about is the addition of morphine prescribed by this doctor. I understand that you are not obligated to tell me anything, but can you just tell me one thing? Is there a possibility of addiction?"

"The doctor has dismissed Jan as a patient," the nurse said. "I can't tell you anything, but you are on the right track."

Still, I was not ready to believe that my daughter was a morphine addict. The drug culture my children had grown up with was making my life a living nightmare. I had no doubt that the drugs they had taken during adolescence could ruin their lives. Jan was so angry and upset at me that I barely heard from her for almost a year afterward. The loss of our close relationship and failure to see my grandchildren left me sleepless with worry until I finally decided to try to bring us back together again.

I ignored her cluttered, dirty apartment when she gave me a tour without showing me the converted garage her boyfriend occupied separately from the family. She was short and uncommunicative when I asked about how her business was doing. The equipment she used in the business was in the living area where her clients came to pick up fliers, resumes, advertising brochures, and documents she produced. The floor was littered with papers, toys, and dirt. I was amazed that she could work in such an atmosphere. How long would customers contend with such a business atmosphere?

After a brief visit, I started to leave, when her boyfriend appeared and ordered me off the premises. Jan became hysterically upset about me being there.

A few months later, Jan moved to an apartment above the busiest intersection in the city, with no yard or place for the children to play. In the few times she allowed me to visit, I was aghast at the chaos in which they lived. The place was filthy. A pet rat escaped to live in the walls, and cat and dog feces, overturned plants, and unwashed dishes pervaded the premises. The odor was overwhelming. I had to get my grandchildren out of that filth and disorder, so I offered to buy them another house. No child or grandchild of mine had to live this way and I was determined to do something about it. In hindsight, it was another irrational decision, but I had to try. I found a small, older four-bedroom, two-bath home in a nice area, and put most of the cash I had down on it, and got a loan for the balance of the purchase price. When I took Jan and the children to approve it, they loved it, thanked me profusely, and agreed to maintain it, keep it clean, and pay the monthly payment.

Jan paid most of the payments the first year, and when she received an inheritance from her grandmother's estate, she repaid me for prior loans I had given her for business equipment and mortgage payments she had missed. The following year, she paid only two or three mortgage payments all year, and the house looked even worse than her prior dwellings. Filth, dirt, and debris were everywhere.

I now was sure that her addiction to pain killers was out of control and begged her to go into a treatment program. She denied any addiction. She was perfectly alright.

Now retired with no income, I had no alternative to evicting her when she received the second payment from her grandmother's estate without paying what she owed. The house was costing me over $1,000 a month which I could not afford on retirement income.

Jan said, "I was ready to write a check," when she received the eviction notice, but she didn't offer to repay the missing payments. Instead, she purchased new stereo and television equipment and a pool and expensive toys for the kids. The value of the property decreased by thousands of dollars, and again, I was forced to hire contractors to restore it.

They moved into a small apartment, only to be evicted for nonpayment of rent in less than three months. Jan invited me to her son's birthday party there and I was appalled to see the filthiest place I'd ever seen.

When I helped load the truck to move and she and the children had no place to go, I could not stand the thought of my beloved grandchildren being homeless. No one would rent to them with their record of filthy housekeeping and failure to pay rent. It appeared that Jan's business had either failed completely or was close to it.

I saw an ad for a nice manufactured home at a giveaway price and rushed out and bought it. I had to register it with Jan as half-owner before the park would agree to rent the space to her.

Within a short time, I started getting complaints from park management—Jan and the kids were loud, uncooperative, and filthy.

They were evicted and I was stuck with paying rent on the space for the seven months they lived there. The carpet was ruined with animal feces in nearly every corner. The home had to be re-painted throughout and the sub-floor replaced and deodorized before new carpet could be installed. The total cost of repairing the premises was thousands of dollars.

What kind of idiot was I to be subjected to one after another punishment from my drug-addicted daughter? I loved her and was determined to save her and especially the grandchildren I adored. But the punishment got worse. When I asked Jan to sign the manufactured home back to me so I could sell it, she refused.

Jan was lying on the couch, stoned out of her mind, "No, I won't sign any documents." She refused to move for six weeks, saying she couldn't find a place to live.

Eventually, she did sign documents restoring my ownership of the property, but she still maintained that she was not addicted. At one point, she admitted in an email that she had trouble controlling the doctor prescribed medications.

In the following year, she was evicted and moved three or four times, moving in with me while she searched for housing. She blamed me for the evictions. I became her worst enemy, even when I allowed her to move in with me temporarily.

Finally, when no one would rent to her, she moved back to Portland, where at times, she had the children slept in the car before finding shelter and a job.

During the following years, I seldom heard from them except through her sister. They lived on unemployment insurance and child support, existing in abject poverty. The sporadic jobs she found were low pay and brief until she was given a grant to re-train in the medical field.

At present, Jan and the children seem more willing to accept our former loving, trusting relationship after all those years, and I pray that another generation may not go down the drain because of drugs.

The heartbreak of dealing with the continual problems of addicted and mentally ill daughters year after year was taking its toll on me. Will there ever be any relief from the pain I had over my beloved children? What did I do to deserve these burdens? I tried to tell myself it wasn't my problem, but it was. Debbie couldn't or wouldn't earn a living for herself. Bob was on medication for Hepatitis C as well as drugs for his bipolar disease, but he was affable and caring to me. Steve and his wife had good jobs and all the comforts of modern America despite spending habits reminiscent of his father's, although much better.

# Chapter 57

I worked on the Crow 30-acre farm for ten years, leveling, improving the driveway, removing old tool sheds and cleaning out blackberries. My dream was to build a big pond to control the spring on the upper hillside and stock it with trout. When I found a cat operator who was willing to dig the pond at a reasonable cost, I was thrilled to hire him. This would be the crowning glory of the beautiful south-facing rolling hills to reflect the new houses we had created. When it was finished and stocked with fish, I experienced a sense of fulfillment and joy. The place was gorgeous. One could watch deer and quail feeding below the houses, watch the fish jump for bugs in the pond and listen to the sound of quail calling to each other and hear frogs singing in the new pond. My ancestor's dream of land ownership was fulfilled, and I could feel secure at last, although I grieved about selling the 160-acre tree farm that I had owned in partnership with my friend, Wanda.

I was thoroughly burnt-out and only wanted peace, tranquility and free time to pursue my life's goal of painting and writing. In a few months, at the age of 62, I could pay off the mortgage with $65,000 that the man who bought the other 20 aces of the property owed me, and I could retire to the Crow farm and watch the world go by.

Best laid plans! The buyer who owed me $65,000 couldn't pay and I could not afford to spend all the cash I had before I retired to pay the debt on the farm that was due. Mournfully, I knew I had to sell my beloved farm where I had spent so many years to restore a productive life. I grieved for the loss, but the handwriting was on the wall: "You do what you have to do."

When I advertised the farm for sale, my first potential buyers were mesmerized with the south-facing atrium that acted as a heat source for the house. They especially loved the new reflective pond full of rainbow trout that had grown to 16 inches or longer. A week after seeing it, they made an offer to buy it for $110,000. I cried as I signed the agreement. The buyers gloated that the place would be worth half a million dollars within five years. They were wrong. It was worth far more than that.

When I computed my taxes after I retired in 1989, I learned that I owed over $36,000 in income taxes, which eliminated most of the profits on my investment. I grieved over the loss of my retirement farm more than the loss of profits.

I retired in 1989 to nurse my wounds and try to restore my soul. I realized the need for the experiences I had that led to my personal growth, and am grateful for them. My early years gave me the toughness I needed to meet life with courage and determination in order to overcome life's trials. Unfortunately, my current anger at the mistakes of my country has not dissipated completely—and won't—until a new administration replaces the worst one since Hoover and Coolidge.

World peace, prosperity, and a budget surplus of the 1990s under President Bill Clinton slowly drew to a close amid constant attacks on his administration from the right during his eight years in office. He was constantly criticized by the main media, Karl Rove's dirty tricks, and harangued by White Water, and he could do nothing right despite most American citizen's support for him. When Clinton's sexual indiscretions became public, followed by impeachment, his supporters were embarrassed. After all, maybe there was some truth to all the allegations against him.

The new century began to roar into view in the person of the arrogant, former alcoholic and cocaine user, George Bush, with his Religious Right, super-rich base that contributed millions of dollars to his election campaign. Speaking in one-syllable sounds bites and mispronounced words; he waved the American flag and demolished every accomplishment of the Bill Clinton eight years. He began to convince the red and blue states that he was a better choice for president than Al Gore.

As an incurable news junkie, I became so aghast at his proposals that I went door to door to try to convince voters of his lies and innuendoes that Bush spouted from his bully pulpits across the nation. He lied or refused to discuss completing his military service in the National Guard after his father used his influence to help him get the appointment over 100,000 on the waiting list. Dan Rather announced on *Sixty Minutes,* the popular Sunday news program, that he had documents to prove it. CBS fired him and forced him to apologize after the news media declared the documents forged. Every "news junkie" in the country knew the documents were accurate—we have seen the signature of his Commanding Officer and statements that Bush had not complied with an order to submit to drug testing. Despite a score of 25% on his pilot entrance aptitude test, Bush was assigned to flight school, then fast-tracked over on the pilot waiting list into the 111th Fighter-Interceptor Squadron. Lt. Col. William D. Harris, Jr. reported that Bush had two full years remaining on his six-year service commitment and on May 15th, 1974, Bush simply left the base and never returned.

George W. Bush immediately reversed Clinton's policies and renewed Reagan's deficit spending, while he showered the top 1% of income earners, (his "base"), some $630 billion (a 24.2% in tax cuts). The Republicans returned the favor by investing well over $200 million to ensure his election and re-election four years later.

Democracy as we had known it vanished. Inexplicitly, the country was in an undeclared war with a country that presented no threat, while terrorists slinked into their mountain caves. The greatest secrecy in history, with the possible exception of Nixon's reign, became the order of the day. When Congress demanded answers, Bush refused to submit the documents they requested. When they tried to reduce some of his power as the Commander in Chief, he simply created 1,000 "signed statements" that he was exempt from them.

The economy lost over 1.9 million private-sector jobs—the worst record since Herbert Hoover in the Great Depression—and paid $9,000 less. Typical family incomes declined by nearly $1500. 1.3 million citizens were unable to find full-time jobs. Since January 2001, the number of part-time workers rose from 3.3 million to 4.7—a 40% increase by 2004.

The top 1% received as much in income as the bottom 65% combined and the gap between the rich and poor exploded.

With U.S. mortgages going into foreclosure at a record pace, it created a crisis with far-reaching implications from the financial markets to the economic health of ordinary Americans. At the same time, banks and mortgage company wealth became greater than ever by selling bundles of their low-quality loans to hedge fund investors. Afterward, many of them were destined to go bankrupt because the bad loans were not paid, and threatened the economy of the entire world.

Health care costs increased by 50%, while gasoline went up even more, and college tuition costs increased by approximately 35%. Despite Bush's "no child left behind" program, education in most public schools deteriorated. Corporate CEO pay exploded, with the average pay package into the millions of dollars, while corporations laid-off workers and shipped jobs overseas.

As the body count increased among the military, Bush created his own mercenary army in Blackwater Corporation then butchered Iraqi civilians "to protect themselves." Backwater's indiscriminating killings of innocent civilians proved to be the cause of much of the Iraqi insurgency, and Iraqis killed and hung Backwater's employees' bodies from bridge railings in protest.

Bush granted his 170,000-private army—larger than the 150,000-military army in Iraq—payments of $500 a day or more, while American military recruits received such inadequate incomes that their families qualified for food stamps to survive.

The melt-down of the financial market in 2007-2008 left America with the highest deficit in history and an economy reminiscent of the Great Depression. Wall Street investors lost up to 45% of their money and 19 banks failed. Congress passed the TARP program to save the worldwide collapse of the monetary system. Apparently, it never occurred to politicians that backing up the millions of mortgage holders who had been scammed by banks that granting home loans that they were not qualified for, i.e., one Mexican who earned $15,000 a year was granted a loan to purchase a $75,000 loan to buy a house!

# Chapter 58

My time was now mostly free to use as I chose after I retired in 1989

For a long while, I poured my prior life onto paper in an effort to purge my regrets, understand my past, and to look forward to hopes of better days ahead. In doing so, I began to appreciate my successes and understand and accept the motives I had in the past for the decisions I had made throughout my life. Those notes were later useful for writing this book.

I was able to concentrate more on painting, entering my work in galleries, making brochures to advertise my work and taking workshops and classes to improve my paintings. In the spring, summer, and fall, I spent hours planting, weeding, growing, and harvesting my vegetables and fruit from the backyard. I had become my mother, without all the poverty and pain she endured with the same thing.

I planted an Asian pear tree, some grapes, and six blueberry bushes and froze, canned, or dried vegetables and fruits until my freezer was filled.

There was time to visit my beloved sisters, read books and exchange them with friends, and soak up the sun. I guarded my time carefully to get the most of it. Time also provided me with an opportunity to keep up my ardent interest in the political world. I followed government decisions in great detail, wrote my congressmen and senators, and joined a political organization to help elect Obama.

I sat up for hours watching the returns of the election come in. I was delighted and celebrated along with the huge crowds that waited for the new president and his family to thank everyone for voting for him.

I was less afraid of the American political system during Obama's eight years in office and rejoiced over the few changes he was able to make against Republican denunciation. Still, I cheered him on when he finally got the Affordable Care Act passed. I felt that it was not good legislation but it was a foot in the door. How could the act help lower healthcare costs when insurance premiums were added to the cost? Sure enough, as a healthy senior who seldom needed a doctor except for an annual checkup, my medical costs soared. But the insurance companies were making money like never before.

How could every major country in the world afford national health care, when the richest country in the world cannot or won't allow it?

But when the arrogant, narcissistic Donald J. Trump and his spoiled rich kids came into power with the assistance of Russia, I knew within a month that America was in terrible trouble. Trump, the man who would be king, almost every time he opened his mouth and hated anyone with brown or black skin and caused babies to be taken away from their parents, locked children in cages and had leaders from other countries put to death.

Will our country ever recover when one branch of the government backs up a tyrant who rules like a mob boss and bribes other countries to dig up dirt on his rival to help him get elected?

Moreover, when the American citizens vote for such a man, is there any hope for our country?

The Holy Roman Empire faded from history for many of the same conditions as America in the present—an unequal distribution of wealth, unemployment, inflation and militarism. We have lost our way, and Capitalism no longer works.

If America fails to remember the lessons of the past, it will repeat the mistakes. Has there been no evolvement in the human soul in the 21st century than in the distant past? Did we learn nothing from the millions of men and women who died in World War Two and the Korean and Vietnam Wars? Could the long, brutal war in Afghanistan ever be won?

Debbie and Jan accuse me of being co-dependent, and apparently, they are right. I loved my children too much. On the other hand, what mother could allow intelligent, beautiful, worthwhile children and grandchildren to go down the tube if she can try to prevent it? Someday, I can only hope their own unique abilities will overcome their problems since they are brilliant, capable, creative, and talented in so many ways. The source of their youthful mistakes was the '60's sex, drugs, and rock and roll culture, and as long as I am alive, I will suffer the consequences along with them and will crusade to change the status quo. The question is how is it possible to eliminate drug use, which even in small doses for pain builds up ever greater demand until it regulates a life completely? I live with this daunting question night and day.

I thought of my youthful poem, in which I asked providence to throw everything into my path that I needed to learn. Those lessons I needed for greater soul growth had been granted. I wanted to experience it all—good, bad, indifferent. As time went on, I developed the belief that reincarnation was more than a theory and that people are placed on the earth to achieve the most wisdom, knowledge, and spirituality possible during life on this plane. The best road to deep understanding is making and correcting the mistakes we made.

While I saw the path that Jesus seemed to make from being born as David forward until his birth as the baby Jesus, ever-repeating life cycles until His soul became perfected and He finally merged with God. While this never occurred to me in my youth, some unconscious need to experience everything life had to offer was the way toward soul perfection in one lifetime. It was logical, practical, and fair. How else could one achieve perfection? But I wanted to make it happen in fewer lifetimes, thus asking for God to "throw it all" at once, and He may have heard my wishes.

My greatest regret is the drug culture appears to get worse every year instead of better, causing violence, incompetence and mental illness, dependency, more and more dysfunctional families, and poverty of the lower class who pay the taxes while one half to one percent own all the money and seldom pay taxes to support their country.

Before I married Bob, I was "born old" and hardly knew the meaning of meeting life in his carefree, casual manner. He taught me that life could be more fun. His lack of responsibility caused me to become more responsible—someone had to be! Having had little demonstrative love in my younger life, he taught me the need to demonstrate love. Although it took some years, I learned that his indiscretions were—for him—uncontrollable and perhaps even unconscious acts caused by a faulty gene or mental illness, rather than malicious ones. I forgave him because he couldn't help it.

I married a second time out of great need, chasing a dream for a father for my children, seeking to fill an empty hole after Curt's death in an effort to replace him. Cal happened to be there when I needed someone, and I overlooked his suspicious, distrusting traits and money needs in a blind effort to fill my own needs. Leopards do not change their spots, and he did what his nature dictated—grab what he could while the grabbing was good. Perhaps the experience did not cure my naivety entirely, but it was a lesson I needed to learn.

I believe the answer to my youthful questionings, "Why are we here? What is the purpose of life?" is that maybe we are here to account for errors in prior lifetimes, and to receive experiences from which we have the most to learn.

My luck and creativity helped earn a good income and a stable future even when I threw it at my daughters' feet. My old poverty-consciousness is still alive and well, and I realize that I am still trying to prove myself. I had little faith the money tree would continue to grow, and I still find it hard to spend for things I need.

I bought more real estate than I could handle and had to sell during the 1980s recession when markets were appallingly poor. When I became emotionally involved in my rentals due to the irresponsibility of my children and grandchildren, I sold them too soon instead of gritting my teeth and hanging on for the income they would bring. Live and learn!

Except when forced to deal with my children's depressed moods and financial problems, I manage to find the beauty in a sunset, from the first seedlings bursting from the earth, the literature I read, and most of all that I usually can learn something new every day.

I am grateful for the way that Steve and Bobby manage their lives while deploring the fact that some of their maturity levels were affected by prior drug use.

My youthful dreams of writing the great American novel and becoming a famous painter never materialized but I have been able to achieve the ability to express my thoughts and emotions—perhaps not eloquently, but adequately, and I am grateful for that. I have achieved sufficient expertise in using oils, watercolors, and pastels, and the ability to draw images I attempt through long trial and practice, and my abilities continue to improve. My work is finally acceptable in juried shows and galleries in spite of failing to command the high prices of a financially successful artist. For now, that is enough, though I shall continue to strive for greater acceptance and recognition.

Mel and Pat continued to be my best friends and supporters. When Pat was 87 years of age, she and her 91-year-old husband moved into a retirement home in Arizona, where she was diagnosed with multiple myeloma—bone cancer. Her attitude is that it could be a whole lot worse, and she would beat it, as she did for over ten years.

Nothing was going to stop her from starting an art group in her retirement center, continue to paint, exhibit, and act as the president of the art group she started. Her macular degeneration left her nearly blind, but she refused to allow it to affect her weekly bridge game with friends, or her many other activities.

But finally, at the age of 97, the death that she had avoided for so long could not be further delayed, and her wish to go into the sunset quickly occurred. She had had bouts of stomach aches for some time although doctors could find no cause for it. That day in December 2017, the pain began when she arose from bed; she called for help and died shortly thereafter. She had time to call her succeeding trustee in time to ask him to take care of her final wishes. It was so typical of her entire life—she, like our mother, always looked after those she loved. She made sure that her final trust was applied to sisters, nephews, and nieces and it resulted in a better life for her loved ones.

Pat was my best friend, mother, caring sister, and even my biggest critic, and I miss her loving kindness and support more than anything.

Mel at 90 years old was still a workaholic who gardened, canned and cooked tirelessly, while in her free time, she took her great-grandchildren to water and snow ski, and entertained relatives and friends tirelessly. Like our mother, her favorite pursuit was fishing when she could. Our lives changed after Pat's death. It was months before I could get through a day without thinking, "I've got to call Pat." All my family still has that thought daily.

Mel contacted a debilitating disease (Parkinson's) and her many interests and activities declined. Now 98 years old, she now has to use a walker to get around and has to hire someone to take care of her. Not one to give up, she still demands that the garden be planted.

The robustness we learned as children of poverty-stricken tenant farmers gave us meaning and a lust for life. We are grateful for the trials and tribulations that taught us to overcome our problems.

In spite of the agony of my children's problems, I have found a measure of peace, acceptance, and joy. Mel was right when she said, "What doesn't kill you will make you stronger."